IREDAFENEVESHO OWOLABI

# IGNITE
# YOUR CREATIVITY

*How to transform your ideas, talents, skills, and gifts
to creative solutions.*

Flip The Switch Exercises Included

**National Library of Canada Cataloguing-in-Publication Data**

Paperback ISBN:       978-1-998118-00-7

Hardcover ISBN:       978-1-998118-02-1

E-Book ISBN:       978-1-998118-01-4

**Other Books by Iredafe Owolabi are:**

- 4D-Thinking
- Unlocking Your Kingdom Creativity
- How to Make Millions as an Author-Preneur
- Profitable Problem Solving
- Kingdom Verities
- How to Enjoy Kingdom Currency (Vol. 1)
- How to Maximize Kingdom Currency (Vol. 2)
- Kingdom Currency for Students, Graduates and Businessmen (Vol.3)
- 15 Hot Markets Where You Can Easily Sell Your Book Anytime
- 10 Ways to Make Money from a Single Book Idea
- How to Self-Publish Your Books Successfully
- Why you should Write a Book
- Profitable Problem-Solving Workbook
- Idea to Profitable Creation Workbook

- To schedule me for a keynote presentation or to have me speak at your seminar, workshop, training, church, or conference, anywhere around the world or virtually, please visit: www.iredafeowolabi.net/invite-me

- To contact me for feedbacks, to share or tell a story perhaps for inclusion in one of my future books, kindly send an email to info@iredafeowolabi.net.

- To get my latest insights and techniques on creativity, innovation and problem solving, check my creativity blog here: www.iredafeowolabi.net/blog

*Disclaimer: Unless explicitly stated, the names used in the non-personal stories provided are fictional in nature, though the events portrayed are true. However, the personal stories shared in this book are factual and may include actual names. Any semblance to actual individuals, living or deceased, in the non-personal stories is purely coincidental. The purpose of these stories is to illustrate certain concepts and ideas and should not be interpreted as specific references to real people or situations unless otherwise stated.*

# TABLE OF CONTENTS

# PREFACE

**How it all began**

Before I made Canada my home, there were various experiences that shaped me into the authority I am today in the realm of creativity and problem-solving. These memories have followed me everywhere I go. Even as I share my knowledge, insights, and techniques from one conference stage to another, and from nation to nation, those moments remain top of mind. My journey into the domain of creativity took a remarkable turn when I was invited to deliver keynote presentations in Katsina, a culturally rich state in northern Nigeria. The thought-provoking 2-day conference, tagged "Think Outside the Box," was held in 2018 and brought together a diverse audience of youth and adults who warmly embraced the unconventional ideas I presented. It was during this event that I realized the pressing need to bridge the gap between having great ideas, gifts, or potential and transforming them into profitable creations.

Before embarking on this speaking engagement, I had observed that a sizable portion of people often fail to fully tap into their creative potential. Many carry untapped reservoirs of gifts, talents, skills, and ideas that often go unnoticed and remain dormant unless ignited. Some have simply outsourced their creativity to God, when, in fact, God has already sourced them with the ability to be creative. He did that so He could ensure that the creative work He initiated in the beginning would continue. However, many potential creatives are yet to take their place in today's world and contribute to the ongoing creation story.

This book is for you if you do not want to take your gifts, talents, skills, and ideas with you to the grave untapped. It is for those who recognize that their God-given potential is not meant to remain dormant here on earth because it is useless in heaven. Many people are simply on their way to heaven, carrying brainchildren that have been gestating in the womb of their minds for years without being birthed into reality. Are you one of those individuals? Do you know anyone in this category? Chances are, you either know someone who belongs here, or you belong to this category of special individuals who have remained the world's best-kept secret because they are yet to unlock their creative potential. The goal of this book is to help you transform your ideas, gifts, skills, and talents into tangible creations. I have crafted this book to transcend barriers such as race, skin pigmentation, religious background, geographical extraction, or societal status. Regardless of who you are, this book is designed to empower you to fully uncover your hidden genius.

## Another pain point

During my research for the presentation at Katsina, I made a profound observation. I noticed that there was a scarcity of information that could sufficiently explain what creativity truly meant. I wanted to grasp a solid understanding of the very fundamentals of creativity and how they can be harnessed intentionally. However, the existing resources were either abstract, disorganized, confusing, or inadequate. The information available online at that time was either half-baked truth or well-baked ignorance. I also noticed another pain point in addition to the lack of reliable resources. There was no packaged resource available to save interested seekers from wasting time on poorly structured free content online. This gap inspired me to create a solution. So, determined to find answers, I embarked on a personal journey of exploration, guided by the Spirit of God. After delivering an exceptional presentation at the seminar, I kept researching and studying the subject of creativity. That year, I wrote a book to document some of the findings I had made titled "Unlocking Your Kingdom Creativity." Two years after publishing that book, another one followed titled "4-D Thinking" or "Fourth Dimensional Thinking."

It will also interest you to know that in a bid to solve the problem which I had identified, I did not stop at writing books and teaching others about creativity. I sought ways to make my understanding of the concepts and principles relatable to the everyday employee or entrepreneur in the corporate world. I wanted to go beyond mere words to truly convince others of my ability to teach, impart, and inspire creativity. To bridge the gap between theory and practice, I embarked on a journey to acquire another skill that demanded a high degree of creativity. I felt it was essential to not only share principles but also put them into action in my own daily experiences. This led me to transition into the realm of computer software programming, where I began writing words in languages that machines can read. By venturing into the corporate world, I gained invaluable insights into the inner workings of globally renowned tech giants known for their innovation. This includes companies like Google, Amazon, Netflix, Apple, Microsoft, and more. Through daily use of my programming skills and an informed study of the tech industry, I immersed myself in their creation processes and witnessed the continuous development of new products on a global scale. This immersive experience further refined my craft, empowering me to wield it as a powerful instrument for teaching and imparting creativity and problem-solving skills.

## Another speaking engagement

Moved by a deep passion to educate and enlighten people about the true essence of creativity, I committed myself to training and teaching others how to discover and harness their creativity and critical thinking skills. As I traveled from one conference to another, from one stage to the next, sharing my knowledge and experiences, a pivotal moment occurred - I made a promise. And this book in your hands is a fulfilment of that promise. Let me tell you how it all happened.

In the year 2019, on a sunny afternoon, as I sat in my bedroom trying to take a nap, my phone rang. As I picked up the phone, I had no idea that the ensuing conversation would go on to weave the threads of destiny. I believe this conversation set me on a transformative path as a thought leader and an established authority in the arena of creativity. The message I received from the caller was nothing short of an invitation—an esteemed opportunity to share my insights and wisdom at a youth conference held in the vibrant city of Benin, Nigeria. The host, Apostle Gordon Jnr., a man I hold in high esteem, reached out to inform me that I had been selected as one of the keynote speakers, joining a distinguished lineup of presenters for the conference. This recognition heightened my sense of duty, fueling a determination to leave a lasting impact on each attendee. By the way, this is my ultimate goal in every keynote presentation, speaking engagement, masterclass, or training I facilitate. The gratifying impact on every audience I get invited to speak to consistently reaffirms my commitment to this mission. The invitation was inspired by the host's encounter with a seminar presentation tagged "Creativity Accelerator," which I had previously facilitated in the bustling city of Abuja, Nigeria. The profound impact of that seminar resonated with him, prompting him to extend an invitation for me to share this powerful talk on creativity with a larger audience in Benin City, Nigeria. Although the setting was not new to me, and "Creativity Accelerator" as a keynote topic was familiar territory, I did not take my preparation lightly. I engaged in deeper reflection, exploring the inner recesses of my heart and mind, in search of profound insights that would ignite a lasting transformation in the lives of the conference attendees. I dedicated extensive time to further prepare my PowerPoint presentation slides, determined to present a reloaded episode of Creativity Accelerator, infused with more insights and profound principles.

The day finally arrived, I cannot forget it, it was September 14th, 2019. On that auspicious morning, the auditorium buzzed with excitement as vibrant young adults, ranging from ages 20 to 45, trooped in. The arena was packed with over 1,200 attendees, their breath bated, eagerly awaiting the insights I was about to share. As I took the stage, the atmosphere became electrified with anticipation. With each concept, technique, and story I shared, the minds of the attendees opened up to the boundless possibilities of creativity and how to unlock it. The energy in the room intensified, reverberating with powerful responses to the message I delivered. Witnessing the transformative effect my talk had on these attendees left me humbled and immensely inspired to this day.

After my presentation, as I settled back into my seat, I turned my attention to the surrounding audience. Just two seats away from me, a gentleman who had been deeply moved by the insights I shared on the platform expressed appreciation for the thoughts I had conveyed. His heartfelt gratitude served as a powerful reminder of the impact of the profound exposition on creativity that I had just presented. However, his gratitude was accompanied by a question that set the wheels in motion for the creation of this transformative book: "Do you have a book that contains what you just shared?" he asked. At that time, I had already established myself as a prolific author with a collection of seven books. His hopes were raised, anticipating that one of those books might hold the timeless inspirations he sought. At that moment, I realized that although I already had a book on creativity titled "Unlocking Your Kingdom Creativity," it did not cover the aspects I had shared on that memorable day. So, while I explained that to him, I recommended the book on creativity that was available, and he got out his phone to order it right there. Nevertheless, his satisfaction remained elusive. He continued to express a fervent desire for what he had just heard me talk about from the podium. He earnestly appealed to me, urging that I should author a book on those profound ideas, recognizing their transformative potential.

## A promise fulfilled

Touched by the enthusiastic plea and the raw desire I could see in his eyes, I made a promise to this gentleman, whom I could consider an elder brother, given his age. I pledged to him that I would author a book that specifically captures the cutting-edge, creativity-laden insights that I had bombarded their minds with during that one-hour presentation. It is my pleasure to announce to you today that the book you now hold in your hands is the fulfillment of the promise I made to that gentleman at the conference.

Throughout the remaining sessions of that week-long conference, the impact of my talk continued to resonate with the attendees. As I walked toward the cafeteria during recess just after my slot, I encountered several people trying to express their appreciation. With heartfelt sincerity, she said, "I wish I could immerse myself in your complete program on creativity." Her words served as an evocative reminder of the life-changing potential the ideas and concepts I had shared held within them. Although at that time, I did not have a dedicated creativity program to offer, her sentiment planted a seed in my mind that eventually sprouted into the creation of various creativity coaching programs and online courses. This encounter, without a doubt, further intensified my drive to craft this book— an all-encompassing exploration of creativity that would not only kindle the flames of inspiration but also release the hidden gifts, skills, and talents within you and a vast multitude of people.

## Another phone call

In the aftermath of that seminar, I received a call from one of my mentors, Professor Sam, a distinguished professor in his mid-sixties at the time, who had graced the conference as a special guest. Brimming with delight, he extended an invitation to me to visit his university, where he held the esteemed position as Head of Department (HOD) in one of the institution's faculties. He believed his students, lecturers, and co-professors needed to hear the ideas I had shared at the recently concluded conference. Weeks later, I found myself delivering another version of the Creativity Accelerator message to PhD, MSc, and BSc students, including lecturers and professors at the University of Benin, Nigeria.

About five years after the seminar, just before the completion of the first draft of this book in your hand, I was having a chat with Professor Sam. That was when he told me that the students who attended that seminar kept thanking him for organizing it and for bringing me in as the keynote speaker. He then went on to say they were fired up by my presentation, and some of them had gone on to become successful entrepreneurs and CEOs. These encounters, along with others, played a significant role in shaping the birthing of this book. Between when I conceived the idea to pen down this book and just over five years down the line, I embarked on a profound journey. I delved even deeper into the insights, gained invaluable experiences, and meticulously evaluated and refined the concepts.

## What kept me going

Could you imagine that it took me over five years to fulfill that promise? A lot happened within the period of conception and the delivery of this masterpiece. Of course, there were days when I felt like aborting this brainchild as it was premature in the womb of my mind. There were stomach cramps of uncertainty, periods of uneasiness, and sleepless nights. I carried this baby bump of ideas wherever I went, feeling the mental kicks of this baby that sometimes left my brain throbbing. Does the question, "What kept you going?" ever cross your mind? You bet it does! Now, the reason I made sure to develop and publish this book, and not abandon it halfway despite the setbacks I encountered in the process, is this: I always remembered the moment when that gentleman requested this book. As I looked into his eyes, I saw you! Yes, I saw you yearning for a book that could help you ignite your creativity. Even when thoughts of aborting this book idea came, all I saw in my mind's eye was you telling me that I could do it, and that we could make this work. And you know what? I believed you! I believed we could make it work. I realized the immense potential of this brainchild and the trans-generational impact it could have on you and countless others. It was this realization that kept me going, pushing through the discomfort, and embracing the growth that came with it. Just like an expectant mother who chooses to nurture and bring forth new life, I made the decision to wholeheartedly embrace the birth of "Ignite Your Creativity." I saw you and millions of others around the world clamoring for this masterpiece to emancipate them from the limiting beliefs that have long hampered their creativity. Yes, I saw you in that gentleman who made the effusive request that fateful day, expressing your need for a book that would help you ignite your creative spark and fan the embers of your gifted innovative mind. That gentleman made a fervent appeal and somehow committed me to make the promise. I believe he did it on behalf of the millions of people who are waiting to ignite their creativity through this book.

Therefore, I am happy to present to you this book—an immersive exploration into the depths of your creativity, carefully crafted to extract your superpowers, and empower you to become a proficient problem-solver in your sphere of influence. It is a guide designed to help you live a purposeful and fulfilling life by making the most of your unique talents and supersonic capabilities. In "Ignite Your Creativity," I invite you to embark on a thought-provoking and creativity-stimulating journey. Together, we will delve into the core principles and practices that will unlock your creative genius, explore the interplay between creativity and spirituality, and equip you with practical tools and strategies to infuse creativity into your daily existence. This book not only draws insights from contemporary examples and practical techniques but also from scriptural wisdom. It offers a comprehensive understanding of creativity and its intersection with spirituality. Through engaging stories, practical exercises, and accessible techniques, you will learn how to tap into your creative reservoir and channel it towards achieving your goals and aspirations.

Get ready to shed the layers of misconceptions, embrace the true essence of creativity, and unlock the boundless potential that lies within you. It's time to ignite your creativity and embark on a remarkable journey of self-discovery and growth.

## My Approach

People often ask me why I make reference to some scriptural truths in my books, training, keynotes, masterclasses, and teachings. Perhaps, this question may cross your mind as you read this book, so I will help you answer it right away. The reason is that as a thought leader, I am duty-bound to rely on authoritative references and well-researched publications when teaching every concept and precept. There are some known facts about the widespread nature of the book we now know as the Bible. These facts qualify the Bible as a worthy source of truth and reference material. First, the Bible is widely considered to be the most read book and the number one best-selling book in the world. The Bible has been translated into numerous languages and has had a profound influence on literature, culture, and religious thought throughout history. While it is challenging to determine the exact number of copies sold or the number of readers, estimates suggest that billions of copies have been distributed worldwide.

Another interesting fact is that despite its widespread acceptance and distribution worldwide, the Bible is still considered by many to be the most misunderstood book in the world. This is the reason that whenever I get the chance, I try to expound on key truths by referring to stories, quotes, and insights from scripture. My intention is to unveil enduring principles and insights that may have either been forgotten or misconstrued by its readers. This approach allows for a wide-reaching impact, as billions of people worldwide, irrespective of religious affiliation, can resonate with the relatable stories contained in the Bible. I also draw insights from contemporary stories and historical facts to give a well-rounded and balanced view to the reader. I have found this to be an effective way to aid a deeper understanding of the ideas expressed in this book.

**Engage, engage, engage…**

Another crucial aspect of this book that you should not take lightly is the "flip the switch" exercises and affirmations. I strongly encourage you to actively participate in these activities, as they have the potential to bring about a true transformation in you and propel you to new heights. **I also want to give you a spoiler alert: no matter what you do, make sure you at least get to the peak chapter - switches of creativity (chapter 4)!** Also, keep in mind that this is not a book you should try to rush through or consume hastily in one sitting. You will find yourself coming back to this book from time to time, even after a first read. See this book as a life manual for creativity because, as you read, you will discover areas in your life and journey that you need to work on. The best way to enjoy this book is to always have a pen and notepad handy. I understand that you may find this book very captivating and may get tempted to skip the exercises just to go through the content. However, if you really want to ignite your creativity, I advise against this approach. I recommend that you have a pen and a notepad ready to take notes of thoughts, ideas, and action plans that will come to you as you engage with the content in this book. If you are reading the hard copy version of this book, take notes in the allotted spaces and document your journey with this book alongside your personal journal or notepad. Through active participation with the worksheets, exercises, and a personal notepad, your creative spark will be ignited, and you will be motivated, challenged, and inspired. It is my earnest hope, prayer, and expectation that as you read this book, you will not only be transformed but also be transported to an elite level in your problem-solving, creativity, and critical thinking skills. The ultimate goal of this book is to empower you and every other reader across the world to learn how to be more creative with the gifts, skills, and potential you currently have. By uncovering the secrets to being more creative with your gifts, skills, ideas, and talents, this book seeks to ignite a flame within you, fan the embers of your mind, and propel you towards a life of purpose, innovation, and vision accomplishment.

Now, I invite you to embark on this voyage of self-discovery and creative empowerment. Take the first step by diving into the chapters ahead and immersing yourself in the exercises and principles presented. Remember, true growth comes from applying what you learn. Embrace the opportunity to unleash your problem-solving skills and let them guide you towards a life filled with fulfillment. I believe in your ability to create a remarkable future with your current ideas, gifts, skills, and talents. Let's embark on this extraordinary adventure together. Happy reading!


Yours truly,
Iredafe Owolabi.
The Creativity Expert.

# INTRODUCTION

**Can't I just Wing it? No?**

This is a question that may have crossed your mind. After all, why bother learning how to ignite your creativity when you can simply leave things to chance and "wing it"? Many people adopt this approach, hoping that their ideas and talents will somehow lead them to success. They get an idea, discover an innate gift or talent, and run off trying to dare anything that comes their way without an intentional approach. They dive headfirst into pursuing their passions without a result-driven strategy, believing that sheer enthusiasm and determination will be enough. But more often than not, this lack of a structured approach leaves them feeling discouraged, setting themselves up for failure, and constantly getting lost along the way. Let's take a cursory look at the story of Moses to illustrate this point. He had a passion and an innate leadership gift that could potentially liberate the Jews from Egyptian oppression. Fueled by his noble intention, Moses rushed into action without considering the importance of creativity in his approach. He tried to wing it, making frantic efforts to bring his idea to fruition without a clear plan or innovative thinking. Unfortunately, his well-intentioned but misguided attempts ended up in disaster. The situation became so dire that he had no choice but to flee from his assignment in Egypt, leaving him disconnected from his inherent creative potential.

It wasn't until the remarkable encounter with the burning bush, forty years later, that Moses finally got his creativity ignited. In that transformative moment, he gained the insight and inspiration needed to fulfill his purpose. The burning bush experience awakened his dormant gift, skill, and talent, setting him on a path of profound greatness. Now, take a moment to reflect: does this describe you in any way? Have you found yourself rushing headlong into your creative endeavors without giving enough thought to cultivating your creativity? This, in my experience, is where many creatives miss it. Have you ever experienced the frustration of feeling lost or discouraged in pursuit of your dreams because you tried to wing it? If so, it's time to recognize the importance of igniting your creativity and embrace a result-driven approach toward releasing your potential.

Now, this is in no way suggesting that you should sit on your gift and get stuck in analysis paralysis, waiting indefinitely for the perfect moment before taking action. As a matter of fact, the idea I'm trying to impart to you through this book is that you can actually flip the switch on your creativity and ignite it. You do not have to sit around waiting for the spark. You just need to use the various switches, which have been well expounded on in the fourth chapter of this book. These switches will help to trigger your creativity as you go from ideas to creative solutions. Igniting your creativity requires a proactive approach, where you seize opportunities and actively pursue your ideas. So, it's crucial to note that this doesn't mean rushing haphazardly without any thought or strategy. Finding the right balance is key. It involves recognizing when to take inspired action, even if things aren't completely perfect, and when to step back, reflect, and infuse your endeavors with creative thinking. It's about embracing a mindset that values both intuition and deliberate planning.

By understanding the importance of igniting your creativity, you can navigate this delicate dance between action and reflection. It's about leveraging your innate talents while incorporating creativity into your approach. This way, you can harness your gifts and talents effectively, allowing them to flourish and bring about meaningful results.

## Did God ignite His creativity?

Even God did not try to wing it when He got the first opportunity to go from idea to creation. If God, the Almighty and all-powerful creator, who brought the universe into existence with His Omnificence, needed to ignite His creativity, why do you think you can wing it? What makes you believe you can bypass the need to ignite your creativity and just take a stab at it? Why do you feel that you do not need that spark of illumination, flash of inspiration, ray of insight, and intentional engagement that triggers and precedes the creative process? You may wonder, 'How did God ignite His creativity?' Let me show you. If you study the creation account recorded in the first chapter of the book of Genesis in the Bible, you will observe something profound. There were two occasions where God called for light. The first scenario was in Genesis 1:3, where God said, 'Let there be light,' and there was light. The second instance can be found in Genesis 1:14, where God said, 'Let there be lights...' The Bible makes it clear that there was light the first time God called it into being. So why did God have to repeat Himself the second time? I will tell you why. If you take a look at the Hebrew words translated as 'light' on both occasions, you will notice they are different. In Genesis 1:3, the word for 'light' comes from the Hebrew word 'or,' which can be pronounced as 'ore.' According to Vine's Expository Dictionary of Old Testament Words, 'or' means to be lighted up[1] and, according to Strong's concordance, it means illumination.[2] On the other hand, in Genesis 1:14, the word translated as 'lights' comes from the Hebrew word 'ma'owr,' pronounced as 'maw-ore.' According to Strong's concordance, it means luminous body or light-giving body, like a chandelier. By virtue of this information, it means that when God said, 'let there be light' in Genesis 1:3, He was not trying to create the sun, moon, and stars as those were created on the fourth day in Genesis 1:14. This brings us back to the question, 'Why did God have to repeat Himself when He called for light?' The reason is that the first time, God was igniting His creativity, but the second time, He was creating the sun, moon, and stars.

Yes! Looking at Genesis 1:3, God was actually saying 'let there be illumination.' The light God was referring to was not the external sources of light like the sun, moon, stars, or any luminary. Those were created on the fourth day. The light God was referring to was the one within, and that internal spark is what you also need to ignite for your talent, gift, and skills to shine forth. Did you notice that this was the very first statement God made when He saw that the earth was empty, without form, and filled with darkness? In fact, that was the first statement recorded to have been made by God in the beginning. **Before God tried to transform His creation ideas into reality, He first ignited His creativity!** Wow… I don't know about you, but I am stirred up and super stoked by this insight! It means that no matter how empty your life may be or how confused you may feel, if you ignite your creativity, you can activate the lost gifts, talents, skills, and potentials hidden within you. You can transform your world into an avalanche of beauty by igniting your creativity. This is why I believe that by reading this book and acting on the insights that come to you, you will be transported into another realm of greatness and fulfillment through creativity. Just as God needed light before initiating creation, we too require illumination to unlock our full creative potential. Illumination, in this sense, represents those moments of clarity, insight, and inspiration that shed light on the path ahead. It is the spark that ignites your imagination and fuels your passion. Without illumination, our creative endeavors may remain stagnant or lack direction. It is the flash of ingenuity that fuels the creative process. Illumination is a vital connection to creativity because it is in these moments of illumination that new ideas flourish, perspectives shift, and innovative solutions emerge.

Whether it is a sudden beam of insight or a gradual unfolding of understanding, illumination acts as a guiding light, leading us towards novel and imaginative creations. Therefore, in the journey of creativity, actively seeking and embracing illumination is paramount. It involves nurturing an open and receptive mindset, inviting inspiration, and actively exploring diverse perspectives. Ultimately, illumination precedes creativity, serving as a foundational element that propels our creative endeavors forward. By leveraging and harnessing the power of illumination, you unlock the vast potential within you, propelling your ideas from the realm of possibility to tangible and impactful realities.

## More on illumination

Just as a flame ignites in darkness, the idea of igniting creativity suggests bringing light or sparking the initial burst of inspiration and imagination. When I talk about igniting creativity, I often refer to stimulating and awakening your creative faculties, breaking through mental barriers, and finding new ways of thinking as you move from idea, gift, talent, or potential to creation. It can involve techniques such as brainstorming, mind mapping, exploring new environments, seeking diverse perspectives, or engaging in activities that foster inspiration and ideation. The concept of illumination refers to the moment when the spark of creativity occurs, leading to the generation of new ideas, insights, or solutions. It signifies the transition from a state of mental stagnation or blockage to a state of illumination or enlightenment, where creative thoughts and possibilities become accessible. Remember that the Bible describes God as light (1 John 1:5), and it also describes us as light (Matt 5:14). This is because we have that candle within us that must be ignited for us to function to the full extent of our creative capacity. God activated the light within Him during creation, and not only did He beam the rays of that illumination toward the darkness, but He also ignited His creativity before taking action. He would come up with an idea and express the ideas behind His next creative endeavor by saying, 'let there be...' or 'let us make...', and after laying out the vision, He would go into action and make, build, or create what He envisioned.

# What is light?

Since the words 'light' and 'lightbulb moment' come up frequently in this book, I would like to give you some insight into the concept of light. Light is what determines how we see things. There are different kinds of light in the world today. For example, what you see with natural light is different from what you see with the light that emanates from an X-ray. With natural light, you see objects like humans, but with an X-ray, you can visualize internal structures, such as bones and organs, as they can pass through soft tissues while being absorbed by denser materials. Have you ever wondered why objects have different colors? It's also because of the light! When light shines on an object, something interesting happens. The object interacts with the light. It absorbs some of the light and reflects the rest. The reflected light enters your eyes and helps you see the object's color. Imagine you have a flashlight; when you shine it on a red ball, the ball absorbs all the colors except for red. It reflects the red light, which enters your eyes and makes the ball look red to you. Now, imagine shining the same flashlight on a blue shirt. This time, the shirt absorbs all the colors except for blue. The blue light is reflected back, enters your eyes, and makes the shirt appear blue to you. The reason objects have different colors is that they interact with light in different ways. Some objects absorb certain colors and reflect others, and that's what creates the colors we see.

Just as the colors you see depend on the light that falls on objects, your creativity or the way you create is influenced by the perspectives, insights, and inspirations that come your way. The more diverse the sources of light, the richer and more vibrant your creative palette becomes. This is why it is important to be open to new experiences, insights, perspectives, and knowledge as you embark on your creative journey. Allow yourself to soak in the inspiration that flows in this book and watch as your creativity blossoms. Remember, just as light reveals the colors of the world, it can also reveal the colors of your imagination. Take advantage of those lightbulb moments that this book will bring your way and see how your creativity will become a phenomenon the world has yet to see.

> *Let your **light so shine** before men, that they may see your **good works,** and glorify your Father which is in heaven.*

> *Matt 5:16 KJV*

The statement in the Bible verse above is one that many recite without knowing how deep and powerful it is. This verse gives another great insight into the connection between light and creativity. The word 'light' as transliterated above is from the Greek word 'phos'. According to Thayer's definition, it means the light emitted by a lamp or a fire. Simply put, light is that which makes visible, reveals, or makes manifest. This word can also be used as a metaphor to refer to that which is exposed to the view of all, openly and publicly. When you put all these together, it becomes easy to understand why Jesus makes it clear that if your creativity is ignited, your good works will naturally become exposed to the view of men openly and publicly. This light can be seen as the flames of your creative spark, which reveals and exposes your inner glory and hidden potential for all to see. Why is this so profound? The word 'good' in the term 'good works,' according to Thayer's Greek Lexicon, means something that is beautiful to look at, that is excellent in its nature and characteristics, and therefore well adapted to its ends, something praiseworthy, suitably useful, and valuable[3]. And the word 'works' in the Greek rendering means a business, job, or enterprise in which one is occupied. It also refers to any product or thing accomplished by hand, art, industry, or mind. By implication, 'works' means any undertaking, be it a business, job, enterprise, or product, that involves the use of your mind, hand, art, economic activity, or industrial process to perform. So, it means that when you ignite your creative spark, you will receive illumination to do elegant work, create beautiful products that are useful, well adapted to solving problems, and you would perform excellently in your business and professional endeavors. Do not take my word for it, go back to the verse above and study it, then do some research of your own to fact-check the exposition I just outlined here. Then come back to this book and continue reading. Just don't read this book without catching a glimpse of the light that will eventually transform your ideas, gifts and skills into tangible results for all to see.

# CHAPTER ONE
# CREATIVITY MYTHS

One morning, I opened up the Canva app in my phone (a Smartphone application for creating graphics). Then I carefully crafted a design that would later find its way onto my social media pages and statuses. Little did I know that this seemingly innocent act would ignite a thought-provoking discussion about the connection between creativity and lack of resources. The graphic design bore a powerful inscription: "Poverty is not a lack of resources but a lack of creativity." With a tap from the tip of my thumb, I shared it on my WhatsApp status, completely unaware of the impact it would have. Within seconds, I witnessed the virtual landscape tremble as if I had not only "shaken a table" but actually "broken it," leaving many people stunned and compelled to reevaluate their beliefs. The profound impact of the graphic design and its powerful message shattered some limiting beliefs that hold many creatives back, unleashing a wave of discussions. Before long, a curious contact in my network challenged the notion, taking a stance that suggested the opposite of what the inscription said. He asked why many talented individuals remain trapped in financial struggles despite their creative abilities. This encounter made me realize that there is a widespread misunderstanding of what creativity truly entails.

Interestingly, I had once grappled with the same question until I embarked on a journey of discovery and unearthed profound truths about creativity. Through conscious research and personal experiences, I learned how to ignite the dormant creative genius within me and saw the transformation that took place. It became clear to me that many people do not know what creativity really means. They fail to grasp the distinction between having innate gifts, talents, skills, or potential and harnessing the true power of creativity. This misconception, among others, limits their ability to manifest their potential and make a significant impact in their lives, careers, or businesses. Motivated by this revelation, I dedicated myself to helping others unleash their creative potential. As I traveled the world, sharing insights and training individuals and organizations, I realized the urgent need to demystify creativity. So, in this chapter, I aim to dispel such myths or false impressions and guide you towards a deeper understanding of this highly coveted skill known as creativity. You might be among those still seeking clarity on what creativity truly means in a bid to develop yourself. You are not alone, as billions of people around the world today still struggle to define and harness their creative capacity. So, let us look at some limiting beliefs and misconceptions that hold people back from truly expressing their creativity and transforming their potential, knowledge, and gifts into something remarkable.

## Myth One: Creativity cannot thrive in lack

Creativity is a powerful human trait that transcends the boundaries of poverty. It is not limited by one's socioeconomic status or lack of material resources. In fact, creativity often thrives better in the face of adversity, as individuals find innovative solutions to overcome challenges and express themselves through various creative outlets. Lack of money may restrict access to certain resources or opportunities, but it cannot suppress the inherent potential within individuals who have the will to harness their creativity. In the absence of conventional tools or materials, individuals have been known to repurpose everyday objects, utilize their imagination, and tap into their resourcefulness to manifest their creative ideas. Furthermore, creativity can serve as a catalyst for personal growth and empowerment, enabling individuals in impoverished conditions to break free from the cycle of poverty. By harnessing your creative abilities, you can develop skills, showcase your talents, and create opportunities for yourself, opening doors to new possibilities and avenues for success. It is important to recognize that creativity knows no bounds and can flourish in any environment, including those affected by poverty.

True wealth is not defined solely by financial resources but rather by an abundance of creativity. Note the qualifying word "true" because there are definitely other ways to attain riches. And poverty is not solely a lack of resources. At its root, poverty is a result of a lack of creativity and resourcefulness. Whenever I have the opportunity to connect with discouraged creatives, I often encounter one common question: "I am creative, but no one wants to fund my ideas. What is your advice on how to get investors?" or "I am creative, but my only problem is I lack funding. How do I raise funds?" These are valid concerns that most creatives confront on a day-to-day basis. However, it becomes an issue when it is used as an excuse to allow your skills, ideas, and talents to waste away. My response to this common question is usually simple yet powerful: "If you possess creativity, that very skill will enable you to compensate for the lack of resources through resourcefulness. The reason you have creativity is to solve problems, and if the lack of funding is a problem for you, tap into your creativity and solve it." It's crucial to understand that creativity possesses a magnetic pull that attracts resources when set into motion through resourcefulness. If money is scarce, then what other assets do you possess that can propel you from an idea, passion, skill, and potential to a profitable solution? If you say that you have nothing, you have subconsciously identified the problem: a lack of creativity. I want you to understand that if you have creativity, you have something because creativity is what brings in every other resource that you require to succeed in turning your dreams and ideas into reality. **Stop letting your gifts, talents, skills, and ideas waste away because you lack funding. Ignite your creativity!** Creativity exists to solve problems. If you encounter difficulties in acquiring finances, resources, or anything necessary to bring your ideas and dreams into tangible reality, it's time to ignite your creativity.

Your creativity can be utilized to address the resource deficiency. It is contradictory to claim you are creative while failing to employ that creative ability to resolve the only obstacle impeding your progress - funding. Creativity extends beyond generating fancy ideas; it requires actions that demonstrate the validity and authenticity of those ideas. If it means doing jobs that may not align with your passion initially but will grant you the resources, knowledge, or connections needed to start or at least keep your head above the water, do not hesitate to seize the opportunity. By being resourceful, tapping into your creativity, and taking practical steps, you can overcome the financial limitations holding you back from living your dreams. Remember, creativity is an invaluable tool for problem-solving and for propelling you forward, regardless of financial constraints. It's time to awaken the dormant creative force within you. Stop suppressing your gifts, talents, and skills because of a perceived lack of resources. True creativity thrives best in the face of lack. You don't need a vast fortune or an abundance of resources to ignite your creative spark. All you need is a belief in your gift or potential and the determination to make the most of what you already have.

Look around you, within the depths of your mind and the depths of your surroundings, and discover the hidden treasures waiting to be unearthed. Use the challenge of scarcity as an opportunity to showcase your resourcefulness. It is in the midst of such obstacles that true ingenuity is born. Let your creativity become the bridge that spans the gap between what you have and what you envision. Remember, some of history's greatest achievements emerged from the humblest beginnings. The world-renowned brands, revolutionary inventions, and timeless works of art all started with a single spark of creativity. Those who dared to act upon their ideas, even with limited means, paved their path to success. Don't wait for the perfect conditions, as they may never come. Instead, gather the fragments of your creativity, piece them together, and boldly step into the realm of possibility. Trust that as you begin, the resources you need will manifest along the way. So, I urge you, rise from your slumber and seize the day. Start with whatever you have—whether it's a pencil and paper, a humble corner of your home, or the burning desire within your heart. Let your imagination soar, innovate, and create. The world is waiting to witness the brilliance that lies within you. Break free from the shackles of this perceived limitation and let your creativity flourish. Therefore, accept the challenge, leverage the lack, and watch as your ideas take flight against all odds. Now is the time to unleash your creative potential. Find the beauty in scarcity and let your true brilliance shine through. Awaken your creativity and let it illuminate your path to greatness. The world eagerly awaits what you have to offer. Go forth and create wonders.

## FLIP THE SWITCH EXERCISE #1

Myth one - Creativity cannot thrive in lack

a) Identify a creative project or idea that you've been putting on hold due to a perceived lack of resources (e.g., financial, time, materials).

_______________________________________________

_______________________________________________

_______________________________________________

b) List the specific resources you believe you lack for this project.

_______________________________________________

_______________________________________________

_______________________________________________

c) Challenge yourself to find alternative ways to acquire or utilize resources. Brainstorm at least three resourceful approaches that could help you overcome the perceived lack.

---
---
---

d) Choose one resourceful approach and create an action plan to implement it. Consider how you can leverage your existing resources, network, skills, or creativity to make progress on your project despite the perceived lack.

---
---
---

e) Document any insights, surprises, or discoveries that arise during this process. Did you find new solutions or approaches that you hadn't considered before? How did embracing resourceful creativity impact your mindset and creative process?

---
---
---

## Myth Two - Creativity is limited to inherent gift or talent

The term "inherent gift" refers to an innate or natural ability or talent that an individual possesses without much external influence or extensive training. It implies that the person has a particular skill that comes effortlessly or more easily to them compared to others. Such individuals are often referred to as "naturals." When someone is described as a natural in a particular area, it typically means that they have an inherent gift or talent for that specific skill or activity. They possess a natural aptitude or ability that allows them to excel well without intense training or regimen. Being "a natural" suggests that the person has an affinity towards the activity in question. This could be in various domains such as sports, arts, music, academics, or any other area where individuals can showcase exceptional skill. People often recognize naturals by their ability to quickly grasp concepts, display proficiency, and achieve notable success without requiring as much practice or formal training as others. However, it's important to note that inherent gifts are not the sole determining factor for success or creativity. Smart work, dedication, perseverance, and a growth mindset also play crucial roles in achieving excellence. While inherent gifts can provide a head start or advantage, they need to be nurtured and developed through learning, practice, and continuous improvement to fully realize their potential. Inherent talent alone may not be enough to reach the highest levels of achievement; it is the combination of talent and effort that often leads to extraordinary success.

Creativity is often mistakenly perceived as a talent reserved for a select few individuals. However, the truth is that creativity is not solely determined by your innate abilities or fixed traits. An inherent gift is a good starting point when harnessing creative potential, but the interesting fact is that creativity transcends the ability to cultivate gifts that are intrinsic to you. It is a skill that can be cultivated and honed with time and effort. Creativity is not a static, inherent, fixed trait; rather, it is a dynamic attribute. It can be developed, nurtured, and improved through practice, exposure to new experiences, and a willingness to explore new ideas. In circumstances where an innate capacity is lacking, a "light bulb" moment can inspire you to do things you never knew you could do. **Therefore, having the right mindset is crucial, as it can jumpstart your creativity and enable you to figure out ways to compensate for any lack of natural gifting, making the story even more beautiful**. When individuals fully embrace their creativity and harness it in a purposeful manner, they can overcome any perceived lack of natural talent or gifting. This idea is exemplified in the Bible, where people who were nothing short of mediocre or living an ordinary and average life underwent transformative experiences when encountering God. A vivid example is Solomon; his "light bulb" moment occurred when God visited him in a dream and offered to grant him any wish. Instead of asking for material possessions or power to conquer more kingdoms like his father, Solomon asked for a creative mind. Although he did not explicitly say, "Lord, give me a creative mind," from the way God responded and the things Solomon accomplished, God understood what Solomon was asking and gave him a creative mind. That was Solomon's light bulb moment and tipping point.

> *God said to him because you have asked this and have not asked for long life or for riches, nor for the lives of your enemies, but have asked for yourself* **understanding to recognize** *what is just and right, Behold, I have done as you asked.* **I have given you a wise, discerning mind**, *so that no one before you was your equal, nor shall any arise after you equal to you.*
>
> *1 Kings 3:11-12 AMP*

One of Solomon's notable creative achievements was the construction of the Temple in Jerusalem. While Solomon was not an architect, his wisdom and creativity in leadership compensated for his lack of civil engineering or architectural design skills. He meticulously planned and designed the temple, incorporating intricate details and utilizing exquisite craftsmen. The Temple became a symbol of Solomon's wisdom, creativity, wealth, and artistic vision. In addition to his architectural feats, Solomon was also renowned for his musical and poetic abilities. He composed numerous songs and poems, including the famous Songs of Solomon, which poetically depicted love and beauty. His poetic expressions showcased his creative flair and artistic sensibilities. Solomon's life exemplifies how creativity can manifest in various forms of expression, encompassing architecture, literature, and music. His accomplishments serve as a testament to the fact that creativity can be nurtured, developed, and utilized to bring forth remarkable works that inspire and impact others. By tapping into your creative potential, you can explore alternative approaches, think outside the box, and find innovative solutions to challenges. This process of compensating for any perceived limitations can lead to remarkable personal growth and creative achievements. The dynamic power of creativity should not be taken for granted, as it has the ability to empower individuals to surpass their initial capabilities and create something truly inspiring and beautiful.

Consider the remarkable journey of Ben Carson, a renowned neurosurgeon, and an avid follower of Christ. In his early years, he faced challenges and was even labeled as a "dummy" during his fifth-grade education. However, Carson's story took a dramatic turn as he embarked on a path of self-discovery and perseverance. Through dedication, hard work, and a thirst for knowledge, Carson transformed himself from an underachieving student to a trailblazing medical professional. He defied the odds and shattered societal expectations by becoming the first black neurosurgeon to rise to the position of chief of pediatric neurosurgery at the young age of 33. He went from being a "dummy" to being the man with gifted hands, capable of performing surgeries like separating conjoined twins. How did he achieve this? He ignited his creativity! Carson's journey serves as a compelling example that creativity and success are not solely determined by initial talent or intelligence. It is the willingness to embrace challenges, learn from failures, and continuously seek personal growth that paves the way for extraordinary achievements.[1]

What about Jim Kwik, who suffered a head injury as a child, affecting his ability to concentrate and remember anything from school? One of his teachers even called him "the boy with the broken brain." For a while, he believed he could never be as good as the other kids when it came to learning, until he experienced his light bulb moment later in life. At this writing, Jim is a brain coach and world-renowned expert in brain optimization, memory improvement, and accelerated learning. He has coached top Hollywood stars to memorize their scripts in movies like X-Men and has worked with big shots like Bill Clinton, Richard Branson, Elon Musk, and more. How did the boy with a broken brain become a man who "fixes" people's brains? He ignited his creativity! Jim taught himself how to read by secretly reading comic books at night when his mom thought he was asleep. Reading about superheroes like the X-Men, who were rejected by society but discovered and developed their superpowers, inspired him to learn how to read. Despite being a misfit and facing ridicule at school, he discovered that he too had a superpower – his mind. This realization flipped the switch on his creativity, and he had his "aha" moment when he asked himself one day, "how can I learn faster?" and "how does my brain work?" This triggered a series of connections that turned him into the brain expert that he evolved into.[2]

Now, let's consider the founder of Kentucky Fried Chicken, Colonel Harland Sanders. He is an interesting example to discuss. While he had a passion for cooking, he did not achieve great success until later in life. Colonel Sanders faced multiple setbacks and failures throughout his early career. He worked various jobs and started several businesses, including a gas station and a motel, which didn't thrive. It was not until his 40s that Colonel Sanders had his "aha" moment. He developed a unique blend of 11 herbs and spices for his fried chicken recipe and started serving it at a small restaurant attached to a gas station in Kentucky, USA. The recipe gained popularity, and as word spread, the demand for his fried chicken grew. The recipe did not come from a natural or inherent gift but from passion, practice, and the light bulb moment he had. So, can we agree that the Colonel ignited his creativity? Despite facing numerous rejections when trying to sell his recipe to restaurants, he persisted and eventually franchised his concept. He traveled across the United States, signing franchise agreements with other restaurants to serve his fried chicken. This marked the beginning of the Kentucky Fried Chicken (KFC) empire[3]. Despite not having a natural gift or early success, Colonel Sanders's perseverance, innovation, and dedication to his craft allowed him to create one of the most successful fast-food chains in the world. His story serves as a reminder that creativity and success can be achieved at any age and through persistence, even without initial natural gifting.

Every individual has the potential to tap into their creativity and unlock their hidden talents. So, let go of the notion that creativity is an exclusive domain of the gifted few. Instead, believe in your own potential to cultivate and expand your creative abilities, regardless of your perceived disabilities. With dedication, perseverance, and a willingness to explore new ideas, you can unleash your creativity and open doors to endless possibilities. Remember, creativity knows no bounds when nurtured with passion and determination.

## FLIP THE SWITCH EXERCISE #2

Myth Two - Creativity is limited to inherent gifts or talents.

   a)  What skills would you like to develop and nurture in order to enhance your creativity?

_________________________________________________

_________________________________________________

b) What courses, books, exercises, or programs do you need to develop your creative skills?

_______________________________________________

_______________________________________________

_______________________________________________

_______________________________________________

c) What time do you intend to set aside for intentional and habitual creative practice?

_______________________________________________

_______________________________________________

_______________________________________________

_______________________________________________

d) Which mentors, friends, colleagues do you want to learn from, while still embracing your unique creative voice.

_______________________________________________

_______________________________________________

_______________________________________________

_______________________________________________

Flip the switch on the myth that creativity is limited to inherent talent and embrace the limitless possibilities of your own creative journey.

## Myth Three: Creativity is limited by physical disability

History is replete with individuals who, despite their physical disabilities, displayed remarkable creativity and problem-solving abilities. Franklin D. Roosevelt is a classic example. In 1921, at the age of 39, Roosevelt contracted polio, which left him paralyzed from the waist down. This life-altering event could have easily stifled his ambitions and creativity. However, Roosevelt refused to let his physical limitations define him or hinder his ability to lead and make a lasting impact. Despite being confined to a wheelchair, Roosevelt became one of the most influential presidents in American history. His creative problem-solving skills and innovative policies played a pivotal role in guiding the United States through the Great Depression and World War II. Through his leadership, he implemented the New Deal, a series of programs and reforms aimed at revitalizing the economy and providing relief to millions of Americans. His creative approach to governance helped restore hope and stability during a time of immense crisis. Roosevelt's story demonstrates that physical disability does not limit one's ability to think creatively, lead effectively, and make significant contributions to society[4]. Despite his paralysis, he harnessed his creativity, resilience, and determination to overcome obstacles and leave a lasting legacy. His story serves as an inspiration to individuals facing physical disabilities, reminding them that creativity knows no bounds and can flourish in the face of adversity.

What about Cobhams Asuquo and Stevie Wonder, who, despite being blind from birth, produced legendary music in their time? While their unique circumstances may have shaped their approach to music, the combination of their talent, ignited creativity, dedication, and hard work allowed them to achieve remarkable success in their lifetime. How did they become so proficient at something that typically requires sight? Some may argue that they surpassed many other musicians with two eyes through sheer talent. However, there are indeed other musicians with talent and sight who may never make contributions like they have, to music. Their stories prove that creativity goes beyond physical abilities. Stevie Wonder's songwriting skills, musical arrangements, and innovative use of various instruments demonstrate this. His ability to convey emotions, tell stories, and connect with his audience through his music is a testament to his artistic genius5.

Similarly, Cobhams Asuquo's accomplishments go beyond having sharp ears. Legendary music creation demands more than just perceiving sound accurately. Playing the piano, for example, requires a deep understanding of music theory, technical proficiency, and the skill to convey emotions through the keys. Connecting with an audience goes beyond simply hearing their applause; it involves tapping into their emotions, creating a shared experience, and leaving a lasting impact. While having sharp ears is an important foundation, true musical greatness and audience connection come from a combination of skill, passion, creativity, and a profound understanding of the art form. Can we now agree on something? They ignited their creativity! You see, creativity knows no limits set by any disability. It finds ways to compensate for any perceived limitations and enables individuals to express their talents and passions fully. **Don't let any physical disability stop you, creativity comes from your spirit.** That's why bodily limitations can never stop anyone who has ignited creativity! What about the story of Nick Vujicic, who was born with a rare condition called Tetra-Amelia syndrome, resulting in the absence of arms and legs? Despite his physical challenges, Nick became a globally recognized motivational speaker, author, and entrepreneur. His journey is a testament to his extraordinary creativity and resilience. Nick learned to adapt and perform various daily activities using his feet and developed innovative ways to accomplish tasks that many would consider impossible without limbs. He got a specially designed wheelchair and even mastered swimming, surfing, and playing sports. Nick's positive mindset and unwavering determination have inspired millions of people around the world. He travels extensively, delivering motivational speeches that encourage individuals to embrace their uniqueness, overcome obstacles, and pursue their dreams[6].

The reason I highlighted these examples is to help you break free from any barriers you may have placed on yourself due to a natural disability you may be facing. I want to encourage you to let go of any mental shackles you might have imposed on yourself because of a physical disability. It could be a disability such as severe hearing loss or any other non-life-threatening challenge. Your creative potential knows no limits, and I urge you not to let your disability weigh you down or hinder your progress. Instead, let it be the catalyst for a transformative journey. Consider this moment as a turning point in your life, where you no longer see your physical disability as a limitation. Rather than dwelling on what you cannot do, focus on what you can do exceptionally well. Hone your unique abilities and harness the power of your creativity to defy expectations and challenge conventional norms. Let your determination and resilience shine through as you overcome obstacles and pave your own path towards success and fulfillment. Remember, your journey is a testament to the strength of the human spirit and the boundless possibilities that exist when we embrace our creativity without limitations. So, rise above your perceived limitations, unleash your creative potential, and show the world the incredible things you are capable of.

## FLIP THE SWITCH EXERCISE #3

Myth Three - Creativity is limited by physical disability

a) What physical disabilities or limitations do you recognize that may have limited your progress as a creative?

_______________________________________________

_______________________________________________

_______________________________________________

b) What negative beliefs or doubts have you held about your creative potential due to your disability?

_______________________________________________

_______________________________________________

_______________________________________________

c) Now that you know that creativity is not solely dependent on physical abilities, what avenues can you explore for creative expression? Research and explore adaptive tools, technologies, or techniques that can support your creative endeavors.

_______________________________________________

_______________________________________________

_______________________________________________

Remember, your physical disability does not define your creativity. Embrace your strengths, adapt to challenges, and let your creativity shine through. Flip the switch on the myth that creativity is limited by physical disability and unlock your full creative potential.

## Myth Four: Creativity only comes via spontaneous inspiration

Creativity is not solely reliant on sudden bursts of inspiration or divine intervention. While inspiration can play a role, cultivating creativity often involves a combination of deliberate practice, curiosity, and active exploration. It's essential to understand that if you are born again and Spirit-filled, you already have the seed of creativity within you. You possess the "dunamis" – the dynamic ability to create. You don't need to wait for some special or divine intervention before releasing your creativity. If sudden bursts of inspiration come, take advantage of them and use them. However, you should never sit idly and do nothing, waiting for inspiration to strike.

This is a common misconception that fails to capture the true essence of the creative process. While moments of sudden insight and divine inspiration can certainly occur, they are not the sole drivers of creativity. Creativity is a multifaceted, yet straightforward phenomenon that can be nurtured and developed through intentional effort. It goes beyond waiting for a lightning bolt of inspiration to strike; it involves actively engaging in practices that foster problem-solving. One of the key factors in cultivating creativity is deliberate practice. Just like any skill, creativity can be honed and refined through consistent and focused effort. It requires dedicating time and energy to explore and experiment with different ideas, techniques, and approaches. By consistently engaging in creative activities, whether it's writing, painting, composing music, or any other artistic pursuit, you can sharpen your creative abilities and expand your creative repertoire.

One inspiring story that exemplifies the myth of spontaneous inspiration and the reality of deliberate practice and active exploration in cultivating creativity is the story of Thomas Edison and the invention of the incandescent light bulb. Contrary to popular belief, Edison did not stumble upon the concept of the light bulb overnight. It was not a sudden moment of inspiration that led to its creation. In fact, Edison went through numerous iterations and thousands of failed attempts before finally succeeding. Edison approached the invention of the light bulb with a mindset of deliberate practice and active exploration. He conducted countless experiments, systematically testing different materials, designs, and configurations. Each failure provided valuable insights and propelled him closer to finding the right combination. Edison's approach was fueled by curiosity and a relentless pursuit of knowledge. He was not afraid to venture into uncharted territory and challenge existing conventions. His determination to find a practical and commercially viable solution for electric lighting drove him to push the boundaries of his creativity. Throughout the process, Edison embraced the philosophy of "genius is 1%

inspiration and 99% perspiration." He understood that creativity was not solely dependent on flashes of brilliance but required persistent effort and an unwavering commitment to the creative journey. Eventually, after countless experiments and years of dedicated work, Edison achieved success. He developed a light bulb that could provide long-lasting, practical electric lighting. His invention revolutionized the world and forever changed the way we live. The story of Thomas Edison's journey to inventing the light bulb serves as a powerful reminder that creativity is not solely reliant on spontaneous inspiration. It highlights the importance of deliberate practice, curiosity, and active exploration in unlocking our creative potential. Edison's story inspires us to embrace the process, persevere through failures, and continuously push the boundaries of our creativity in pursuit of groundbreaking ideas and innovations. Creativity involves stepping out of comfort zones, embracing uncertainty, and adopting a mindset of experimentation. This can mean venturing into new territories, trying new approaches, and taking calculated risks. By exploring uncharted territories, individuals can push the boundaries of their creativity and uncover new insights and possibilities. Now, do you see that creativity is not solely dependent on divine intervention or elusive moments of brilliance? It is a process that can be cultivated, nurtured, and refined through deliberate practice, curiosity, and active exploration. By embracing these elements and integrating them into your creative endeavors, you can unlock the full potential of your creative self and embark on a journey of continuous growth and innovation.

## FLIP THE SWITCH EXERCISE  #4

Myth Four - Creativity only comes via spontaneous inspiration

a)  Choose a project or idea that you've been wanting to pursue but have been waiting for sudden bursts of inspiration.

_______________________________________________

_______________________________________________

_______________________________________________

b)  Identify specific actions or practices that can help you cultivate inspiration intentionally. These could include activities, rituals, or strategies that have worked for you in the past or new approaches you'd like to try.

_______________________________________________

_______________________________________________

_______________________________________________

c)  Create a schedule or routine that incorporates these intentional practices into your creative process. Set aside dedicated time each day or week to engage in activities that stimulate your creativity and provide inspiration.

_______________________________________________

_______________________________________________

_______________________________________________

## Myth Five: Creativity guarantees perfection or instant success

Creativity does not guarantee perfection or immediate success. This is another common misconception that can hinder individuals from fully unlocking their creative potential. The reality is that creativity is a dynamic and iterative process that sometimes involves trial and error, learning from mistakes, and continuous improvement. One notable example that dispels this myth is the story of the famous author J.K. Rowling and her journey to bringing the Harry Potter series to life. Before achieving global fame and acclaim, Rowling faced numerous rejections from publishers who failed to see the potential in her manuscript. Rather than succumbing to discouragement, Rowling persevered and continued to refine her writing and storytelling skills. She embraced the feedback and criticism she received, using it as an opportunity for growth and improvement. Her commitment to her craft and willingness to learn from her mistakes allowed her to develop a captivating narrative and a well-imagined world that resonated with millions of readers. Rowling's experience demonstrates that creativity is not about achieving perfection or instant success7. It is about embracing the process, learning from failures, and continually refining one's skills and ideas. Creativity requires resilience, adaptability, and the willingness to take risks and learn from setbacks. The creative journey is often marked by moments of frustration, setbacks, and uncertainty that may make immediate success unlikely. However, it is through these challenges that individuals can grow and evolve as creative beings. The ability to learn from mistakes, make adjustments, and persevere in the face of obstacles is what ultimately leads to the realization of creative visions. Understanding the truth that creativity does not guarantee perfection or instant success allows you to approach your creative endeavors with a growth mindset. It encourages you to view failures and setbacks as valuable learning opportunities and to continuously strive for improvement and innovation. By embracing the iterative nature of the creative process, you can unlock your true creative potential and achieve meaningful and impactful results.

## FLIP THE SWITCH EXERCISE  #5

Myth Five - Creativity guarantees perfection or instant success

a)  Reflect on your own expectations when it comes to creativity. Do you believe that creativity should guarantee perfection or instant success?

__________________________________________________

__________________________________________________

b)  Consider any past experiences where you felt discouraged or disappointed because your creative endeavors didn't meet your expectations of perfection or instant success.

__________________________________________________

__________________________________________________

c)  Think about any fears or beliefs you may have around making mistakes or experiencing setbacks in your creative process.

__________________________________________________

__________________________________________________

Take the first step towards your creative goal, even if it feels imperfect or incomplete. Start creating and allow yourself to make mistakes along the way. Focus on progress rather than perfection.

## Myth Six: Creativity needs external validation to thrive

One of the misconceptions that holds people back is the idea that they need external validation of their creativity before they can create. There is nothing wrong with seeking feedback or conducting market research. However, what I am trying to address is the attitude of potential creatives who seek people's approval before they embrace and showcase their gifts, talents, and skills. Particularly in today's era, where the craving for social media "likes" and "shares" often drives the creative process, overshadowing genuine ingenuity. Do not allow social media metrics to steer you away from the driver's seat of your creativity. Rekindle the joy of creating for the sake of self-expression, personal growth, and fulfillment. Let your creativity be a reflection of your true self, untouched by external judgments. The desire for external validation, seeking approval and recognition from others as a measure of one's creative worth, is not needed. Here are some reasons why seeking external validation for your creativity is unnecessary to prove that you are creative:

a) **Diverse Perspectives:** Creativity thrives on diversity and individuality. When seeking external validation, there is a risk of conforming to societal norms or popular trends, stifling originality, and limiting the exploration of new ideas. True creativity often involves breaking boundaries and challenging existing paradigms, which may not always align with prevailing external validation criteria. When I wrote my first book, I sought validation from one of my former mentors. He kept dragging his feet and going around in circles, and when I persisted, seeking his endorsement for my work, he subtly gave me signals that he did not like my writing style. I have nothing against him because I recognize that artistic expression is subjective, and different individuals have diverse preferences and tastes. I felt broken, though, but thankfully, I was undeterred because I knew that my ideas and unique approach did not need validation to make a difference in the lives of people around the world. Do not wait for some individual who poses as an "authority" to give you the green light before you turn your ideas, gifts, passion, and talents into creative solutions. Identify those whom you are called to serve with your gifts and begin to share your talents, gifts, and skills with them. That is the best way to get real validation.

b) **Authentic Expression:** External validation can inadvertently lead to a focus on meeting the expectations of others rather than staying true to one's own creative vision. Authentic expression requires the freedom to explore and experiment, even if it deviates from what is traditionally validated. Emphasizing external validation can hinder this exploration and compromise the integrity of creative work. Shift your perspective on feedback from seeking validation to embracing opportunities for growth and improvement. Seek constructive criticism from trusted mentors, peers, or creative communities that can help you refine your craft. Use feedback as a tool to learn and develop your skills, rather than solely relying on it for validation.

c) **Intrinsic Motivation:** Creativity is fueled by intrinsic motivation, the internal drive to create for the sake of personal fulfillment, curiosity, and passion. Relying solely on external validation as a measure of creativity can diminish the intrinsic joy and satisfaction that comes from the creative process itself. Overemphasis on external validation can lead to a constant need for validation, potentially eroding one's confidence and diminishing the intrinsic motivation to create. Sometimes people who you look to for external validation are out to extinguish your creative spark, so you want to be careful. While it is natural to seek some form of recognition or appreciation for creative work, it is important to remember that external validation should not be the driving force behind your creativity. The true essence of creativity lies in self-expression, personal growth, and the joy of exploring new ideas. Recognizing the intrinsic value of creativity and focusing on the process itself can liberate you from the myth of external validation and allow your creativity to flourish in an authentic way. Embrace the joy and satisfaction that comes from the act of creating, rather than solely seeking approval or recognition from others. Find fulfillment in the journey of exploring your ideas, experimenting, and honing your skills.

d) **Evolving Standards:** External validation is often based on prevailing standards, trends, or opinions that can change over time. Relying on external validation alone may lead to a constant chase for approval, as standards and tastes can be fickle and unpredictable. True creative fulfillment lies in staying connected to one's own unique voice and vision, rather than relying solely on external measures of success. A conventional business coach will tell you to validate your idea in the market first before creating. I believe that is a good thing to do for the sake of awareness. However, keep in mind that sometimes, even the market cannot validate your idea until it sees the tangible product because they may not even know what they want until you trigger it with your product, service, or creative solutions. So, while I encourage market analysis, be cautious with the findings you make during your "market research," so you do not mistakenly abandon your brainchildren. Steve Jobs once said that most times, clients or buyers don't know what they want until you create it for them or show it to them. How true! Henry Ford once said, "If I'd asked customers what they wanted, they would've told me 'A faster horse.' People don't know what they want until you show it to them. That's why I never rely on market research. Our task is to read things that are not yet on the page."[8] Hear this: **the value and impact of creative work cannot be solely determined by external opinions or validation**. Having validation from external sources is great, but it is not a requirement for creativity to thrive.

Understand that the people you look to for validation may not appreciate your unique approach, and that bias could deny you their validation.

## FLIP THE SWITCH EXERCISE  #6

Myth Six - Creativity needs external validation to thrive

a)  What are the motivations that drive your creativity?

_______________________________________________

_______________________________________________

_______________________________________________

Remind yourself that your creative journey is primarily fueled by your own passion and inner drive, not external validation.

b)  What specific objectives are meaningful to you, regardless of external validation.

_______________________________________________

_______________________________________________

_______________________________________________

## Myth Seven: Creativity is complexity

Many people mistake creativity for complexity. Whenever they are faced with problems, they look for complex methods to solve the problems rather than exploring the simpler solution that usually do not appear to be obvious at first. **You do not need complexity to display creativity**. Creativity is often best demonstrated through the use of simple, everyday solutions to tackle complex problems. This may seem counterintuitive to some, but the reason behind this perspective is clear. By focusing on the fundamentals of problem-solving, we can truly grasp the essence of creative thinking. It is through understanding and appreciating the power and impact of what we might consider ordinary that we can achieve extraordinary outcomes. Consider the remarkable possibilities that arise from just the 26 letters of the alphabet or the seemingly "ordinary" 9 digits of the number system. These foundational elements serve as the building blocks for countless creations and innovations. They remind us that extraordinary achievements are constructed upon layers of what we might perceive as ordinary. Similarly, complexity itself is often a combination of simpler components and concepts intertwined. By adopting this mindset, we can strip away the veil of complexity that often shrouds problems. We gain the ability to see through intricate layers and identify the underlying simplicity that exists within. This understanding enables us to approach problem diagnosis and solution-finding with clarity and effectiveness. Leveraging the power of simplicity and acknowledging the interplay between the ordinary and the extraordinary empowers us to unravel complex challenges and unlock our creative potential. It encourages us to focus on the core elements, master the fundamentals, and discover innovative solutions that have the capacity to make a lasting impact.

As a software engineer, I encounter complex problems daily. When the complexity of the moving parts begins to overwhelm me, I sometimes find myself diving deep into complex solutions and losing sight of the essence. However, I then realized this fundamental truth: creativity does not equate to complexity. As a result, I became intentional about applying a different approach when faced with a complex task. I break it down into simpler steps or components, allowing me to tackle each one individually. By focusing on smaller manageable elements, I gradually build a solution on solid foundations. This method has proven effective in navigating intricate problems, offering straightforward solutions, and maintaining clarity.

Taking it one step at a time, I make progress and piece together a comprehensive solution that addresses the complexity. This approach emphasizes the power of simplicity and highlights the effectiveness of breaking down complexity into manageable pieces for successful problem-solving. Creativity thrives when we simplify the complex. It is the ability to distill intricate concepts or convoluted problems into their essential elements that allows for innovative breakthroughs. Complexity often arises from a web of interconnected details, layers of information, or overwhelming factors. However, true creativity lies in finding elegant solutions amidst this complexity. In the pursuit of creative problem-solving, it is crucial to embrace the power of simplicity. This process of simplification not only aids in comprehending the problem but also paves the way for imaginative solutions. Moreover, simplicity fosters accessibility and inclusivity. Complex ideas or products often create barriers, limiting their reach and impact. On the other hand, simplicity enables broader understanding, engagement, and application. By distilling complex concepts into simpler forms, we empower individuals from diverse backgrounds to participate, contribute, and benefit from the creative process. Embracing simplicity does not imply disregarding depth or sophistication. It involves finding the balance between complexity and accessibility, homing in on the core essence while preserving the richness of ideas. This allows for the creation of elegant, user-friendly solutions that can be appreciated by a wide range of people.

In summary, when we debunk the myth of complexity and embrace the power of simplicity, we unlock new dimensions of creativity. By simplifying the complex, we open doors to innovative thinking, inclusive solutions, and the potential for impactful change.

## FLIP THE SWITCH EXERCISE  #7

- Myth seven – creativity is complexity

Instruction: Take a pen and a piece of paper or a journal

- Choose a creative project or idea that you consider to be complex.

- Write down all the elements, features, and aspects that contribute to its complexity.

- Take a step back and identify the core message or essence of your project or idea.

- Now, imagine simplifying your project or idea by removing non-essential elements and focusing on the core message.

a) How does the simplified version of your project or idea resonate with your intended audience? Does it still capture the essence of your original concept?

_______________________________________________

_______________________________________________

_______________________________________________


## Myth Eight: Craftiness is creativity

This is where some people miss the true essence of creativity. There is a very thin line that demarcates creativity from craftiness, and it is extremely easy to cross that line without knowing. Many people set out on their journey to greatness with a good degree of inventiveness, perspicacity, originality, and pure genius. However, some let greed and avarice corrupt their brilliance, and before long, they slide from being genuinely creative to becoming crafty. One thing I have noticed from close observation and the study of both successes and failures in my day is the tendency to become crafty, dubious, and devious if not checked. That is why I have decided to mention this here, to either inform, remind, or prepare you against such tendencies.

> *Now the serpent was **more crafty** than any of the wild animals the Lord God had made. He said to the woman, "Did God really say, 'You must not eat from any tree in the garden'?"*

> *Gen 3:1 NIV*

Even the Bible recognizes that craftiness and cunningness, in the negative sense of the word, are corrupted forms of creativity. The term "crafty" in the verse above comes from the Hebrew word "arum," which means to be shrewd, sly, cunning, and crafty. To be crafty means to be deceitful in a way that leads someone into error. It represents the duplicity and double-dealing nature of a trickster who takes advantage of unsuspecting victims for selfish gain or to bring them to a disadvantage without their knowledge.

It would interest you to know that the serpent being referred to in the above verse was also known as Lucifer. He was described as an excellent angel, full of wisdom, and a very creative musician until he corrupted his wisdom and let greed and pride get the better of him. As a matter of fact, the reason Lucifer lost his exalted place in Eden was because he corrupted his nature and became crafty. Imagine that God Himself described him as "perfect in beauty" and gave him an exalted position, but Lucifer turned the wisdom he possessed into craftiness. The verse below will give you a better picture:

> *You were the **seal of perfection, full of wisdom and perfect in beauty**. You were in Eden, the garden of God; every precious stone was your covering... The workmanship of your timbrels and pipes was prepared*

*for you on the day you were created. You were the anointed cherub who covers; I established you; You were on the holy mountain of God; You walked back and forth in the midst of fiery stones. You were perfect in your ways from the day you were created, till iniquity was found in you.* **By the abundance of your trading, you became filled with violence** *within, and you sinned; therefore I cast you as a profane thing out of the mountain of God; And I destroyed you, O covering cherub, from the midst of the fiery stones. Your heart was lifted up because of your beauty;* **you corrupted your wisdom for the sake of your splendor**; *I cast you to the ground, I laid you before kings, that they might gaze at you. You defiled your sanctuaries by the multitude of your iniquities,* **by the iniquity of your trading**; *therefore I brought fire from your midst; It devoured you, and I turned you to ashes upon the earth in the sight of all who saw you.*

*Eze 28:13-18 NKJV*

Imagine the greatness Lucifer possessed before he corrupted his creative wisdom and became foolishly crafty. What more could he have desired? Was it truly worth risking the splendor he already possessed? This serves as an explanation for why crafty individuals cannot provide sensible reasons for their unscrupulous wickedness. Crafty people actually possess the potential for exhibiting creativity in its purest form, utilizing their intelligence for good. However, they actively choose to embrace evil with their creative gift. The reason for this is that their creativity has been corrupted. Their very nature has been infected like a virus, rendering them incapable of doing any good for those they encounter, unless they purge themselves of their evil intentions and motives.

> *But He **perceived their craftiness**, and said to them, why do you test Me?*

> *Luke 20:23 NKJV*

The word 'craftiness' in the above verse is from the Greek word 'panourgia.' According to Thayer's definition, it means 'a specious or false wisdom.'[10] While in Strong's Greek lexicon, the same Greek word is said to mean 'trickery or sophistry.'[9] All these words describe craftiness as something founded on deceit and must not be mistaken for smartness or creativity. Creativity is pure, but like every good thing God created, it can be corrupted. History is littered with stories of great men and women from both ancient and contemporary times who, through pure genius and creativity, became known for their significant contributions to the world. However, just when fame and stardom embraced them, they became devious and succumbed to the subtle cravings of their own greed. They were found to have taken advantage of people who held them in a place of honor due to their astute display of creativity when they first emerged. I have witnessed individuals who, due to their creative endeavors, became overwhelmed with power, leading them astray. Whether through an invention, a groundbreaking discovery, or significant progress, the newfound fame stemming from their creativity became a driving force with potentially negative consequences.

> *That we should no longer be children, **tossed to and fro** and carried about with every wind of doctrine, by the **trickery of men**, in the **cunning craftiness of deceitful plotting**,*

> *Eph 4:14 NKJV*

Some corporate scandals that have rocked a couple of big firms across diverse industries and geographies are attributable to having crossed the fine line between being creative and crafty. Most times, at the bidding of the policy makers and power brokers in such enterprises, either to make more revenue or to outrank their competitors, a lot of shady and crafty things are done. In the year 2015, Volkswagen, a renowned automobile manufacturer, was involved in a scandal where they installed software in their diesel vehicles to cheat emissions tests. This deceptive practice allowed the company to meet regulatory standards while exceeding pollution limits in real-world driving conditions.[11] Indeed, it may seem tempting to exploit or deceive others when we find ourselves in advantageous positions. It's worth acknowledging that even the most virtuous among us may harbor such tendencies and proclivities. That's precisely why I aim to help you distinguish between the creative and the crafty. By providing this understanding, my goal is to empower you as you embark on your own adventurous and impactful journey towards an accelerated future filled with creativity.

> He **frustrates the devices of the crafty**, *so that their hands cannot carry out their plans.*
>
> *Job 5:12 NKJV*

This verse serves as a reminder that there is a higher power that can thwart the intentions of the crafty, ensuring that their plans do not come to fruition. Never believe that craftiness pays. Despite the allure of momentary gain and fleeting pleasure that may accompany sophistry, it ultimately leads to frustration and disappointment. **The short-term benefits of deceit and manipulation pale in comparison to the lasting fulfillment that comes from embracing the purest form of creativity**. Always remind yourself of the creative potential that God has instilled within you. Success can be achieved by harnessing your innate creativity and using it with integrity and authenticity. Understand that your creative endeavors, rooted in truth and guided by moral principles, have the power to bring about meaningful and enduring outcomes.

In a world where craftiness may appear advantageous, stay steadfast in your commitment to use the creativity bestowed upon you honorably. Reject the allure of manipulative tactics, and instead embrace the path of genuine creativity. With this mindset, you can navigate your journey with confidence, knowing that your actions are aligned with your values and guided by the transformative power of true creativity.

## FLIP THE SWITCH EXERCISE  #8

Myth Eight: Craftiness is creativity.

1. Reflect on your current understanding of craftiness and creativity. What preconceived notions or beliefs did you have about the relationship between the two?

___________________________________________

___________________________________________

___________________________________________

2. What ways can you expand your creative horizons, explore new ideas, and push beyond the boundaries of craftiness?

___________________________________________

___________________________________________

___________________________________________

## Myth Nine: Creativity involves big thinking with no doing

When I discovered that creativity was a subject I was passionate about, I did a lot of research on the topic but was disappointed to find out that there was not enough insight out there. Most articles I came across online could not do justice to the definition of creativity. They seemed unable to distinguish between creativity and big thinking. That's why, in all my interactions, be it speaking engagements or day-to-day conversations with friends, family, and people in general, I always make sure to differentiate between having great ideas and being creative. Having bright ideas is fantastic, but it does not amount to creativity. Creativity is an action word. You can think passively, but you cannot create passively. You must take a step, act, and make that change you have always imagined in your mind to truly be creative. I've heard people say, "If I had more money, I would be creative." As nice and sincere as that sounds, the reality is that if you were truly creative, you would find ways to generate more money. Creativity is the propelling force that helps you overcome the very obstacles that try to bring you down. When you point your index finger, blaming external factors for your downfall or failure, remember that the other fingers are pointing right back at you for not finding creative solutions to those same blockers.

## FLIP THE SWITCH EXERCISE   #9

Myth Nine: Creativity involves big thinking with no doing.

a) Do you find yourself getting caught up in grand ideas without following through with concrete actions? What are the underlying reasons or challenges that may contribute to this pattern.

___________________________________

___________________________________

___________________________________

b) Choose one specific big idea or project that you have been contemplating but have yet to take significant action on. Write it down and describe the desired outcome or goal associated with this idea.

___________________________________

___________________________________

___________________________________

c) Break down the big idea into smaller, actionable steps. Create a list of practical actions or tasks that you will take to move closer to the realization of your idea. Be specific and consider realistic timelines for each step.

___________________________________

___________________________________

___________________________________

d) Evaluate any potential obstacles or barriers that may hinder progress in executing your big idea. Identify strategies or solutions to overcome these challenges and ensure forward momentum.

___________________________________

___________________________________

___________________________________

e) Why is this idea important to you and what drives your desire to see it come to fruition. Clarify your personal purpose and connection to the idea.

_________________________________________

_________________________________________

_________________________________________

## Myth Ten: Certification brings creativity

Another prevalent myth in the realm of creativity is the belief that certifications automatically bring creativity. Many individuals erroneously assume that obtaining certifications or formal qualifications will make them more creative in their chosen field. However, this notion overlooks an important aspect of creativity: the ability to create unique experiences and ideas based on the knowledge and skills you already have. Let me be clear: **"educational certification does not equate to creativity."** No doubt, formal education has made notable contributions to modernization and civilization. However, many people have put limits on their creativity, placing too much value on the certificates and titles that come with graduating from an educational institution. If you are a good student of history, you would notice that most of the greatest men of both ancient and contemporary times were individuals who made a difference by cultivating creative ways to educate themselves, with or without going through a formal educational system. You see, there are many people brimming and burning with creative potential who never manifest their creativity. They have refused to venture into the journey of personal discovery that awaits them because they are waiting to get certified, finish multiple courses, or get chartered. There is nothing wrong with acquiring these accolades in your field of interest. However, in their absence, if you become afraid to take a chance on your creativity because you think people would not give you an opportunity, then you are missing the point. Hear this: **If you do not believe in yourself now that you are not certified, you would not believe in yourself when you get certified**. If you cannot create your own unique experience based on the knowledge you already have in your chosen field because you lack confidence, you will still struggle with confidence even after obtaining certification. This phenomenon is commonly referred to as "imposter syndrome." Imposter syndrome is characterized by a persistent feeling of inadequacy and the fear of being exposed as a fraud, despite evidence of one's competence and achievements. It can affect even the most accomplished individuals, causing them to doubt their abilities and hold back from fully embracing their creativity. Therefore, I believe that if you don't feel confident in your creative abilities and unique perspective before obtaining certification, the certification alone is unlikely to magically boost your confidence or unlock your creative potential. Improving self-esteem is crucial in this regard, and it can be achieved with or without formal education or prestigious degrees. Creativity comes from within, derived from personal experiences, insights, and the way you connect and interpret information. While certifications can provide valuable knowledge and technical skills, they do not guarantee the emergence of innovative ideas or a creative mindset.

It is a different matter when you belong to a regulated profession. Many professions require specific regulated knowledge before obtaining a license to practice. However, even in such cases, if you do not incorporate creativity into your formal training and education, you may remain average, fail to make a difference in your field, or end up as a licensed failure. Therefore, it's essential to understand that being certified, chartered, or licensed does not guarantee creativity. Creativity is what unleashes your potential, enables you to stand out in your learned skill, and makes a significant impact. Consider the birds of the air; they do not need licenses, certifications, or charters to fly. Take the eagle, for example, the young eagle learns through observation, watching its mother fly in and out from the comfort of the nest. The mother eagle then subtly encourages or teaches her young to fly by making the nest uncomfortable and pushing them out. Often, what we need is that push, not another fancy degree! Otherwise, we will keep learning and gaining new knowledge without acting on any ideas and opportunities that come our way. The eaglets may fall in the process, they might even crash land or lose their balance, but the mother eagle picks them up, and they repeat the process until the eaglet grasps the fundamentals of flying like an eagle and using the storms to soar even higher. Once it clicks, the young eagle unlocks the flying potential within its being with the help of the mother eagle. It's truly amazing!

Even though academic intelligence and creativity are related, they are not the same thing. While intelligence dwells on convergent thinking - finding the one solution to a problem, creativity is deeply entrenched in divergent thinking - generating multiple possible solutions to a problem. **"Having a certificate and receiving recognition for completing an educational program does not necessarily demonstrate creativity, nor does it serve as proof of your problem-solving abilities."** Shocking as it may sound, it is an undeniable truth! In the 21st century and beyond, many recruiters and employers no longer base their hiring decisions solely on certificates. They have come to realize that creativity and problem-solving skills are often lacking in many applicants. Sometimes, even when individuals possess all the required certifications for a position, they may not be the right fit. Regrettably, it's disheartening to discover that most educational institutions, as of the time of this writing, do not prioritize teaching students how to be creative or how to unleash their inherent creativity. Even more surprising, they fail to teach them how to think critically. Isn't it amazing? It's no wonder why numerous people attend universities, graduate, and find themselves deep in debt with no job prospects. This phenomenon is not limited to underdeveloped economies. While the ratio may be relatively higher in such regions compared to more developed ones, this trend transcends geographical boundaries and affects people worldwide. How can individuals possess all that knowledge from school and still end up financially strained? Most broke and unemployed graduates have never even considered this question. Sadly, many of them never learned how to think effectively in the first place.

Bob Proctor, the founder of Proctor Gallagher Institute, once said, "A lot of times, we confuse mental activity with thinking," and I wholeheartedly agree with him. Some people return to school because they believe they need certificates to demonstrate their capacity and skills, but that couldn't be further from the truth. For the record, I have no bias against pursuing education or further research. However, if pursued without incorporating creativity, one could attend school endlessly, earn numerous degrees, and still end up broke, frustrated, unfulfilled, and lacking inventiveness. Education without creativity renders a person helpless, with the knowledge they cannot utilize or convert into tangible currency.

Five years before I published this book titled 'Ignite Your Creativity,' something significant happened - particularly when I conceived the vision for this book in your hands. I had already begun to read and research extensively on the subject of creativity and problem-solving to support the growth of this brainchild in the womb of my mind. I realized that, apart from being a published author of about 16 books and possessing authoritative insight into the subject of creativity through extensive research, one of the best ways to convince people that I could teach them creativity was to acquire another skill that demanded a high degree of creativity. My intention was not merely to impart principles that I had not put into action for myself or explored in my daily experiences. I wanted to "walk the talk" so that I could better relate to the average person who aspires to understand and become more creative. Thus, I ventured into not only writing books for the human mind but also composing 'books' and 'scripts' for computers to read in the form of code. Yes! That's when I started writing computer software programs.

However, during my transition into this field, I almost fell victim to the same trap I experienced as a software engineer trying to get my foot in the door. I enrolled in courses and classes but never felt fully prepared. Not because I wasn't competent enough, but because I was focusing on the wrong things. I prioritized earning certifications over learning to create and build real-world projects using my knowledge. It was then that a friend of mine, who had learned to code independently, advised me against chasing certifications. Despite holding a bachelor's and post-graduate degree in Computer Engineering, he ended up mastering computer programming by seeking answers on the web. He pointed out that the school program made computer engineering needlessly complicated, emphasizing unnecessary theory to pass exams and earn degrees while neglecting hands-on skills essential for solving real-world problems. His advice was candid and assertive when he shared this with me. He said, 'Dafe, focus on building projects and don't waste your money on certifications.' I found that difficult to understand because, like every self-taught engineer, I had the imposter syndrome that kept telling me I did not have a degree or at least a certification, hence could not be a great developer. After heeding my friend's advice, I discovered for myself the importance of adding creativity to learning. I followed his counsel and went on to work as a professional software engineer in different great firms. This gave me the opportunity to network with some of the smartest minds from different countries around the world while surfing the web for answers and deploying my creativity and problem-solving skills. Ninety percent of the recruiters or hirers I interviewed with in the various tech roles I landed did not care much about my paper certifications. All they wanted to know was what I had built or created with my creativity and experience, and how I could add value to their firm. So, if you have the time, resources, and opportunity, go for formal education but infuse some creativity into your educational pursuit. On the flip side, in the absence of time and resources to go back to school, **focus**

**on being resourceful by harnessing your creativity because, at the end of the day, manifesting your creativity trumps acquiring certificates**. If you have not had the chance to attend school, take advantage of the internet and pursue self-education in professions that are not rigid with formal regulations and licensing. Investigate non-certification-based resources, such as workshops, online courses, mentorship programs, collaborative projects, and self-guided learning opportunities. Embrace diverse sources of inspiration and knowledge to broaden your creative horizons.

Alternatively, if you genuinely want to pursue a regulated profession and have the chance, go to school, but do so smartly, like a creative individual!


## FLIP THE SWITCH EXERCISE #10

Myth Ten: Certification brings creativity

1.  What role have certifications played in your creative pursuits so far in your journey?

    _______________________________________________

    _______________________________________________

    _______________________________________________

2.  If you are currently in a traditional degree or certificate program or you plan to start one in the foreseeable future, how do you plan to inject creativity into your formal education?

    _______________________________________________

    _______________________________________________

    _______________________________________________

3. What gifts, talents, skills, and potential do you currently possess and did not learn from a formal institution?

_______________________________________________

_______________________________________________

_______________________________________________

4. What alternative pathways have you considered to nurture and enhance your creativity apart from the traditional path of earning or acquiring certificates?

_______________________________________________

_______________________________________________

_______________________________________________

5. Are there specific certifications or degrees that align with your goals, career aspirations, and personal growth? Consider whether they offer practical skills, industry recognition, or access to networks and opportunities that complement your creative journey. List them.

_______________________________________________

_______________________________________________

_______________________________________________

Remember, the goal of this exercise is to challenge the myth that certification is the sole or primary source of creativity. Embrace a broader understanding of creativity and the multitude of pathways that can lead to creative expression and innovation. Emphasize self-discovery, personal growth, and a passion-driven approach to nurture and unleash your creative potential.

## Myth Eleven: Creativity is exclusive to certain special people

Creativity is not limited to a select group of individuals or specific professions. It is a trait that exists within all of us, and everyone has the potential to tap into their creative abilities. When God created mankind, He deposited the creative seed within all humans and programmed them to be fruitful. Throughout history and across cultures, humans have demonstrated a capacity for creative expression. This universality suggests that creativity is a fundamental aspect of human nature, accessible to all. It is also important to understand that creativity is not limited to extraordinary acts or grand endeavors. It manifests in everyday life through problem-solving, innovative thinking, and finding novel approaches to challenges. From cooking a new recipe to devising a unique solution at work, people engage in creative acts regularly, showcasing that creativity is a part of ordinary human experiences.

> *For we are God's handiwork, created in Christ Jesus to do good works, which God prepared in advance for us to do.*
>
> *Eph 2:10 (NIV)*

The above verse reminds us that each person is uniquely created by God with creative intent, value, and purpose. It affirms that we are God's handiwork, designed with creative potential to accomplish good works that He has specifically prepared for us. It reinforces the notion that creativity is not limited to a select few but is a divine gift bestowed upon every individual. It encourages us to embrace our creativity, explore our unique talents, and engage in meaningful endeavors that contribute to the betterment of the world.

Les Brown, a famous American speaker, said something profound: 'You were created by the Creator to create.' In other words, every single human out of over 8 billion unique individuals on the planet today was created by the Creator to create. Yes! No wonder the very first attribute God displayed when He introduced Himself to the universe was creativity. The very first verse of the first chapter of the first book of the Bible records that in the beginning, God displayed creativity! In fact, that means He introduced Himself as the Creator before revealing Himself to us as the Savior. Why? Because God is the epitome of creativity in every sense of the word. He displayed it in the way He carefully brought the entire creation into being. God did the first phase of creation and then brought mankind into the picture to continue from where He stopped. This means that every human being can be creative. You have the unfettered capacity to create and recreate. No wonder when God created man, the first thing He said to us was, 'Be fruitful'! How instructive. So, there was no question as to whether mankind is 'seed full.' All God wanted from us was to allow the seed of ideas, gifts, and talents He buried in each one of us to gain tangible expression, flourish, and produce fruit. So, you see, the problem is never with ideas. If you think you lack the ideas for productivity and creativity to manifest through you, then think again, because it is already in you to be creative. **God has created each one of us with the versatility and the flexibility to create a new reality every time we face an obstacle.**

Before becoming one of the most successful authors of all time with the "Harry Potter" series, J.K. Rowling was a struggling single mother living on welfare. It was during a delayed train journey that the idea for Harry Potter and his magical world came to her. Rowling's creative spark emerged during a difficult phase of her life, showcasing that creativity can flourish even in challenging circumstances7. I find this interesting because I grew up thinking that the great inventors and creators of our times were "special" or belonged to an esoteric class. However, as I delved into their life stories and explored historical accounts, I came to a profound realization. These renowned figures were, in fact, ordinary men who became creators because they accessed their hidden reservoirs of extraordinary potential. Most of them were nobody before they manifested their creative genius through deliberate and consistent practice. Some deliberately sought this wellspring of creativity through persistent longing and intentional efforts, while others stumbled upon it by sheer chance or circumstance. Either way, they earned their spot in the halls of fame by turning their ideas into tangible and valuable creations. Their lasting impact, marked by their significant contributions, serve as a testament to the power of their creative endeavors. However, it is important to recognize that their achievements were not a result of being inherently superior to you or anyone else. The key factor that set them apart was their ability to ignite their creativity and unleash their imaginative potential. By harnessing their creative spark, they were able to leave indelible footprints on the sands of time.

## FLIP THE SWITCH EXERCISE #11

Myth Eleven: Creativity is exclusive to certain special people

a) Do you have any personal experiences or societal influences that have shaped this myth and contributed to your perspective? Outline them here.

________________________________________________

________________________________________________

________________________________________________

________________________________________________

________________________________________________

________________________________________________

b) Identify and list below any self-imposed barriers or beliefs that may be hindering your creative expression.

_______________________________________________

_______________________________________________

_______________________________________________

_______________________________________________

_______________________________________________

c) Engage in a self-assessment exercise to recognize and appreciate your own creative strengths and talents. Identify the unique ways in which you express creativity, whether it's through writing, visual arts, music, cooking, problem-solving, or any other form of creative expression.

_______________________________________________

_______________________________________________

_______________________________________________

_______________________________________________

_______________________________________________

d) Dedicate regular time to engage in creative activities that resonate with you and give yourself permission to experiment and make mistakes along the way. List the actions you plan to take to achieve this.

_______________________________________________

_______________________________________________

_______________________________________________

_______________________________________________

_______________________________________________

## SAY THESE WORDS

My creative potential is not limited by any lack; I find innovative solutions in any situation. Creativity flows through me, and I nurture it with practice, exploration, and growth.

I believe in the notion that creativity is not only reserved for a chosen few; it is within me to express. My creative expression is not defined by my physical abilities but by the depth of my imagination. My creative well is always flowing, ready to be tapped into whenever I choose.

External validation is not a requirement for my creative fulfillment and joy. I create for myself, finding fulfillment in the act of creation rather than seeking external approval.

I break down complex ideas into manageable steps, unlocking my creativity along the way. I refuse to be crafty and fraudulent; my creativity will not be corrupted by greed and avarice. I combine big thinking with purposeful action to bring my creative ideas to life.

I recognize that certifications do not define or limit my creative abilities. I believe that creativity is not reserved for an exclusive reserve of people; it is a God-given power that is now working within me.

I arise, I shine because the light has come, my creativity is ignited, and I am ready to impact my world with my refined gifts, processed skills, and divine talent. Thank you, Lord!

# CREATIVITY WORKSHEET #1

**Instructions:**

Use this worksheet to challenge common creativity myths and release your creative potential. Grab a pen and a personal journal or notepad.

a)  Myth Reflection:

Take a moment to reflect on each of the following creativity myths and consider how they have influenced your perspective on creativity. Tick beside whichever one has influenced you the most.

- Myth 1: Creativity cannot thrive in lack.
- Myth 2: Creativity is limited to inborn gifts or talent.
- Myth 3: Creativity is limited by physical disability.
- Myth 4: Creativity only comes via spontaneous inspiration.
- Myth 5: Creativity guarantees perfection or instant success.
- Myth 6: Creativity needs external validation to thrive.
- Myth 7: Creativity is complexity.
- Myth 8: Craftiness is creativity.
- Myth 9: Creativity involves big thinking with no doing.
- Myth 10: Certification brings creativity.
- Myth 11: Creativity is exclusive to certain special people.

b)  Mindset Shift:

Choose three myths that resonate with you the most and complete the following exercises to shift your mindset and release your creativity.

a)  Myth _______________________________________________

Exercise: Reflect on a time when you felt limited by this myth. How did it affect your creative pursuits? How can you challenge this myth and redefine what is possible for yourself? Write your answers on your personal notepad.

b) Myth ________________________________________

Exercise: Explore examples of individuals who have defied this myth and achieved remarkable creative success. What can you learn from their stories? How can you apply their mindset to your own creative journey? Write your answers on your personal notepad.

c) Myth ________________________________________

Exercise: Identify a personal belief or assumption that aligns with this myth. How has it held you back from fully expressing your creativity? What steps can you take to break free from this limiting belief? Write your answers on your personal notepad.

3. Creative Exploration:

Choose one myth that has held you back the most and complete the following exercise to explore new possibilities and expand your creative expression.

a) Myth ________________________________________

Exercise: Engage in a creative activity or project that challenges this myth head-on. Push yourself to experiment, take risks, and embrace the process without seeking external validation or approval.

Remember, this worksheet is designed to help you challenge and overcome creativity myths, empowering you to embrace your creative potential fully. By shifting your mindset and taking intentional steps, you can ignite your creativity and tap into the endless possibilities that await you.

# CHAPTER TWO

# WHAT IS CREATIVITY?

It was a blazing hot summer day by a beautiful lake on the south side of Calgary, Canada. The sun's rays turned the water into a sparkling mirror, while laughter and friendly conversations filled the air. The aroma of sizzling barbecues permeated the surroundings, making our stomachs growl in anticipation. A gentle breeze brushed against our skin, carrying the melodic sounds of birds chirping. As I stood on the sandy beach, my heart raced with a mix of excitement and curiosity. This team-building event was organized by the big shots of a US-based Fortune 100 company where I worked at the time, presenting immense networking possibilities. The presence of directors, the big bosses, wearing shorts and mingling eagerly with everyone, made the atmosphere buzz with energy. It was a chance to connect and learn from key people within the firm. Among the crowd, I couldn't help but notice my new director, a figure of authority and accomplishment in the industry. Our paths finally crossed as he approached me, accompanied by some colleagues. At that moment, my curiosity began to unwind, eager to make the most of this networking opportunity. I started asking him some insightful questions that triggered interesting responses. Thus, we delved into a conversation that felt like a gateway to new insights and ideas. In that moment, the lake faded into the background as our discussion took center stage. As our conversation continued, we got to know each other better, and we both spoke about our visions and career aspirations. The next question I asked him sparked a fresh inspiration. I inquired, "What were you looking for when you handpicked me from a different team division to help with one of your critical projects?" His answer struck a chord within me. He said, "I was not looking for or targeting a specific person; I was searching for someone with a particular attitude, and your name came up." He then went on to say, "You can teach anybody technical skills, but there are some skills you just cannot teach, and that is what I was looking for." I immediately understood what he meant.

## Soft skills vs. Hard skills

You see, hard skills and soft skills are two distinct types of abilities that individuals possess. Hard skills refer to specific, measurable capabilities, such as using Microsoft Excel or writing code in C-sharp. These skills are relatively easy to acquire or teach because they are job-specific and easily quantifiable. On the other hand, soft skills are more abstract and require more expertise to teach compared to hard skills. Creativity is a soft skill, and it is essential to remember that teaching a hard skill is generally easier than teaching a soft skill. Some even believe that a soft skill like creativity can only be caught through inspiration, making it impossible to teach. However, I believe that creativity can be both taught in a structured manner and caught through impartation or inspiration. Despite its abstract nature making it difficult to impart, I firmly believe that anyone can become more creative, including you. So, even though soft skills are harder to teach compared to hard skills, I have designed this chapter to help you develop increased creative capabilities. Let's begin by understanding what creativity is.

This is a question I sought answers to years ago, and I couldn't find any authoritative insight into it. Therefore, in this chapter, I have presented some of the most complete and life-transforming definitions of creativity. I believe that grasping these definitions of creativity is fundamental to catching the spirit of creativity and learning beyond the surface. By understanding and applying these different definitions, you should expect to experience a significant improvement in your creativity. So, what is creativity?

## 1. **Ability to Create:**

As the word implies, creativity is the ability to create. When most people hear the word 'creativity,' the first thing that comes to mind is being able to think of great ideas. While that is a good quality and a necessary part of the creative process, it does not completely portray the true meaning of creativity. Everyone has ideas, whether good or not-so-good ones, but not everyone can transform those ideas into tangible creations. That's the gap that needs to be filled. The cycle of creativity is not complete until you transform your ideas, skills, and talents into creative solutions. Just as a pregnant woman must deliver her baby for the cycle of procreation to be fulfilled, the creative process requires more than just conceiving ideas. It is the act of transforming those ideas into reality that truly defines creativity.

Consider this analogy: If a woman conceives multiple pregnancies but none of them come to term for whatever reason, her family may remain childless unless they adopt a child. Similarly, many individuals harbor brilliant ideas worth billions, yet if they remain unexecuted and buried away, they will not reap the benefits of their creativity. To be truly creative, it is essential to give birth to the ideas you carry within you. You must nurture them, develop them, and bring them to life so that the world can witness their impact and benefit from their existence. Creativity thrives when your ideas are translated into action, making a tangible difference in your life and the lives of others. So, do not merely conceive remarkable ideas; commit to bringing them to fruition. Just as a mother experiences the joy of holding her newborn child, you can experience the fulfillment of creativity when you deliver your ideas and brainchildren for the world to see and benefit from. Let's also look at this from a biblical perspective. God's definition of creativity has been the most absolute and definitive reference. No material makes a successful attempt to explain the origin and source of creativity without recourse to scripture, because God is the source of creativity. That is why I would like to show you some important references that will help solidify the concepts below.

> *God spoke to Moses: "See what I've done; I've personally chosen Bezalel son of Uri, son of Hur of the tribe of Judah. I've filled him with the Spirit of God, giving him skill and know-how and expertise in every kind of craft to create designs and work in gold, silver, and bronze; to cut and set gemstones; to carve wood — he's an all-around craftsman. "Not only that, but I've given him Oholiab, son of Ahisamach of the tribe of Dan, to work with him. And to all who have an aptitude for crafts I've given the skills to make all the things I've commanded you:*

> *Exodus 31:1-6 MSG*

Please read the above verse again and take note of the letters in bold text. If you have read it a second time, you can agree with me that it was really powerful. Did you know that the first time God filled men with the Spirit of God, it was for creativity, and this happened in the old dispensation, even before the era of speaking in tongues? By virtue of what God said to Moses in the scripture above, it is safe to say that creativity is the ability to create useful designs, art, craft, products, and services of any kind through unique combination of skill, know-how, and expertise.

It may shock you to know that the first time a reference was made to someone being filled of the Spirit of God in the Bible, it was not for them to speak in tongues but for them to be creative. The scripture above in Exodus 31:1-6 where God Himself said He had filled a man named Bezaleel with the Spirit of God, represents the first place in Bible where it is recorded that someone was filled of the Spirit of God. This is very profound because we have many Christians who are filled with the Spirit of God but do not know the immense creativity which that confers on them. They only speak in tongues as a sign of being filled and that is really where it ends. I have nothing against speaking in tongues as that is something I enjoy in my own relationship with God. Nonetheless, I find it concerning that most believers were never taught how the fullness of God's Spirit in them can translate to being creative. The above verse also describes how God gave wisdom, understanding, and knowledge to the craftsman Bezalel, allowing him to create beautiful and intricate works of art. It suggests that wisdom can enhance a person's ability to create and innovate. That means that creativity is a product of wisdom, understanding and knowledge in the right combination. Based on this understanding, it is safe to say that the spirit of creativity comes from God and He endows us with the ability to create. Right now, receive a divine impartation and inspiration to create designs with your gifts, talents, skills and craft in Jesus' name!

> **SAY THESE WORDS**
>
> I believe that creativity is a divine gift bestowed upon me by God. I am confident that as I deploy my gifts, skills, and talents, I receive supply from God's unending wells of inspiration. I receive daily loads of innovative ideas that flow from the divine source, and I put it to work by the power of the Spirit of God at work in me. I embrace my role as a vessel of creativity, ready to unleash my unique gifts, talent, skills, and abilities to create and make a positive impact in the world.

## FLIP THE SWITCH EXERCISE #12

- Creativity as the ability to create

Instructions: Take a pen and a notepad

1. Select one of the ideas from your idea bank that you find particularly inspiring.
2. Break down the idea into smaller actionable steps or milestones that can lead to its realization. Consider what would be required to turn the idea into a tangible creation.
3. Identify the first three practical steps you can take to start bringing your idea to life. These could include conducting research, sketching a design, creating a prototype, or exploring available resources.
4. Write down these three steps and commit to completing them within a specific timeframe. Set realistic goals that allow you to make progress while fitting into your schedule.
5. Begin working on the first step immediately after completing this exercise. Take action and immerse yourself in the process of creating.

Through this exercise, you will experience the transformation of your idea into a tangible creation. By taking deliberate steps and committing to the creative process, you will bridge the gap between imagination and realization. Remember that the journey of creation involves not only the initial idea but also the iterative process of refining and shaping your creation.

## 2. Ability to solve problems:

Creativity, in its simplest and purest form, is about providing solutions to the problems in your surroundings. Remember, the first act of creativity ever recorded on Earth was performed by God Himself when He created the heavens and the earth. The Bible records that the earth was in a chaotic mess, and God brought order into the universe by engaging His creative prowess. Everything was a mess; the whole earth was submerged with water, and darkness was upon the face of the deep. That was when God began to display creativity. Therefore, creativity is all about problem-solving, and problem-solving is all about creativity. This is why I always make the effort to emphasize that creativity does not stop at having great ideas whenever I get the chance. Your creativity is yet to manifest until your ideas have been implemented to solve a problem successfully. No wonder, when God created the first man, the first ability He tried to test was not his obedience but his problem-solving and creativity skills. That shows you how important it is to God that you function as a problem-solver and a creator. The reason creativity exists in the first place is to solve problems. In fact, creativity brings about problem-solving through the resourceful use of the ideas, skills, and talents you possess. Problem-solving provides the avenue and platform for you to bring your ideas to fruition. Creative ideas get translated into practical and innovative solutions for problems to be solved. If you have ideas, skills, and talents, you must be able to map them to specific problems that represent a pain point you want to address. Through creativity, you can then develop and build solutions for those specific problems with your ideas, skills, and potential. Problem-solving fuels creativity by serving as a catalyst for innovation. It presents opportunities to challenge assumptions and bridge gaps between existing knowledge and desired outcomes.

From the beginning, when God made man, His delight was to see man display creativity just as He would. When the first man, Adam, was created, God gave him the opportunity to display this attribute in several ways, and interestingly, Adam did not disappoint. The original default setting of man was to see a problem and find a solution, not run away from the problem or say, "God will do it." As a matter of fact, when God created the first man, He gave him three tests. Out of those three tests, one was a test of man's problem-solving ability, and Adam passed it. The other was a test of man's creativity, and he passed it, while the third one, which he failed, was a test of his obedience.

In the first test to check man's problem-solving ability, God gave man work and asked him to dress and keep the garden. In other words, to deal with the problem of weeds and all other challenges that come with cultivating, tilling, and tending a garden. This test would require man to display problem-solving skills for him to succeed, and as you know, Adam did the job very well. This proves that the original intent of man's existence had problem-solving built into it. The concept of work only exists when there is a problem to be solved. No business or company exists without a problem they are trying to solve for the market they serve. No entrepreneur will be in business if they are not trying to solve a problem. No company hires you for the fun of it. If anyone gives you work or a job, they are effectively asking you to put your problem-solving skills to the test. That is exactly what God did when He gave Adam work – made him engage his inbuilt problem-solving ability.

> *The Lord God took the man and put him in the Garden*
> *of Eden to work it and take care of it.*
>
> *Gen 2:15 NIV*

The second test was to check man's creativity. God gave man the task of coming up with names for all the animals. This is similar to the "find x" kind of problems we encounter in elementary schools. Adam successfully solved the problem by deriving creative and unique names for each animal. You will agree with me that this required a considerable degree of creativity to figure out, especially because Adam had never named animals before, nor had he taken a course on "animal-naming" prior to that moment. He had to study each animal as they were brought to him and come up with names seemingly out of thin air. Then, God examined each name to see if they were appropriately given to each animal. As you know, Adam did not disappoint because God had already deposited that capacity in Adam to be a productive and creative problem-solver.

> *Now the Lord God had formed out of the ground all the beasts of the field and all the birds of the air. He brought them to the man to see what he would name them; and whatever the man called each living creature, that was its name. So, the man gave names to all the livestock, the birds of the air and all the beasts of the field.*

> *Gen 2:19-20 NIV*

The third test was to check Adam's obedience, and since it required him to use his freewill, he did not pass that test. The reason for Adam's disobedience was that he thought he could be as wise, intelligent, discerning, and creative as God (Gen 3:6). He had witnessed God's witty display of creativity and desired to possess the same wisdom as God, not realizing that he had already been created in the image and likeness of God. I won't delve into the details surrounding the third test as that is beyond the scope of this topic. However, it is evident how God had already instilled problem-solving and creativity into man's DNA from the very beginning.

Every competent IT engineer, manufacturer, creator, producer, or developer subjects every product they create to rigorous testing to ensure its proper functionality. As a professional software engineer who has worked in reputable tech companies around the world, I can attest to this practice. After gathering requirements, my software development process usually revolves around testing. I have come to understand the significance of testing in the world of software development, and it helps ensure that the product meets its intended purpose. I can also better comprehend why God decided to put the first man He created through some tests. Just like great companies thoroughly test their products before delivering them to customers, tests allow creatives to identify and address any issues that may arise. Moreover, it enables them to ensure that their solutions, inventions, or products will work exactly as intended. This is essentially what God was doing when He assigned these three initial tasks to man after creation.

**SAY THESE WORDS**

I was created by God to be a problem-solver. At my home, place of work and business I deploy this skill efficiently every day. My creativity empowers me to see beyond limitations and find inventive ways to solve problems. I thrive in problem-solving scenarios, using my creative thinking to unlock effective solutions. My problem-solving abilities complement my creativity, allowing me to navigate challenges with confidence and ingenuity. Glory to God!

## FLIP THE SWITCH EXERCISE #13

- Creativity as the ability to solve problems

Instructions: Think of a current challenge or problem in your life, whether personal or professional, that could benefit from a creative solution. Brainstorm and write down at least three creative approaches or ideas to address the problem. Use a personal notepad if you need more space.

1. Develop an action plan to implement one of the creative solutions you generated. Consider the following:

a) What steps do you need to take to put your creative solution into practice?

_______________________________________________

_______________________________________________

_______________________________________________

b) Are there any obstacles or potential challenges you anticipate, and how will you overcome them?

_______________________________________________

_______________________________________________

_______________________________________________

2. How do you currently perceive problem-solving in relation to creativity?

_______________________________________________

_______________________________________________

_______________________________________________

a) Can you recall a specific problem or challenge that you successfully solved through creative thinking?

_______________________________________________

_______________________________________________

_______________________________________________

b) How did you feel when you were able to apply your creative problem-solving skills to overcome the challenge?

_______________________________________________

_______________________________________________

_______________________________________________

c) What specific skills or qualities do you possess that contribute to your problem-solving abilities?

_______________________________________________

_______________________________________________

_______________________________________________

## 3. Ability to be unique in state and approach

Creativity is the wellspring from which uniqueness flows, giving birth to ideas, perspectives, and creations that are distinctly original and individual to you. Uniqueness is the outcome of nurturing your ideas, talents, gifts, and creative impulses. It results from identifying your individuality and allowing it to shine through in the creative process. Each person possesses a distinct set of skills, talents, perspectives, and life experiences, which become the building blocks of their unique creative expression. Uniqueness in this context refers to the inherent characteristics, experiences, and perspectives that make each person one-of-a-kind. It acknowledges that your individual background, talents, and personality shape the way you perceive the world and approach creative endeavors. By embracing your unique state or identity, you tap into a wellspring of creativity that sets you apart and allows you to offer fresh perspectives and innovative ideas. Stop trying to be like someone else. It is great to learn from others, but refuse to fall victim to copying them mindlessly. When you copy others, you bury your unique state and identity in the process. On the other hand, uniqueness in approach relates to the distinct manner in which you approach and tackle creative tasks. Your unique approach, if allowed to gain expression, infuses your personal style, values, and passions into your creative pursuits.

In today's world, many individuals shy away from living out their originality. They fear embracing their true selves and instead choose to emulate people they admire, seeking to replicate their notable achievements. It's important to remember that even the best photocopy of an original remains just that— a copy, not the authentic or original version. Being unique does not require reinventing the wheel; it simply involves recognizing and leveraging your strengths in a distinct way. For instance, uniqueness in your approach to work can stem from identifying the special attributes you bring to the table that set you apart from others. Once you discover this, it becomes your unique selling point. Cultivating a unique selling point that is not a mere replica of someone else's experience requires creativity.

One trend most creatives follow is trying to replicate someone else's results without preserving the value of their unique style and diversity. This tendency can easily overshadow your unique qualities. It compels them to cloak their gems with the peculiarity of others, denying the world the chance to experience their originality. If you genuinely wish to unlock your creativity to its fullest potential, you must never deny yourself the opportunity to be "you." Embracing your distinctiveness is what sets you apart and makes you exceptional. Attempting to blend in without standing out will prevent others from recognizing and appreciating your true creative potential.

Creativity is the mother of uniqueness and distinction. It generates results that distinguish good from great. Creativity is the one thing that separates originals from counterfeits. You may copy the work of a creative person, but you can never produce results like a creative person would. That is what sets geniuses in a class of their own. They are ingenious, inventive, and resourceful in whatever they produce. Consider this: With over 8 billion people on the planet, no two individuals possess the exact same DNA. Even among identical twins, there exists something that differentiates and distinguishes them. Therefore, understand this truth: No one else will produce your product, write your book, or start your business exactly like you. Why? Because no one else is precisely like you. That is why it is imperative to bring your unique qualities to the forefront with unwavering commitment and authenticity. You were wired uniquely for a specific purpose. So, abandon the pursuit of becoming someone else, for no one else could ever be like you. No matter how hard you try, the best copy of an original remains nothing more than a copy. When I talk about geniuses, what comes to mind? The names of renowned scientists, artists, or great celebrities like Albert Einstein, Ngozi Okonjo-Iweala, Marie Curie, William Shakespeare, Chimamanda Adichie, or Michael Jackson, I guess. These individuals have displayed ingenuity in their own way. As right as it could be for your mind to respond in that manner, it would be totally erroneous not to think of yourself as a genius who has the capacity for such brilliance in your own unique way. There is nothing stopping your name from being mentioned alongside theirs because you are just as unique. These great names that always pop up when we talk about genius men and women are no better than you. The moment you ignite your creativity and begin to express your unique perspectives and approach in everything you do, you will marvel at the results. It is an infallible fact that we are all potential geniuses, a fact even Albert Einstein himself expressed in his writings.

So, have you discovered your unique skills, gifts, and talents? Would you give that genius in you the opportunity to creatively express its uniqueness? Reflect on this as you move forward.

## Idea Thieves

People can steal ideas and intellectual property all they want. The best they can do is milk the potential of that idea for a while if they are crafty enough. Eventually, there would come a point where creativity would be needed for the wells not to dry up. In the absence of such creativity, the wells would dry up. This is what happened to Isaac in the Bible when he dug wells. The people, out of envy, fought over the wells with Isaac's servants. Instead of fighting back, he would simply go and dig another well until the people got tired of striving with him over his wells (Gen 26:19-33). These wells represent the creativity of Isaac. Just as no one could steal the ingenuity of Isaac, the same goes for a creative person. You can steal the product of a person's creativity, but you can only go so far with it. For example, Steve Jobs was removed from Apple, a company he founded and after a while, the company revenue began to tank. Why? They lacked creativity to sustain the vision and brand because they weren't the originators. They probably had fancy business degrees but lacked what Steve Jobs had - creativity for Apple. They had to bring him back and when he came back, he set Apple back on course. You see, you can't fire a man from his creativity!

If you are truly creative, it would not matter if someone stole your ideas or resources because you already possess in you the engine for creating and executing fresh ideas and producing new resources. This is not to say that you should not protect your intellectual properties in every way possible. Far from it! This is only to make you understand that if you are creative, even when your wells run dry or get taken from you forcefully or unjustly, you can dig up another well that would spring forth fresh water. So, it makes no difference that the market is saturated, and your "wells of sales" are running dry. Through creativity, you can dig up a new well, unique to you, and find a new segment of the market that is untapped.

## SAY THESE WORDS

My creativity shines through the unique way I perceive and interpret the world around me. I celebrate my uniqueness and understand that it is the source of my creative power. I confidently explore uncharted territories, knowing that my unique approach can lead to remarkable discoveries. I honor my individuality and refuse to be confined by conventional norms or expectations. I embrace the freedom to think differently and to challenge established ideas with my unique perspective. I am helped by God as I distinguish myself creatively via my gifts, skills, and talents.

## FLIP THE SWITCH EXERCISE #14

- Creativity as the ability to be unique in state and approach

1. What are some defining moments or qualities that make you unique? How can you leverage these attributes in your creative endeavors to bring a fresh perspective?

________________________________________

________________________________________

________________________________________

________________________________________

2. How can you explore new methods or unconventional techniques to add a unique touch to your work or business?

________________________________________

________________________________________

________________________________________

________________________________________

3. How can you incorporate your unique and distinctive qualities into your creative projects?

________________________________________

________________________________________

________________________________________

________________________________________

________________________________________

4. How can you combine your distinct approaches to create something innovative?

________________________________________

________________________________________

________________________________________

________________________________________

________________________________________

## 4. A propelling force:

Creativity operates like a force that pushes you to act on ideas in a way that produces visible and tangible results. When you release the hidden creative gem shut up within you, it thrusts you into action with bursts of enthusiasm like a propellant force. You cannot activate your creativity and yet be docile or passive about the ideas that burn within. In other words, creativity and inactivity are mutually exclusive.

> *You know well enough how the wind blows this way and that. You hear it rustling through the trees, but you have no idea where it comes from or where it's headed next.*
>
> *John 3:8 MSG*

Creativity is a force that nobody sees where it comes from, but when it hits you from within, you immediately see the impact in and around you. You cannot claim to be creative and remain stagnant or static in whatever it is that you do. It is a propelling force that drives innovation and transformation. When creativity is nurtured and channeled effectively, its impact becomes visible and tangible. It is also important to note that the propelling force of creativity can be hindered or diminished through misuse or neglect. Imagine windmills standing tall in an open field with their blades ready to capture the power of the wind. The wind represents the propelling force of creativity that surrounds us. When harnessed properly, the windmills rotate gracefully, converting the wind's energy into useful power. Consider what happens when the windmills are neglected or misused. If the blades are left idle, stagnant, or in disrepair, they no longer capture the full potential of the wind's force. The wind blows right through them, untapped and wasted. Similarly, when we fail to engage our creative abilities or misuse them, it's as if we neglect the "windmills" of our minds. We let the force of creativity go unnoticed or unutilized. The ideas, innovations, and transformations that could have been generated remain dormant. To fully benefit from the force of creativity, you must actively engage and nurture it. You need to keep your creative blades sharp, open yourself to inspiration, and embrace a mindset of exploration and experimentation. Just as windmills require regular maintenance, you must continuously fuel your creative spirit, allowing it to propel you forward.

## What kept them going?

When you see rockets move at incredible speeds as they blast into space, it makes you gape in awe. Rockets have powerful engines that allow the spacecraft to escape the Earth's gravitational pull and fly into space with no restraint. The propulsion mechanism that gives the rocket engine such power and escape velocity is produced via the internal combustion that takes place in its chamber. When the fuel gets mixed with an oxidizer and is ignited in the combustion chamber, hot exhaust gas is generated, and that is used to propel the rocket. Even though this is a rather simplistic illustration of how rockets get propelled from the Earth into space, it speaks volumes of how creativity can propel anyone into higher dimensions of performance when ignited. This further shows that creativity is a propelling force when fired up in you or ignited. Think about some of the greatest inventors who embarked on an exploratory journey to birth an innovation. What do you think kept them going in the face of setbacks? What makes a person who fails the first time keep going until the one thousandth time when they get it right? When you truly ignite your creativity, you will come to understand what kept people like Thomas Edison going. That same force would propel you to heights of undaunted accomplishments that you never knew you could ascend into.

Creativity, when ignited, burns within you in a way that keeps you moving with gusto. It makes you transform your ideas into tangible creations no matter the external forces trying to stop you.

## Talent without the propelling force

There are so many people who lack this force that could push them to reach out for their dreams with gusto. That is why you can hire the best coaches in the world, attend all the greatest seminars, or read all the good books. You could even take all the popular courses in your field, but if none of these can ignite the fire of creativity within, you may end up feeling more demotivated, frustrated, and depressed. This is because you have talent but lack the fire that ignites the passion within you. It is that fire that transforms your raw talent into refined gold. One thing that is common among true creatives is that they have a sense of urgency that thrusts them into definite actions, yielding remarkable results. These individuals are always motivated to get out of bed in the morning or even at odd hours to work on their ideas until they turn them into tangible creations. They weather the storm, withstand the pressures of discouragement, and overcome the inertia forces of disappointments until they watch the fires of their creativity burn and refine their raw ideas into finished products and services.

As you read this book, I see the engines of your creativity jerking and thrusting you unto greatness. You will rise with determination each morning, ready to work on your ideas and bring them to life! An unseen force from within will stimulate the willingness you require to put in extra effort in honing your craft and serving your gift. Even during challenging times, you will excel where others have lost steam without feeling burnt out in Jesus' name! Your dedication and perseverance will be the fuel that drives your creative journey. Take advantage of the resources available to you, whether it's learning from the best coaches, attending seminars, reading books, or engaging in relevant courses. But always remember that the true spark of creativity lies within you. It is your internal fire that will propel you towards remarkable results. So, I charge you to ignite that fire within. Believe in your ideas, trust in your abilities, and take bold steps forward. Embrace the passion and inspiration that comes from the creative force within you. Let it guide you towards tangible creations, turning your dreams into reality. Don't let your talents or your ideas remain dormant and unused. Step into action, seize the opportunities that come your way, and watch as your creativity unfolds its full potential.

## SAY THESE WORDS

I embrace challenges as opportunities for my growth, using them to propel me to new heights. Each day, I tap into my limitless creative potential, propelling myself closer to my goals. I am a catalyst for positive change, using my skills, talents, and creative abilities to propel my life upward and forward only. I am fueled by inspiration and imagination, propelling me to push the boundaries of what is possible. My creativity is an unstoppable force, propelling me past obstacles and towards breakthrough moments day by day. Hallelujah!

## FLIP THE SWITCH EXERCISE #15

Creativity as a propelling force:

1. What do you do to maintain momentum and follow through on transforming your ideas, gifts, and talents to creative solutions?

________________________________________

________________________________________

________________________________________

2. Do you have set goals and a system of accountability to ensure you follow through on your creative ideas? What are they? Use a notepad if more space is needed.

________________________________________

________________________________________

________________________________________

3. How can you learn from setbacks and use them to propel your creativity forward?

________________________________________

________________________________________

________________________________________

## 5. A dynamic change of state:

Creativity, as a dynamic change of state, refers to the ability to adapt and evolve one's skills, gifts, and talents in response to changing times and seasons. It recognizes that creativity is not a fixed or static trait, but a dynamic and ever-evolving process. Just as the world around us undergoes constant change and transformation, creativity too thrives on navigating these shifts. It involves the capacity to observe, learn, and adapt to new circumstances, ideas, and trends. By being attuned to the changing times and seasons, you can harness your creative potential and use it as a tool to navigate and thrive in a dynamic world. Adapting your skills, gifts, and talents to challenging times and seasons requires a willingness to step outside of your comfort zone and take on new challenges. It may involve learning new technologies, acquiring additional knowledge, or exploring different creative avenues. This adaptability enables you to remain fluid, relevant, innovative, and responsive to the evolving needs and demands of your environment. When you ignite your creativity, you initiate a process of dynamic change. This process mutates and transforms your raw talents, gifts, skills, and potential. Just as raw materials are refined into something new; creativity brings about a similar change in your creative abilities. During the creative process, your raw materials, such as ideas, inspirations, and skills, undergo a dynamic change. In their raw state, your ideas may not make sense. You may appear as an impostor when you first get your foot in the door as a professional. The process of refining and transforming your raw gifts, ideas, and skills is what propels you forward, leading to the manifestation of new and impactful outcomes.

Many successful individuals have experienced this dynamic change of state through creativity. Ben Carson, once called a dummy, soon became known as the man with the gifted hand. Jim Kwik, once referred to as the boy with the broken brain, became the celebrity brain coach known for fixing people's brains and optimizing their memory. Myles Munroe, once told he was a monkey and could never learn, later became a transformational speaker and author. When you ignite your creativity, it is as though you get transfigured into another person. Your attitude changes, your yearnings change, the way you see things changes, and limiting beliefs no longer have a grip on you. You just become like a 'rock star'! You captivate your market, inspire people with your refined products, gifts, skills, and achieve remarkable results. From being known as a dummy, you become the star girl or wonder boy. From being referred to as a poor teacher, you become the renowned student mentor. From feeling like an impostor at work, you become the maverick in the room. The word 'dynamic' describes something characterized by continuous activity, movement, or progress. When applied to creativity, it implies that the creative process is not static or fixed, but rather fluid and ever-evolving. Creativity involves exploring different perspectives, adapting to new circumstances, and embracing change to generate innovative outcomes. It will interest you to note that the term 'dynamo' comes from the word 'dynamic.' While the word 'dynamic' originated from the Greek word 'dunamis,' meaning power or strength.

### *Dynamo => Dynamic => Dunamis*

**Where the arrow => represents "is derived from."*

Dynamo is a specific term that refers to a type of electrical generator that converts mechanical energy to electrical energy. Creativity involves the conversion of energy from one state to another, as creators use their energy and resources to bring about meaningful change and give form to their ideas or visions. In a broad sense, creativity can be seen as the process of transforming existing elements, ideas, or resources into something new or different. This process often requires the conversion of various forms of energy, such as mental energy, emotional energy, physical energy, or even the other external forms of energy. Creativity involves taking raw materials, whether they are physical materials, thoughts, emotions, concepts, ideas, skills or potential and recombining them in novel ways. This transformation requires the use of energy. It could be energy dissipated through mental exertion, experimentation, emotional investment, or physical action. By channeling this potential energy, creators can transform ideas, produce artistic works, solve problems, or innovate in various domains. The energy is harnessed and redirected to manifest the desired outcome or creative expression.

> *But ye shall receive power, after that the Holy Ghost is*
> *come upon you: and ye shall be witnesses unto me both*
> *in Jerusalem, and in all Judaea, and in Samaria, and*
> *unto the uttermost part of the earth.*

*Acts 1:8 KJV*

The word "power" in the above verse comes from the Greek word "dunamis." That is the same Greek word we just examined previously in relation to the words "dynamic" and "dynamo." According to Thayer's Greek Lexicon, the word 'dunamis' is described as "inherent power. That is, power residing in a thing by virtue of its nature, or the power which a person or thing exerts and puts forth."[1] It is amazing that the very last words that came out of Jesus' lips before His ascension were to let them know they would receive "dunamis," in other words, inherent ability, creative power, or dynamic ability to effect changes. I recognize that many have only been taught about the Holy Spirit's power in connection with the working of physical miracles. But this also proves that beyond physical miracles, the power of the Spirit can work mind miracles in you. If you can pause for a second and read this section again from the top, it will become clear to you that the Holy Spirit was also given to you to endow you with inherent potential for dynamism and creativity.

## Thoughts are things

According to Aristotle's philosophy, "dunamis" refers to potentiality or the capacity for change and transformation. He also spoke about "dunamis" in connection with another Greek word known as "energeia." This word represents actuality or the realization of that potential[2]. If creativity can be understood as the combination of potential and action, or idea plus execution, it means that "dunamis" is a word that also describes creativity. This is why I believe that creativity is a dynamic ability to effect change. It is that dynamic energy that helps you transform an idea into a tangible solution or profitable creation. This explains why it is said that "thoughts are things." The idea that thoughts are things suggests that thoughts have the potential to manifest in the physical world and can have tangible effects. Everything you see today was once a thought in the mind of somebody. Every creative exploit you will ever do will first be a thought in your mind. Thoughts contain ideas, concepts, and possibilities that have the power to bring about a change that manifests in the physical world. The dynamic energy of creativity enables the transformation of the state of an idea into a tangible solution or creation. It propels the process of taking thoughts, refining them, and bringing them to life through concrete actions and manifestations.

Now is the time to unleash your creative potential and bring about tangible change in the world. Release the dynamic energy within you and let your ideas take flight. Recognize that your thoughts have the power to become real, tangible things. It is not enough to have brilliant ideas; it is the dynamic execution that transforms them into impactful creations. Receive the dynamic power of creativity and let constant change and progress become your allies. Step out of your comfort zone and fearlessly pursue your vision in Jesus' name! Remember, your creative energy has the potential to bring about solutions, innovations, and positive transformations. Seize this moment to make a difference, whether in your personal life, your community, or the world at large.

> **SAY THESE WORDS**
>
> I embrace the dynamic nature of creativity and embrace change as an opportunity for growth. I thrive in a state of constant evolution and transformation, adapting my creative approach as I explore new ideas and possibilities. I am open to change and allow it to fuel my creativity, unlocking new insights and innovative solutions. I embrace the inherent fluidity of creativity, knowing that it thrives in a state of constant change and adaptation. Those who mocked me in my raw state will see the new me and marvel at what I have become since I ignited my creativity!

## FLIP THE SWITCH EXERCISE #16

Creativity as a Dynamic Change of State:

1. How can your skills, gifts, and talents adapt and evolve to meet changing times and seasons?

   _______________________________________________

   _______________________________________________

2. Are there any limiting beliefs or fixed notions that hinder your ability to embrace the dynamic nature of creativity?

   _______________________________________________

   _______________________________________________

## 6. Ability to be divergent:

To be creative is to be divergent, and being divergent means being unpredictably admirable. It entails thinking and acting in a positively different way from the norm. When I think about divergence, it reminds me of the lady who played a significant role in the popular award-winning movie titled "Divergent." In the movie, people were assigned to factions based on their qualities, skills, and abilities. The female protagonist, named "Tris," possessed uncanny abilities that set her apart from others in different factions. However, like many inherently creative individuals struggling with their identity, she had to battle the fear of standing out because of her differences. Eventually, she learned that she was divergent, but she was also told that she needed to conform in order to survive; otherwise, she would face death. In an attempt to fit in and ensure her survival, she tried to suppress her uniqueness and become convergent with other people's expectations and standards. This internal struggle persisted until her loved ones were in grave danger, and it was her unique abilities that she had feared to manifest that became her only means of defense. Fortunately, she took the risk and used her divergence to help those she cared about, breaking free from the fear of judgment. This situation captures what many gifted, talented, and potentially creative people experience. They fear standing out from the crowd, worried that they might be perceived as too different. Their minds operate from a divergent plane of reasoning, leading them to think differently. However, they are often made to believe that there is something wrong with them for daring to think outside the box. Sometimes the people you look up to, such as teachers, guardians, parents, and even so-called mentors, may inadvertently instill fear in you. They may genuinely believe that stepping out of the crowd and embracing your divergence could lead to failure, danger, or even death. Their intentions might stem from love or concern for your well-being. Nevertheless, these misplaced fears can turn potential world changers into mediocre, causing them to settle for a survival mentality and forego any plans for growth and improvement. Rather than standing out and unleashing their unique potential, they choose to blend in with the masses. In doing so, they forsake the opportunity to make a distinctive and transformative impact on the world. They become too afraid to express divergent suggestions and ideas that might challenge stagnant creatives and lead to progress and innovation.

If only you knew that embracing your divergence is the key to unlocking your true potential, you would wholeheartedly invest in nurturing and developing your unique qualities. Your divergence holds the power to bring you financial success, luxury, freedom, and fulfillment, all of which you were meant to experience freely. Do not be afraid or ashamed of your divergent qualities; instead, make a conscious decision to channel them in a positive direction. But how can you identify when your divergence is positive? You will know this when your motivations are rooted in a genuine desire to usher in a new season, when you consistently bring a breath of fresh air to any situation. Your influence should be aimed at liberating others from physical, mental, emotional, and spiritual bondage caused by outdated traditions, overused methods, and poorly thought-out policies. Every human being carries within them deposits of positive divergence, intentionally placed by the omnificent creator, God. These unique qualities are meant to make you an effective problem solver in your specific time and place. Your task is to recognize, nurture, and celebrate your distinctiveness. Never allow anyone to belittle you based on the color of your skin, the shape of your head, your body configuration, or muscular build. All physical traits and mental abilities were intentionally designed by God, making you a wonderfully made individual with the capacity to diverge from the conventional and limiting norms of the world we live in.

Your world needs positively divergent entrepreneurs, divergent scientists, divergent inventors, divergent engineers, divergent programmers, divergent leaders, divergent politicians, and divergent preachers. People who by nature would manifest creativity in its finest form. These are people who chart new courses, take on new challenges, overcome tradition, and create new and better futures for their generation. Sometimes, they go as far as making heavy sacrifices, they suffer criticism and rejection despite their positive contributions to humanity and society. The good thing, however is that despite the rejection they suffer, their daring act of creativity always pays off and brings about paradigm shifts in the way people think and do things. Positively divergent people are not self-seeking, rather, they seek the betterment of all. When you become divergent, you bring forth the infinite and limitless potential within through your thoughts and actions, no matter what field or industry you belong.

**SAY THESE WORDS**

With God's guidance, I embrace my unique perspective and allow His divine inspiration to fuel my creative divergence. I celebrate the beauty of thinking outside the box, knowing that God's power working through me enhances my results. I receive the grace to explore unconventional paths and ideas, aligning myself with God's purpose as I manifest my brilliance. I refuse to fear! I trust in the power of God's inspiration to lead me to innovative solutions through divergent thinking.

## FLIP THE SWITCH EXERCISE #17

Instructions: grab a pen and notepad.

1. Idea Association: Take a random idea, object or concept and brainstorm as many diverse associations and connections as possible. Challenge yourself to think beyond the obvious and explore unexpected connections that may lead to fresh and innovative ideas.

2. Unconventional Combinations: Select two unrelated concepts or ideas and find ways to combine them in a novel and imaginative manner. Encourage yourself to explore the potential of unexpected combinations and embrace the power of divergent thinking.

3. Question Assumptions: Identify commonly held assumptions or beliefs in your field or area of interest and challenge them. Ask yourself why these assumptions exist and explore alternative perspectives that diverge from the status quo.

Engage in these exercises regularly to nurture your ability to think divergently and embrace the power of divergence as a key aspect of creativity.

## 7. Ability to be productive:

Creativity begets productivity. You cannot claim to be creative until you have produced the unique ideas and visions you have had in their simplest form for others to benefit from. Production takes place through the conversion of source material into resource material. Production aids the change of state from one form to another form considered more attractive, useful, and valuable. You see, wealth only comes to those who convert their raw source material into resource material through processing. As a matter of fact, God created the world to work in such a way that everyone would be co-creators and co-producers. So, everyone has something that can be productized, that is, something that can be converted to a product and monetized. It could be a piece of property, it could be your time, it could be your skill, it could be the empty room in your apartment, it could be the stories and the knowledge you have, and it could even be your past failures. If only you could process these raw materials, you would create value for your property, time, skills, talent, knowledge, room, and stories. That is what entrepreneurs and intrapreneurs do!

> *The slothful man roasteth not that which he took in hunting: but the substance of a diligent man is precious.*
>
> *Prov 12:27 KJV*

The Bible describes one who does not process the raw meat he got from hunting as a lazy person. Productivity is not a product of activity but of diligence. If you do not process your skill, knowledge, expertise, experience, stories, or whatever it is that can be a source material for your resourcefulness, the Bible says you are being lazy. According to the above scripture, it is not enough to go into the field, set a trap or hunt down a wild animal and bring it home. If you do not roast it, you have performed activity without productivity. And this is the situation of many potential creators in the world today.

## If trade by barter were still a thing

Imagine a world where paper and digital currencies are no longer accepted as legal tender, and trade is solely based on bartering. What would you offer in exchange for the things you would typically buy with money? Imagine that a policy was made that before you consume anything, you must produce something you could give in exchange for what you desire. What refined skill, gift, talent, or resource would you trade or do business with? This tells you how important it is for every individual, organization, and nation to begin to take productivity seriously.

In countries where people are paid by the hour, the concept of productivity is easy to communicate. However, it becomes more challenging to understand the true meaning of productivity if you live and work in a system that provides something for nothing. Unproductivity or receiving wealth without effort can be detrimental to creativity and innovation. Merely going through the motions of work without achieving true productivity can stifle one's creative potential. Some individuals may appear busy all day, but their output lacks genuine value and innovation. Merely sitting behind a desk from 9 am to 5 pm does not automatically signify productivity. It is crucial to assess whether your work leads to personal growth, evolution, innovation, and the transformation of your skills and personality. Every day, I become a better person, learning something new about creativity, and getting to display my inborn creativity. I have been fortunate to find a path that keeps me mentally challenged. Mind you, my current career as a software engineer was not the traditional path I took. I didn't find my degree from my alma mater interesting or stimulating enough, so I decided to transition to another industry. Learning how to write code with no computer science background was a painful process, but I persevered because it resonated with what I wanted to do. The choice of a career path is not just about the job title; it's about finding what truly resonates with you and brings out your creativity in a productive manner. So, if you find yourself needing to go through the pain of transitioning to another field for a new challenge, I encourage you to do so. Simply staying in the same spot for decades without making any significant progress or development does not align with claiming to be creative or productive. True creativity thrives when we actively seek growth, push boundaries, and constantly evolve our skills and perspectives. It's only when you utilize the resources at your disposal to create uniquely finished goods and services that can help others that you become truly productive as an individual, regardless of your field, business, or profession.

Production is the result of completing the cycle of creativity. Therefore, its significance cannot be over-emphasized. The reason why it is crucial to bring your creative ideas to fruition by developing tangible products or offering valuable services is simple. People have problems, and they are in need of solutions. By creating and delivering packaged products and services, you can address those needs and provide value. Remember, your creations have the potential to make a positive impact on others.

Consider what you can create or produce for your community or locality, as it is through productive output that your creativity can truly make a difference. As you embark on your creative journey, remember that your productivity is a powerful force that can transform ideas into reality and inspire others. The world eagerly awaits the fruits of your creative endeavors. Now, go forth and leave an indelible mark with your productivity and creativity!

> **SAY THESE WORDS**
>
> I effortlessly tap into my creative potential, allowing it to fuel my productivity. I find joy and fulfillment in being productive through my creative endeavors. I am a master at combining creativity and productivity to bring my ideas to life. Each day, I harness my creative energy to drive my productivity to new heights. I am inspired by the limitless possibilities that creativity brings to my productivity. My creativity fuels my motivation, helping me stay focused and productive.

## FLIP THE SWITCH EXERCISE #18

Productivity booster

1.  Are there any limiting beliefs or patterns that might be hindering your creativity and productivity? Write them down and identify one belief or habit you want to change.

_______________________________________________

_______________________________________________

_______________________________________________

_______________________________________________

_______________________________________________

2. Write down three goals that excite and motivate you and create a plan with actionable steps to achieve them.

_______________________________________________

_______________________________________________

_______________________________________________

_______________________________________________

_______________________________________________

3. Write down affirmations or positive statements that reinforce your growth mindset in relation to your creativity and productivity.

_______________________________________________

_______________________________________________

_______________________________________________

_______________________________________________

_______________________________________________

Remember to approach these exercises with an open and curious mindset.

# CREATIVITY WORKSHEET #2

**Instructions:**

Use this worksheet to explore and deepen your understanding of creativity based on the various definitions discussed in Chapter 3. Engage in the activities and reflections below to expand your perspective and ignite your creative potential. This worksheet will help you explore different dimensions of creativity and how they relate to your own creative journey.

1. Ability to Create:

a) Reflect on your own creative abilities and skills. What are some specific areas or domains in which you excel in creating? Write them down below.

___________________________________________

___________________________________________

___________________________________________

___________________________________________

___________________________________________

2. Ability to Solve Problems:

a. Identify a current problem or challenge you're facing in your personal or professional life. Write a brief description of the problem below.

___________________________________________

___________________________________________

___________________________________________

___________________________________________

___________________________________________

b.  Brainstorm at least three creative solutions or approaches to address the problem. Be open to unconventional ideas and perspectives.

    1.  _______________________________________________

        _______________________________________________

    2.  _______________________________________________

        _______________________________________________

    3.  _______________________________________________

        _______________________________________________

c.  Choose one of the solutions you brainstormed and create an action plan to implement it. Set specific goals and deadlines to track your progress.

3.  Ability of Uniqueness in State and Approach:

a.  Reflect on your own creative style or approach. What sets you apart from others in your creative endeavors? Write down three unique aspects of your creative expression.

    1.  _______________________________________________

        _______________________________________________

    2.  _______________________________________________

        _______________________________________________

    3.  _______________________________________________

        _______________________________________________

b.  Choose one of the unique aspects you identified and think of ways to further enhance and embrace it in your creative work. Write down your ideas below.

    1. ________________________________________

    ________________________________________

    2. ________________________________________

    ________________________________________

    3. ________________________________________

    ________________________________________

4.  A Propelling Force:

a.  Reflect on moments in your life when you felt truly inspired and motivated to create. What were the factors or experiences that propelled your creative energy? Write them down below.

    1. ________________________________________

    ________________________________________

    2. ________________________________________

    ________________________________________

    3. ________________________________________

    ________________________________________

b.  Identify one action or practice that you can incorporate into your daily routine to maintain and nurture your creative energy. Write it down and commit to implementing it.

    Action/Practice:

    ________________________________________

    ________________________________________

6. Dynamic Change of State:

a. Think about a recent creative project or endeavor you undertook. How did the project transform or evolve throughout its development? Reflect on the changes and growth you experienced.

_________________________________________

_________________________________________

_________________________________________

b. Choose one aspect of your creative process that you want to focus on refining or improving. Set specific goals and strategies to facilitate dynamic change and growth in that area.

_________________________________________

_________________________________________

_________________________________________

7. Ability to Be Divergent:

a. Explore different sources of inspiration and creative influences outside of your usual comfort zone. Choose one new source or medium and spend time immersing yourself in it. Reflect on how it expands your creative thinking and possibilities.

Source/Medium:

_________________________________________

_________________________________________

b. Engage in a divergent thinking exercise. Take a common object or concept and brainstorm as many unique and unconventional uses or interpretations for it as possible. Write down your ideas below.

Object/Concept:

_______________________________________

_______________________________________

Unconventional Uses/Interpretations:

1. _______________________________________

_______________________________________

2. _______________________________________

_______________________________________

3. _______________________________________

_______________________________________

(Continue the list with as many ideas as you can generate.)

8. Ability to Be Productive:

a. Reflect on your current creative habits and routines. Are there any areas where you can enhance your productivity and focus? Write down one specific improvement you want to make in your creative productivity.

Improvement:

_______________________________________

_______________________________________

b. Identify any potential distractions or obstacles that hinder your creative productivity. Develop strategies or actions to minimize or overcome those challenges.

Remember, this worksheet is designed to deepen your understanding of creativity and help you explore different dimensions of your creative potential. Feel free to add any additional reflections or insights as you work through the exercises.

# CHAPTER THREE

# WHERE DO YOU BELONG?

## A question on creativity

One day, a lady approached me with an intriguing request: she wanted me to explain the concept of creativity to her without using the direct terms "creative" or "create." She sought a deeper understanding of what I meant when I referred to her own inherent creativity. In response, I offered her an analogy which I believe captures the essence of creativity. I said to her, "Your creativity is like a refined gift at work—a masterpiece of untapped potential, well-furnished for display. It's a learned skill in motion, representing ideas that come alive through purposeful action." I went further to say, "Think of it as your unprocessed food ingredients getting transformed into a well-cooked meal, teasing your senses with their flavors and aromas. Your creativity is what turns raw meat into a tasty, finger-licking chicken soup." I guess she could relate more to this analogy because, by her own admission, she loved cooking.

When I refer to your creativity, I am also talking about that book idea of yours that blossoms into a published work, cherished, and celebrated by readers worldwide. Your creativity has the power to turn your unsung melody into the harmonies and rhythms of a mesmerizing musical composition, captivating hearts, and minds. It's what propels you to turn dreams into reality, to explore the depths of your imagination, and unleash the superpower within. Also, your creativity has a remarkable ability to turn passion into profit—a catalyst that transforms what you love into a business. This business not only brings you satisfaction but also puts food on your table and caters to others through you. It's the alchemy that turns raw talent into a polished product, ready to be shared with the world. Creativity is a dynamic force that breathes life into your visions and aspirations. It manifests as a building plan brought into tangible reality—a mere blueprint transformed into a finished house, embodying the dreams and aspirations of its creator, architect, or builder.

After the explanation, she not only gained clarity about creativity, but she also got a vivid picture, and a clear understanding of what creativity could mean for her. She got into a personal and intimate knowledge of the subject. This understanding came with active participation, and she came up with her own definition of creativity.

I have a question for you, and I want you to give it serious thought based on what you have read so far. The question is: what does creativity mean to you? The reason I shared my response to that lady with you is so you can grasp the essence of your own creativity. My goal is to help you define what creativity means to you and translate that into a tool that ignites your creativity, converting your ideas, skills, talent, and potential into valid opportunities that produce tangible results. With these words, I aim to trigger your imagination, spark a newfound understanding, and instill appreciation for the creative potential within you. As you read this book, you will not just acquire fresh knowledge about creativity, but you will also get fired up with insights that ignite your creative spark. As you read through this book, do well to observe as your hidden gifts gets reawakened, your passion realigned, and that innate talent of yours rediscovered. You will find yourself on the fast lane of purpose fulfillment and become a person of multiplied impact. Creativity is a powerful force that resides within every one of us, including even the least likely among us, waiting patiently to be activated and harnessed.

The moment I came to the realization that every living, breathing human being on Earth can be creative, I began to ask questions. And the answers I discovered are what I intend to share with you in this chapter. Here's the question that provoked some of the insights I have shared in the following pages: If truly everyone is creative, why do most people find it difficult to deploy their creativity? Why do many potential creatives struggle to turn their passion, skill, or talent into tangible results, finished products, or profitable businesses? Why does it appear almost impossible for people who carry brilliant ideas to go from ideas to creative solutions, profitable creations, or tangible results? Why do individuals with potential for life-transforming books, trail-blazing technologies, disease-curing antidotes, awe-inspiring music, or impactful works end up taking their creative geniuses to the graveyards with them?

The answer I got as I pondered these thought-provoking questions is that not everyone has ignited their creativity. This is largely because most people do not even know that they have it in them to be creative. Some people, who may know they have it in them to display creativity at an elite level, do not know how to go about their journey. In other words, some people once ignited their creativity, but somehow, the flames of their gifts, skills, and talents got quenched, so they need to re-ignite their potential. While some don't even know they have it in them and, thus, never ignite their creativity.

## Seven types of potential creatives

Now, in addition to discovering the answers to these questions, I also found that there are seven categories of people who either need to ignite or re-ignite their creativity. You may find that you identify with one or more of these categories, and that is perfectly fine. Either way, you will learn how to ignite or re-ignite your creativity through the insights you will find as you read on. Everyone whose creative fire was either extinguished or who never had any spark to begin with belongs to one or more of these categories that I am about to show you. Even if you discover that you fall into one or more of these seven groups of creatives, do not let that discourage you. I say that because in this book, you will find the keys to release yourself from the clutches that may have kept you in any group. The reason for this is to help you identify where you are on this journey so that, by the time you are done reading this book, you will be able to see the impact and progress you have made. If you feel you do not fall into any of these categories, you could benefit from reading through it as well. I encourage you to even take the exercises because you may know someone who would need help in any of these areas. So, feel free to read on curiously if that's where you belong. The seven main groups of potential creatives are:

1. The Dormant Creatives
2. The Lost Creatives
3. The Unrecognized Creatives
4. The Suppressed Creatives
5. The Stagnant Creatives
6. The Discouraged Creatives
7. The Fearful Creatives

Now, take a moment to reflect upon your own life's journey as an individual. Are you a dormant creative who is yet to tap into your full potential? Or perhaps a lost creative who is searching for that vibrant spark of talent that once burned passionately within you? Maybe you are an unrecognized creative, grappling with the pain of seeing others steal your shine while you watch the tremendous talents and gifts that lie within you wither away. You may have even suppressed your creative instincts due to external pressures or fear, making you a part of the suppressed creatives group. Are you a fearful creative who may be paralyzed by apprehension? Or do you feel trapped in a creative plateau, not knowing there is more beyond being a stagnant creative? Lastly, are you a discouraged creative who has faced adversity and criticism, leading to a loss of confidence in your abilities, gifts, talents, and potential? No matter which category resonates with you, this chapter is a steppingstone towards reigniting your creative fire. Therefore, you are on track to transforming your skills, gifts, and talents into tangible solutions and profitable creations. Once you can identify yourself in any of the seven categories that I have introduced to you, you will be on your way to success. It will mark the beginning of a life-transforming journey towards releasing your gifts, talents, and ideas, and transforming them into creative solutions and tangible creations.

This is important because throughout our lives, we often find ourselves caught up in the external world—busy schedules, and the pressures of everyday life. Amidst the chaos, we sometimes lose touch with the essence of who we truly are and the potential that burns within us. Nevertheless, within each of us exists an untapped wellspring of creativity waiting to be discovered. This is an invitation for you to embark on a transformative inspection of your inner landscape. This is a call to embrace self-reflection as a powerful tool for self-discovery, allowing you to unlock the hidden doors that lead to your creative potential. It is my belief that by understanding these categories and their unique challenges, you will find the guidance and inspiration needed to unlock your gift, talent, skills, or creative potential and thrive in your endeavors. By peering into the depths of your being, you will discover the raw materials that fuel your creative fire and the true essence of your artistic spirit. Each step will bring you closer to uncovering your authentic self and igniting the creative spark that may have remained dormant within you. But keep in mind as we dive in, that cross-examining yourself with each of the seven categories can be an intense and revealing process. It may unearth long-forgotten dreams, passions, and aspirations, as well as fears, doubts, and insecurities. However, it is through this honest exploration that you will rediscover your passion, reclaim your gift, redefine your creative identity, and reconnect with the vast reservoir of creativity that resides within your soul. Prepare yourself to navigate uncharted territories, confront your innermost fears, and embrace the power of self-discovery. Are you ready to embark on this journey of introspection? Let us delve into the world of creativity and unleash the power that lies within you. Now, I invite you to carefully examine yourself as you study these seven categories and figure out where you belong.

## 1.  Dormant Creatives

Do you feel a growing sense of dissatisfaction or unfulfillment in your life, suspecting that your creative potential is being left untapped? Have you experienced moments of inspiration, but haven't taken any action? Did you ever dismiss your own creative ideas or talents as insignificant or unworthy of attention? Do you feel a sense of regret for not giving yourself permission to explore your passions? Have you always felt a deep sense of untapped creative potential within yourself? Dormant creatives are individuals who have never fully tapped into their creative potential. These are people who possess creative potential but are yet to fully explore or express it. They are literally sitting on a goldmine but have no clue that the raw gem they possess can become so valuable if properly harnessed. These individuals may feel a longing or desire to engage in creative pursuits but find themselves stuck, uncertain, or disconnected from their creative side. Dormant creatives often have various reasons for not fully embracing their creativity, some of which are founded on myths and misconceptions. While others might have prioritized other aspects of life, such as career or family, with little or no time or energy for any creative endeavors. Sometimes, fear of failure, self-doubt, or comparison with others can contribute to the dormancy of their creative abilities.

### The gifted singer

Sarah had always been a gifted singer but had never pursued it seriously. She believed her vocal abilities were just a hobby and not something she could truly excel in. One day, she attended a local music concert and was captivated by the power and emotion conveyed by the singers on stage.

Inspired, Sarah decided to take singing lessons. As she explored her voice and practiced diligently, she discovered a hidden talent within her. The lessons ignited her passion, and Sarah soon found herself singing at every opportunity, awakening her dormant creativity and bringing it to life. She joined a community choir and experienced the joy of harmonizing with others. Sarah's voice blossomed, and she gained confidence to perform in front of a small audience. Her friends and family were amazed by her talent and encouraged her to pursue a career as a professional singer. Sarah embraced her dormant creativity and started performing at local cafes and open mic nights. Her soulful voice touched the hearts of those who listened, and she began receiving invitations to perform at larger venues and events. Sarah's talent brought her joy and fulfillment, and she realized that she had underestimated her own potential for greatness as a singer. Discovering her dormant creativity not only allowed Sarah to express herself fully but also connected her with a vibrant music community. She began collaborating with other musicians, recording her own songs, and even released an album that resonated with listeners worldwide.

Sarah's story reminds us that sometimes our greatest passions lie dormant within us, waiting to be unleashed and shared with the world. Does Sarah's journey resonate with you? Have you ever felt a deep longing or desire to pursue a creative passion that lies dormant within you? Sometimes, we can find ourselves in a similar situation to Sarah, where we have talents or creative inclinations that we've overlooked or underestimated. It's easy to push aside our passions due to fear, self-doubt, or the belief that they are merely hobbies and not worth pursuing seriously. Reflect on your own life and consider if there's a creative spark within you waiting to be ignited. Is there a dormant talent or passion that you've kept hidden or neglected? If so, what steps could you take to awaken and nurture that creativity? Igniting dormant creativity by exploring that gift you call a mere hobby can bring immense joy, fulfillment, and a deeper sense of self-expression. If this describes you, then this book is the answer to your burning desire for help. It's never too late to tap into your creative potential and allow it to flourish.

Dormant creatives have a vast mass of uncultivated potential, but they often look at those who have already cultivated theirs and try to be like them or wish to be like them. In doing so, they neglect their own creative edge. Have you noticed a yearning or longing to express yourself creatively but have been unsure of where or how to start? Have you neglected or overlooked your own creative edge while comparing yourself to those who have already cultivated their creativity? Have you found yourself hesitating to explore your interests due to fear of failure or judgment? Dormant creatives may feel overwhelmed or intimidated by the accomplishments of others, causing them to doubt their own abilities and potential. They may believe that creativity is something reserved for a select few or that they need to emulate the creative expressions of others to be considered successful. However, it's important for dormant creatives to realize that creativity is not a competition or a fixed standard. Each person has their own unique set of talents, perspectives, and creative potential waiting to be discovered and nurtured. If this describes you, hear this: By accepting your own individuality and exploring your interests and passions, you can unlock your creative edge and tap into your true potential. By nurturing your own creative abilities and developing your unique voice, you can awaken your dormant creativity and make meaningful contributions in your own authentic way.

Gideon was a mighty warrior, but before he could release that potential, he needed an "aha moment," or what you can call a mind shift. He had a very poor sense of self-worth, and until he had his light-bulb moment through the signs God gave him, he could not release his potential. Gideon and his 300 men defeated a seemingly uncountable Midianite army through creative strategies inspired by God. While the story of Gideon in the Bible primarily focuses on his role as a military leader and judge, Gideon initially exhibited qualities that align with the concept of a dormant creative—a person with untapped creative potential. Dormant creatives usually see a compliment as flattery because they are not confident in their ability, capacity, gift, potential, or skill. That was why Gideon found it difficult to accept the angel's compliments and salutations. He thought, "Hey, I am nothing close to a mighty warrior. I am no mighty man, I am from a poor background, and my creative battle strategies will stay dormant." A dormant creative would rather die with his or her gift being only a hobby. They prefer to sing or sculpt in their closet or backyard rather than impact their generation. However, a light-bulb moment can ignite their creativity and awaken the sleeping giant within them.

> *The Lord turned to him and said, "Go in the strength you have and save Israel out of Midian's hand. Am I not sending you? "But Lord," Gideon asked, "how can I save Israel? My clan is the weakest in Manasseh, and I am the least in my family." The Lord answered, "I will be with you, and you will strike down all the Midianites together." Gideon replied, "If now I have found favor in your eyes, give me a sign that it is really you talking to me. Please do not go away until I come back and bring my offering and set it before you."*

> *Judg 6:14-18 NIV*

In the biblical narrative, Gideon starts off as an ordinary individual, unsure of his abilities and feeling insignificant compared to the challenges he faced. When called upon to lead the Israelites against their oppressors, Gideon expressed doubts about his capabilities, highlighting his dormant state of self-belief and leadership potential. However, as the story progressed,

Gideon went through a transformation. He received a sign from God, which instilled confidence in him and awakened his inner genius for creative battle strategies. Gideon was finally persuaded, tapped into his leadership gift, and then utilized his strategic thinking and creative problem-solving abilities to achieve victory over the Midianites. From a creative perspective, one can view Gideon's transformation as an awakening of his dormant leadership and creative potential. Just as dormant creatives often need a catalyst or moment of realization to unlock their creative potential, Gideon's encounter with God and the subsequent signs served as a catalyst for his transformation, that was the light bulb moment that flipped the switch for him. It is through this awakening that Gideon discovered his gift, potential, inner strength and tapped into his creative problem-solving abilities. If you identify with this group, be rest assured that your "aha moment" is already here. As you read this book, you will be fired up for exploits and see yourself unearthing the goldmine of potential, talent, or gifts you have been sleeping on.

**SAY THESE WORDS:**

"I am gifted, I am talented, I am full of creative potential, and from this day forward, I refuse to let my inherent abilities and capacities lay fallow and uncultivated. I was born as an answer to the cry of millions, and I will not fail my generation. I will serve my gift to the world in ways that will blow my mind. Therefore, I refuse to back down!"

Note: Remember, affirmations and self-talk are powerful tools to shift your mindset and reprogram yourself for success in your creative journey.

## FLIP THE SWITCH EXERCISE  #19

   a.  Do you identify as a dormant creative?

   b.  If not, what can you do to avoid ever becoming a dormant creative if you do not identify as one?

   c.  If yes, what do you think is responsible for this? (Try to avoid the blame game and take responsibility where possible).

   d.  What aspects of dormant creatives stand out to you most?

## 2. Lost Creatives

Have you ever felt like you used to have a strong passion to express your talent, skill, or potential in a particular area of interest but now struggle to reconnect with it? Have you experienced setbacks or challenges that have dampened your enthusiasm and belief in your creative abilities? Have you faced moments of self-doubt where you question your creative talents or fear that your ideas aren't good enough? A lost creative is an individual who once possessed a vibrant creative spark, but somewhere along the way, lost their connection to it. They may have encountered setbacks, faced self-doubt, or found themselves trapped in a monotonous routine that gradually stifled their natural gift, potential, creativity, and talent.

## The talented photographer

Damian was a photographer who had once captured breathtaking images that attracted attention and compliments. His great eye for composition and ability to capture fleeting moments made his work stand out. However, as the digital age took hold and photography techniques rapidly evolved, Damian found himself struggling to keep up with the changing industry. The demands of mastering new equipment, software, and social media platforms overwhelmed him, leading to self-doubt and a loss of confidence in his abilities. Feeling disheartened and disconnected from his once-beloved craft, Damian gradually set his camera aside. He couldn't bear the thought of producing work that didn't live up to his own high standards. Months turned into years as his camera collected dust, and the passion that had fueled his creativity seemed to fade away.

Then, one morning, Damian decided to embark on a peaceful nature hike. As he walked along a winding trail, the golden rays of the sun began to peek through the dense foliage. The symphony of birdsong filled the air, and a gentle breeze rustled the leaves. The natural beauty surrounding him stirred something deep within his soul. Without thinking, Damian reached for his Smartphone and launched the camera app almost instinctively. As he peered through the lens, framing the awe-inspiring scenery, he felt a flicker of excitement and anticipation. With every click of the shutter, he rediscovered the joy of capturing the essence of nature, freezing moments in time that seemed to tell their own stories. In that moment, Damian realized that his love for photography had never truly disappeared; it had merely been overshadowed by the pressures of an evolving industry. That was his "aha moment." Inspired by the beauty of the world around him, he made a decision to embrace his own artistic journey on his own terms, and that was all he needed to reignite his lost creativity. Damian began to experiment with blending traditional and digital photography techniques, allowing his skills to flow freely. He sought out unique perspectives, chasing the interplay of light and shadow, and capturing the hidden beauty in everyday scenes. Through his newfound approach, he started to develop a distinctive style that merged his technical skills with his artistic vision.

Driven by his passion, Damian sought out like-minded photographers and joined local photography communities. He engaged in collaborative projects and attended workshops, finding inspiration and support from fellow creatives. These connections not only helped him grow as an artist but also provided a sense of camaraderie and encouragement on his creative journey. As Damian shared his work with others, he began to receive positive feedback and recognition once again. Exhibitions and gallery showings became opportunities to showcase his unique perspective and reignite his creative fire. The profound impact of his images on viewers confirmed that he had found his way back to his true calling. Damian's story serves as a reminder that even in the face of uncertainty and self-doubt, rediscovering one's creative passion is possible. By reconnecting with the beauty of the world and embracing one's unique vision, a lost creative can overcome obstacles and reignite their artistic spark, forging a path that is true to their own voice.

## The burning flames of rediscovery

Did you know that Moses, the great prophet of old, was a lost creative for 40 long years until he rediscovered his assignment and reignited his passion, vision, and creativity? Moses initially exhibited great potential and creativity but experienced a period of disconnection and self-doubt (Exo

2:11-15). In the wilderness, Moses found solace and reflection, spending forty years away from the people he was called to lead. During this time, he tended sheep and lived a quiet, humble life. However, the people he was destined to lead kept crying to God for help. God sought him out and appeared to him in the form of a burning bush, commissioning him once again to fulfill his divine purpose. You see, the reason you must rediscover your lost passion, vision, gift, and creative potential is that a lot of destinies are at stake. The future of many people around you and around the world is dependent on your ability to ignite your creativity. Have you ever imagined what life would be like if no one got creative enough to invent airplanes, lightbulbs, cars, the internet, and all the other wonders of modern civilization? Who knows if you are the next creative that would take the world into the next wave of industrial revolution? But here you are possibly lost in the wilderness of mediocrity, with a lost passion and disconnected from the zone where you manifest your creative potential and gift. It is time to wake up! It is time to rediscover that lost passion and reignite your creativity.

Moses' story exemplifies the journey of a lost creative who experiences periods of doubt, isolation, and disconnection from their creative potential. It shows that even when one feels inadequate or uncertain, divine intervention and self-reflection can reignite the spark of creativity and propel one back into their purpose. By rediscovering their identity and reconnecting with their creative gifts, lost creatives can overcome self-doubt and embrace their calling, just as Moses did when he found the strength to lead the Israelites out of slavery and into a new chapter of their journey. It does not matter how long you have lost your passion, connection, and focus. For Moses, it had been forty long years since he lost focus on his assignment. He was even eighty years old when he rediscovered himself. If Moses could reclaim his lost passion, realign with his life's vision, and reignite his gift, you can too. No wonder the Bible says that the gifts and the callings of God are irrevocable (Rom 11:9). There is a caveat though, Moses lived till the age of one hundred and twenty, so he had forty years to fulfil his assignment with the gift he had. You, on the other hand, have no idea how much time you have left. So, you must take this even more seriously, as a matter of urgency. If you feel disconnected from your creativity, know that the creative potential within you is innate and enduring, waiting to be reignited, but time is of the essence. All you need is one encounter, one light bulb moment, one conversation, one chance, one revelation, and one word to trigger the process that will reignite your creativity. And I believe that as you read on, your creativity will begin to burn like liquid fire, ready to erupt from within you with a volcanic force that will transform your life.

When God wanted to help Moses rediscover his gift and assignment, all He did was re-ignite Moses' passion through a burning bush (Exo 3:1-6). The burning bush can be interpreted as Moses' "light bulb moment" or a pivotal turning point in his journey of rediscovering his gift and reconnecting with his creative potential. All you need to regain and reignite your lost creativity is one "aha moment"! When Moses initially fled from his assignment and abandoned his role as a leader, he found himself in a state of isolation and uncertainty. It was during this period in the wilderness that he encountered the burning bush—a tipping point that reconnected him with his vision and gifting. The burning bush captured Moses' attention and drew him closer. Your own burning bush might be this book! As you read this book, you will find your passion burning inside of you once again. It may even be a conversation or a need that triggers that lost gift and helps you trace your steps back to where you will find fresh inspiration to release your potential. As Moses approached the bush, God spoke to him and reaffirmed his calling, reminding him of his unique gifts and purpose. In that sacred encounter, Moses experienced a profound realization—an awakening of his creative and leadership potential. The burning bush served as a powerful symbol of divine inspiration and guidance, igniting the flame of Moses' creativity and reigniting his passion to serve the people of Israel.

Look at all the problems Moses had to solve to get the children of Israel out of Egypt. It tells you how important it was for Moses to rediscover himself in the wilderness before going back. I pray for you that, as you read this, your lost gift, passion, potential, and visions will be rediscovered with fresh zeal and new unction to excel in Jesus' name! From that moment onward, Moses accepted his role as a leader and embraced the creative solutions he could provide to free the Israelites from bondage. He demonstrated his creativity and problem-solving abilities through the miracles and signs he performed, guiding the people, and leading them on a journey towards liberation. The burning bush served as a catalyst for Moses to reclaim his gift, passion, and talent for leadership and creative solutions. It symbolized the moment when his lost creativity was rediscovered, and he finally found his calling once again. It marked a significant turning point in his life and set him on a path of fulfilling his purpose and making a profound impact on the lives of the Israelites. Just as the burning bush sparked Moses' creative reawakening, lost creatives can also seek moments of inspiration and divine guidance to reignite their own creative flames. Whether it be through a profound encounter, introspection, or a series of events, these light bulb moments have the power to awaken the hidden gifts, talents, and passions, propelling them toward a renewed sense of purpose and the fulfillment of their creative potential.

**Over to you**

Maybe you are a fashion designer who has always been known for your unique fashion styles and innovative designs. But a period of personal loss and financial struggle dampened your spirit, leading you to abandon your craft. The pressures of life overshadowed your creativity, leaving behind an unfulfilled longing to express yourself through your fashion designs and creative dress styles. Or perhaps you are a talented graphic designer who once had a natural flair for visual communication. The specific craft or area of gifting that once piqued your interest and fueled your need for creativity isn't really important. What matters is that you feel you have lost it. If you recognize or resonate with the description so far, then you belong to this category. But don't worry; you are about to rediscover your lost treasure and reignite your passion, mission, and vision. If you find yourself in this group, it is crucial to embark on a journey of self-reflection. By delving into introspection, you can begin to uncover the underlying reasons for your creative slump and pave the way for rediscovering and reigniting your creative fire. This process may involve examining past experiences, identifying any limiting beliefs or external influences that contributed to your disconnection from your creativity, and exploring new avenues for self-expression. I pray for you that you will receive divine stimulation right now and find your creative spark in Jesus' name!

> **SAY THESE WORDS:**
>
> I am a creative, with unique gifts and talents waiting to be reignited, rediscovered, and served to my world. My past setbacks and doubts do not define me. Every day, I am taking steps towards reconnecting with my creative passions and reigniting the fire within me. Every day, I receive new ideas, fresh inspiration, and divine experiences that will reignite my creative spirit. I am reclaiming my creativity, making a positive impact with my unique gifts every day.

## FLIP THE SWITCH EXERCISE  #20

    a.  Do you identify as a lost creative?

_________________________________________________

_________________________________________________

_________________________________________________

b. If not, how can you support and encourage lost creatives around you, fostering an environment of creativity and growth.

_______________________________________________

_______________________________________________

_______________________________________________

c. If you identify as a lost creative, consider the following questions to guide your self-reflection:

    i. What are some specific moments or experiences in your life where you felt most connected to your creativity?

_______________________________________________

_______________________________________________

_______________________________________________

    ii. What were the factors or circumstances that led to your disconnection from your creative pursuits?

_______________________________________________

_______________________________________________

_______________________________________________

    iii. How have these experiences influenced your beliefs and self-perception as a creative individual?

_______________________________________________

_______________________________________________

_______________________________________________

d. Embrace a mindset of growth and possibility:

i. What steps can you take to create a nurturing and supportive environment for your creativity to flourish?

_________________________________________________

_________________________________________________

_________________________________________________

ii.　What resources, tools, or communities can you seek out to reignite your talent, creative passion and expand your skills?

_________________________________________________

_________________________________________________

_________________________________________________

iii.　How can you incorporate regular creativity practices into your routine to foster a consistent and vibrant creative mindset?

_________________________________________________

_________________________________________________

_________________________________________________

Remember, you have the power to flip the switch and reignite your creativity. Embrace the journey of self-discovery, and intentional action, as you reconnect with your lost creative self and embrace a renewed sense of purpose and joy in your creative pursuits.

## 3. Unrecognized Creatives

Here is how to identify an unrecognized creative. These are individuals who are not recognized or compensated adequately for their creativity. They may be undervalued, overlooked, or not given the recognition they deserve for their creative talents and contributions. They may face challenges in gaining visibility, finding opportunities, or receiving fair compensation for their work. Unrecognized creatives are individuals whose creative talents and contributions should get them seen, heard, and paid but often go unnoticed, undervalued, or unrewarded. They possess a wealth of creative potential, but their work may not receive the recognition and compensation it truly deserves. Have you often felt that your creative talents and abilities go unnoticed or underappreciated? Have you struggled to gain recognition or opportunities to showcase your creativity? Do you feel that your creative work is undervalued or not adequately compensated? If this describes you, do not despair because you can create your path to recognition and fulfillment amid all this. Unrecognized creatives often find themselves in a situation where their creative potential remains hidden or underutilized. Many unrecognized creatives possess a strong passion for their creative pursuits but never receive the acknowledgment or compensation they deserve for their contributions. This could cause the creative fire within such creatives to be put out without the individual even realizing it. If this is you, you must not allow that fire to get extinguished by this unfortunate circumstance. You need to reignite your creativity and turn the narrative in your favor.

The story I am about to share with you will show you why you must not back down in the face of being unrecognized, unrewarded, or unappreciated. Rather, that is the time when you should reignite your creativity and figure out a better way to handle the situation.

## The poor high school teacher

There was a poor but creative high school teacher who remained unrecognized until he ignited his creativity and achieved success. Mark was an unappreciated teacher who always poured his heart and soul into his profession. He was dedicated to his students' growth and aimed to inspire a love for learning within them. Mark went above and beyond, developing creative lesson plans, integrating technology, and incorporating real-world experiences to make the curriculum engaging and relevant. Despite his tireless efforts, Mark found himself in an education system that failed to fully recognize and compensate for his contributions. He could barely afford to pay his bills as he earned a minimum wage and never got a promotion despite his commitment. The innovative and student-centered approach that Mark brought to his classroom was overlooked. Mark's colleagues and administrators did not fully grasp the depth of his impact on the students' lives. His ability to connect with students, understand their individual needs, and provide meaningful support often went unnoticed. The personal sacrifices he made, such as spending extra hours preparing lessons or staying late to help struggling students, were unseen by many. The lack of recognition and appreciation took a toll on Mark's motivation and job satisfaction. He questioned whether his efforts truly made a difference, and the feeling of being undervalued dampened his enthusiasm for teaching. While he sat on his bed one Saturday evening, feeling frustrated, he came across an advert about an online course program. A surge of inspiration coursed through Mark's veins as he listened. "I can do that," he said to himself with a glimmer of excitement. The idea of packaging his wealth of knowledge and experiences into an online course seemed like the key that could unlock a world of possibilities. Perhaps this was his opportunity to break free from the confines of traditional recognition and reach a wider audience. Driven by his newfound idea, Mark delved into the world of online education. He immersed himself in learning the art of creating captivating video lessons, designing comprehensive course curriculums, and building a platform to showcase his expertise. With every passing day, his confidence grew as he realized the potential impact he could have on aspiring teachers and students far beyond the walls of his classroom.

As Mark's online courses gained traction, his visibility and influence expanded exponentially. Word of his engaging teaching style and insightful content spread like wildfire across social media platforms and educational communities. People from all corners of the globe sought his courses, drawn by his passion, expertise, and genuine desire to make a difference. What started as a quest for recognition soon transformed into something greater. Mark's online presence not only brought him the visibility he had longed for but also opened doors to unexpected opportunities. Invitations to speak at conferences, collaborate on educational projects, and even consult for renowned institutions poured in, all stemming from the impact he was making through his online courses. But it wasn't just recognition and financial gains that fueled Mark's fulfillment. The true reward lay in witnessing the impact his teachings had on the lives of his students. The flood of messages, emails, and testimonials pouring in from individuals who found inspiration, acquired new skills, and discovered their own passion for teaching reaffirmed that his journey had been worth it. In embracing the digital realm, Mark had not only found visibility and a wider reach but also unlocked a profound sense of purpose. His decision to step beyond the confines of traditional recognition led to a fulfilling path where his creativity thrived, and his impact knew no bounds.

> *Now there lived in that city a man poor but wise, and he saved the city by his wisdom. But nobody remembered that poor man. So, I said, "Wisdom is better than strength." But the poor man's wisdom is despised, and his words are no longer heeded.*
>
> *Eccl 9:15-16 NIV*

The above verse speaks of a poor, wise man who delivered a city through his skill, intelligence, and creativity. However, despite his significant contribution, the verse states that "no one remembered that same poor man." This passage highlights a common theme where the wisdom, talent, or creative contributions of individuals, particularly those who are not recognized or valued by society, may go unnoticed or unappreciated. Have you encountered challenges in finding a supportive and rewarding environment that recognizes and celebrates your creative contributions? Have you experienced frustration or disappointment in not receiving the recognition you believe your creative abilities deserve? Unrecognized creatives may encounter challenges in finding the right opportunities to showcase their work and gain the exposure needed to be noticed. They may face barriers in accessing platforms, networks, or communities that can provide the visibility they seek, and this can impact their confidence and hinder their creative growth. Even though the lack of recognition can lead to feelings of frustration, self-doubt, and a loss of motivation, this is still no excuse to allow the embers of your creativity to burn out. Do not question your worth and the value of your creative contributions, based on these external factors. Rather stay consistent and figure out ways to document your brilliance.

## Another perspective

Unrecognized creatives can also face the unfortunate experience of having their ideas stolen by others, which further compounds the lack of credit and acknowledgement they suffer. This act of idea theft deprives them of the recognition and validation that should rightfully accompany their creative contributions. When unrecognized creatives have their ideas stolen, it can be deeply disheartening and demoralizing. Seeing someone else take credit for their original concepts or works can leave them feeling robbed, both creatively and emotionally. It can undermine their confidence and sense of ownership over their own creations, potentially leading to a loss of motivation and a reluctance to share their ideas openly. The impact of idea theft goes beyond the loss of credit and acknowledgment. The path of an unrecognized creative can be filled with frustration and feelings of being overlooked or underappreciated. Despite their immense talent and dedication, they may find themselves working in the shadows, their creativity hidden or unacknowledged by a wider audience.

## Steps to overcome lack of recognition

As an unrecognized creative, there are steps you can take to address the problem and gain the recognition you deserve. Here are some actions you can consider:

### a. Keep Record

One crucial step for unrecognized creatives is to keep a record of their contributions. In many businesses and organizations, I have witnessed incredible displays of problem-solving skills and creativity go unnoticed. One common factor in these situations is that the individuals involved often fail to document their own contributions. This is something Mordecai could have done differently, instead of leaving his compensation to chance. It is important not to expect rewards or compensation for every act of creativity or for every help rendered to others. However, in the corporate world, it's necessary to ensure that your contributions are not overlooked because no one heard about them. Deploying your talents and gifts silently may be suitable for charitable purposes, but within the corporate and business domain, it's crucial to make your value known. As an employee, it's essential to maintain a dedicated repository where you document your successes and achievements. Additionally, do not be afraid or shy to share and discuss the valuable impact of your work with your colleagues, managers, or superiors in a creative way. Take every opportunity to highlight your successes, whether it's during team meetings, performance evaluations, or networking events. By actively recording and promoting your contributions, you increase the likelihood of being acknowledged and appreciated for your creative efforts.

Remember, it's not about seeking rewards, but rather ensuring that your creative contributions are recognized and valued by others.

## b. **Self-Promotion:**

Take an active role in promoting your work and showcasing your creativity. Utilize social media platforms, create a professional website or portfolio, and share your projects, achievements, and creative process with others. Engage with relevant communities and networks to expand your reach and visibility. You must understand that it is not about who does it best, it is about who is loudest about what they do. This is what it takes to get your name out there, and you cannot leave that to chance. This is something the poor wise man in Ecclesiastes 9:15-16 was probably not intentional about. Joseph never left his marketing and promotion to chance. Whenever he interpreted a dream for a prisoner, he would ask them for a 'referral' or a 'review'. This was how he got a recommendation in the palace while he was yet in prison. The verse below shows how Joseph promoted himself after interpreting the dream for the king's officers in the prison:

*But when all goes well with you, remember me and show me kindness; mention me to Pharaoh and get me out of this prison.*

*Genesis 40:14 NIV*

The above verse emphasizes the importance of seizing opportunities and actively seeking recognition. If you identify as an unrecognized creative, now, more than ever, it is crucial for you to take the reins of your own destiny. Don't wait for others to discover your talent or recognize your creative potential. Ignite the flames of your creativity and let your unique abilities shine. Let your ideas burn through the fabric of obscurity that tries to hide your creative spark. Seek out opportunities to showcase your work, collaborate with like-minded individuals, and share your creations with the world. Remember, it is within your power to rise above the shadows of obscurity and make your mark. The journey to recognition starts with you. Dare to ignite your creativity and unleash your boundless potential.

**c.  Network and Collaborate:**

Build connections with other creatives, professionals, and influencers in your field. Attend events, workshops, and conferences where you can meet like-minded individuals and potential collaborators. Collaborations can help amplify your work and introduce you to new audiences.

**d.  Seek Feedback and Constructive Criticism:**

Share your work with trusted peers, mentors, or professionals in your field and actively seek their feedback. Constructive criticism can help you refine your craft and improve your creative output. Use feedback as a learning opportunity and a way to grow as an artist.

**e.  Educate Yourself:**

Continuously develop your skills, knowledge, and understanding of your craft. Invest time in learning new techniques, exploring different mediums, and staying updated with industry trends. Attend workshops, take online courses, or join creative communities that offer educational resources.

**f.  Find Supportive Communities:**

Seek out communities and groups that appreciate and support unrecognized creatives. Surrounding yourself with like-minded individuals who understand the challenges you face can provide encouragement, inspiration, and opportunities for collaboration.

### g. Be Persistent and Resilient:

Recognize that gaining recognition takes time and perseverance. Keep creating and pushing forward even in the face of setbacks or lack of immediate recognition. Stay committed to your artistic vision and believe in the value of your work.

### h. Explore Alternative Avenues:

Look for alternative channels to showcase your creativity and gain recognition. This could include participating in local art exhibitions, submitting your work to online platforms or publications, seeking out independent galleries or venues that promote emerging artists, or even organizing your own showcase or event.

---

**SAY THESE WORDS**

The world is ready to recognize and appreciate my creative contributions. I am stepping into the spotlight and claiming my rightful place as a recognized creative. I am worthy of acknowledgment and appreciation for my creative work, and nothing can change that. I attract the people, materials, circumstances, network, and opportunities that will pave the way for me, bringing honor into my life. I am heard, seen, paid, sought after, and recognized for my gifts, talents, and creativity in every place and every day.

## FLIP THE SWITCH EXERCISE  #21

    a.  Do you identify as an unrecognized creative?

_________________________________________________

_________________________________________________

_________________________________________________

    b.  If not, what steps can you take to ensure you gain the recognition you deserve and avoid being unrecognized in the future?

_________________________________________________

_________________________________________________

_________________________________________________

    c.  If yes, what do you believe has contributed to being unrecognized? (Take responsibility where possible and avoid the blame game).

_________________________________________________

_________________________________________________

_________________________________________________

    d.  What aspects of being an unrecognized creative stand out to you most?

_________________________________________________

_________________________________________________

_________________________________________________

## 4.  Suppressed Creatives

Suppressed creatives are individuals who possess creative talents but find themselves in situations where their creative expression is restricted, hindered, or limited. These individuals may face various obstacles that prevent them from fully expressing their creativity and sharing their work with the world. These obstacles could be external, such as societal constraints, censorship, organizational restrictions, lack of resources or opportunities, or internal struggles, such as self-doubt, fear of judgment, or creative blockages. These constraints cause them to cover their creativity with a mental cloak and suppress it from gaining expression. This mental cloak represents the psychological and emotional defenses that individuals develop in response to the challenges, limitations, or societal pressures they face. It's how suppressed creatives may feel the need to shield their creativity, as if wrapping it in an invisible garment, to navigate the constraints imposed upon them. This mental cloak also symbolizes their inner struggles and the conscious or subconscious decision to hide their creative potential. If you find yourself in this group, you need to ignite your creativity, embrace your true self, and reclaim your creative voice, so that you can unleash your full creative potential.

> *Neither do people light a lamp and put it under a bowl. Instead, they put it on its stand, and it gives light to everyone in the house. In the same way, let your light shine before men, that they may see your good deeds and praise your Father in heaven.*
>
> *Matt 5:15-16 NIV*

This verse above conveys the message that the light within you should not be hidden or suppressed but rather ignited, shared, and utilized to benefit others. In the context of suppressed creatives, it emphasizes the importance of allowing your creative light to shine brightly instead of concealing it out of fear, self-doubt, or external pressures. Whatever it takes to give expression to your suppressed potential, you should explore these avenues to allow creativity to shine forth from within you. As long as it does not entail abusing yourself or others or violating God's will and purpose for your life, it is time to display the wonderful deeds that you are capable of. Just as a lamp's purpose is to illuminate its surroundings, suppressed creatives have a unique gift or talent that deserves to be expressed and shared with the world. By embracing their creativity, stepping out of the shadows, and letting their light shine, they can inspire and positively impact others, much like the light from a lamp brightens a room. This scriptural passage also encourages suppressed creatives to overcome their inhibitions and take pride in their creative abilities. It serves as a reminder that their talents are meant to be shared openly, enriching the lives of others, and bringing beauty and inspiration to the world.

## The suppressed interior designer

Suppressed creatives only need a light bulb moment to break out of whatever seems to be repressing their creativity. This story will give you an idea of what I am talking about. Jessica had always possessed a natural flair for interior design. However, growing up, she encountered significant resistance and criticism from her family and friends, who dismissed her creative passion as a frivolous pursuit. Believing their judgment, Jessica suppressed her desires and pursued a more conventional career path, burying her true creative instincts. For years, Jessica worked in a corporate job that left her feeling unfulfilled and disconnected from her authentic self. Deep down, she longed to express her creativity and make a tangible impact through interior design. However, the fear of judgment, societal expectations, and self-doubt kept her creativity locked away.

One day, a chance encounter with an inspiring interior design exhibition sparked a fire within Jessica. The beauty and innovation she witnessed reawakened her suppressed creative spirit. Determined to break free from the chains of conformity, Jessica embarked on a journey of self-discovery and creative reawakening. She sought therapy to address her deep-rooted insecurities and fear of failure, gradually building the confidence to embrace her creative talents. Jessica started attending design workshops, networking with like-minded individuals, and immersing herself in the world of interior design. Despite facing resistance from those around her who questioned her decision to veer off the conventional path, Jessica persisted. She refused to let their doubts and her own self-imposed limitations hold her back any longer. Through persistence, dedication, and unwavering belief in her abilities, Jessica eventually launched her own successful interior design firm. Today, Jessica is not only living her dream but also empowering others to embrace their own suppressed creativity. Through her designs, she strives to create transformative spaces that reflect her clients' unique personalities and aspirations.

Jessica's story serves as a powerful reminder that even in the face of suppression, it is possible to reclaim one's creativity and find true fulfillment by following one's passion.  Can you relate to Jessica's journey of suppressing her creative passion and yearning to break free, just as she did? Take a moment to truly connect with Jessica's story. Allow it to resonate within you. Are there aspects of your own life where you have hidden your creative desires, talents, or passions, much like Jessica did? Can you feel the weight of unexpressed potential within you, the longing for something more? Picture the moments when you held back, when you silenced your creative voice out of fear or a sense of obligation. Feel the emotions that arise as you consider the dreams you may have set aside, the artistic endeavors left unexplored. Acknowledge any regrets, frustrations, or missed opportunities that may surface. But let these emotions serve as a turning point, a catalyst for change. Let them fuel a fire within you, igniting a powerful conviction that it is time to break free from the chains of suppression.

**How to overcome the suppression of your creativity**

In the book of Genesis, Joseph was a young man with big dreams and visions given to him by God. However, his creative potential was suppressed by various circumstances he faced. Joseph's own brothers were envious of him and plotted to get rid of him. They sold him into slavery, and he ended up in Egypt, far away from his family and everything familiar to him. As a slave, Joseph's creative abilities may have been stifled, as he was subject to the control and demands of his masters, but he refused to let that stop him. Later, Joseph's situation worsened when he was falsely accused and thrown into prison. He endured years of confinement, which could have easily dampened his spirit and suppressed his creativity. Despite these setbacks, Joseph remained consistent in displaying his creativity. Whether he was a housekeeper or a prison keeper, he did not let that deter him; he infused excellence into every task he was assigned. He displayed his gift every chance he got. It was during his time in prison that Joseph's creative gifts emerged once again. He interpreted dreams for his fellow prisoners, showcasing his ability to discern and understand the meaning behind these visions. Eventually, Joseph's gift of interpreting dreams caught the attention of Pharaoh, the ruler of Egypt. Pharaoh summoned Joseph and sought his wisdom in interpreting a troubling dream. Empowered by God's guidance, Joseph interpreted the dream accurately and offered a creative solution to save Egypt from a devastating famine.

Pharaoh recognized Joseph's wisdom and appointed him as a high-ranking official, giving him authority and the opportunity to exercise his creative problem-solving skills. Joseph's story illustrates the journey from suppression to recognition of creative abilities. Despite being oppressed and facing numerous challenges, Joseph's creative potential could not be extinguished. His faithfulness and perseverance led to his eventual rise to power, where his creativity was fully utilized for the benefit of others. This example reminds us that even in times of suppression or adversity, our creative potential can still find a way to shine through. It encourages us to remain steadfast in our gifts and trust that God can elevate us from suppression to recognition, opening doors for us to express our creativity and make a positive impact. If you find yourself in an organization, association, or company where your creativity is always being suppressed, you should have an exit plan because not only your fulfillment, but the destinies of millions of people are tied to the potential inside you. That brainchild must not be suffocated in the womb of your mind and denied expression. You owe it to yourself, your brainchild, and God to share your creativity with the world. Sometimes, it could even be your religious affiliations with a church denomination or mosque that seem to suppress and stifle your creativity. You must rise and shine because the light is coming unto you, reigniting that suppressed creativity. It is time to move from under the bushel where you have been covered and take your place strategically in locations where the world can benefit from your creative spark.

Another major reason for suppression is that some people may think creativity is only possible in certain areas like art and science. So, they subconsciously tell the giant within them, 'stay asleep because there is nothing for you out there, nobody will buy into my gift.' This is a blatant lie! Some people cover their light with a bushel because those around them erroneously believe that if you are not building a spaceship going to Mars or developing the next tech-savvy invention, you are not creative. This mindset can also lead to the suppression of your creativity, and many people in this category go through life being average and mediocre, with minimal impact. If you find yourself in this category, recognize that creativity is expressed in problem-solving, communication, and even daily tasks. You can begin to unlock your own creative potential. Granting yourself permission to explore, experiment, and make mistakes, without worrying about what people will say, is a great step toward removing the suppressors of your creativity. It is time to open your eyes to the limitless possibilities that await you.

## The immigrant chef who tried to numb her gift

There was a talented chef named Adaora, who possessed a remarkable gift for preparing authentic Nigerian dishes. Before she migrated to Canada, she had mastered the art of making local dishes from her grandmother. Whenever you tasted her prepared dishes like jollof rice and dodo, pounded yam and egusi soup, fufu, banga soup, and afang soup, it transported you to the heart of Nigeria with every bite. However, Adaora chose to suppress her culinary talents, believing that her traditional Nigerian cooking skills might not be embraced in the foreign land she had migrated to. After settling in a new country, Adaora faced a barrage of doubts and insecurities. She was worried that the people in her new community might not appreciate the bold flavors, vibrant colors, and unique ingredients that defined Nigerian cuisine. These fears led her to suppress and bury her cooking gift and conform to the local food culture in Canada. Every time she ate at a restaurant, deep within her, she knew there was a void that needed to be filled. She would feel her gift kicking inside of her like a baby in the womb of a pregnant woman. Whenever she felt this way, she would numb the feeling by binge-watching movies on Prime and Netflix just to get those visions off her mind.

One day, while attending a multicultural food festival, she stumbled upon a booth that showcased diverse cuisines from around the world. Adaora's eyes sparkled as she noticed a small crowd gathered around a stall serving various exotic dishes. Curiosity compelled her to approach the stall and inquire about the chef behind the tantalizing aromas. To her surprise, the chef turned out to be an immigrant from a different country, showcasing the flavors of his homeland fearlessly. Adaora's heart swelled with inspiration as she realized that she, too, could share her beloved Nigerian cuisine with pride. In that moment, it felt like a light bulb suddenly got ignited within her. She became filled with the confidence and determination to break free from the chains of suppression. She said to herself, 'If that Mexican chef could express his cooking gift in a strange land, I will not suppress my gift.' At this point, she knew there was a market for her cooking gift. She believed she could target fellow immigrants who wanted to relish the taste of Nigerian food in Canada.

With her creativity ignited, Adaora embarked on a personal journey of self-discovery and culinary reawakening, ready to share her gift with the world. She reconnected with her Nigerian roots, immersing herself in the vibrant flavors, cultural traditions, and age-old cooking techniques. With each dish she prepared, Adaora infused it with her passion, love, and unwavering belief in the power of her cooking. Word of Adaora's culinary prowess began to spread within her new community. Beyond what she had expected, people from various backgrounds yearned for authentic, homemade Nigerian food, eager to savor flavors they had never experienced before. Encouraged by the positive feedback and the growing demand for her dishes, Adaora found the courage to establish her own catering business, specializing in Nigerian cuisine. Through her vibrant and flavorful creations, Adaora became a cultural ambassador, introducing her community to the richness and diversity of Nigerian food. Her fufu, pounded yam and egusi soup, jollof rice, banga soup, and afang soup became the talk of the town, captivating the palates of food enthusiasts far and wide. Adaora's light bulb moment not only transformed her own life but also ignited a newfound appreciation for Nigerian cuisine within her community. By refusing to suppress her cooking gift and sharing the authentic flavors of her homeland, she bridged cultural gaps, broke down stereotypes, and inspired others to celebrate their own unique culinary heritage.

Adaora's story serves as a powerful reminder that suppressing one's creative gifts only hinders personal growth and limits the world's exposure to unique talents. Through her courage and unwavering belief in her abilities, Adaora not only found success as a Nigerian chef but also rekindled a sense of pride in her cultural identity. What gifts or talents have you been suppressing or hiding from the world because of fear or self-doubt? Have societal expectations or cultural norms prevented you from fully embracing and expressing your true creative potential? How would your life be different if you had the courage to break free from suppression and share your unique talents with the world?

These questions are designed to provoke introspection and encourage you to reflect on your own life, passions, and creative aspirations.

---

**SAY THESE WORDS**

I reclaim my creative power and refuse to hide my talents any longer. My unique perspective and creativity have the potential to make a meaningful impact. Therefore, I break free from the constraints that have tried to suppress my creativity. I let go of any limiting beliefs that others have imposed on me and embrace my own creative journey. I am worthy of success and fulfillment through my creative pursuits. I step into the light, confident in my abilities, and ready to share my creativity with the world.

---

## FLIP THE SWITCH EXERCISE  #22

a.  Are you currently feeling suppressed in your creative pursuits?

_________________________________________________

_________________________________________________

_________________________________________________

b.  If not, how can you support and uplift suppressed creatives around you, fostering an environment of creative freedom and expression?

_______________________________________________

_______________________________________________

_______________________________________________

c.  If you identify as a suppressed creative, consider the following questions to ignite self-reflection and empowerment:

i.  What are the specific creative talents or passions that you have suppressed or held back from expressing fully?

_______________________________________________

_______________________________________________

_______________________________________________

ii.  What are the underlying reasons or obstacles that have contributed to the suppression of your creativity?

_______________________________________________

_______________________________________________

_______________________________________________

iii.  How has this suppression affected your sense of fulfillment and overall well-being?

_______________________________________________

_______________________________________________

_______________________________________________

c.  Embrace the power of self-liberation and creativity:

i.    What steps can you take to reclaim and unleash your suppressed creativity?

__________________________________________________________

__________________________________________________________

__________________________________________________________

ii.    How can you surround yourself with a supportive network or community that encourages and celebrates your creative journey?

__________________________________________________________

__________________________________________________________

__________________________________________________________

d.  Believe in your creative worth:

i.    How can you challenge and overcome the limiting beliefs or negative self-talk that have held you back?

__________________________________________________________

__________________________________________________________

__________________________________________________________

ii.    How can you celebrate and honor your creative accomplishments, no matter how small, as milestones on your journey of self-discovery and fulfillment?

__________________________________________________________

__________________________________________________________

__________________________________________________________

Remember, as a suppressed creative, you have the power to flip the switch and reclaim your creative potential. Reflect on these questions, and let them guide you towards a path of purpose fulfillment.

# 5. Stagnant Creatives

Do you find yourself repeating familiar patterns and ideas, avoiding risks, or staying within your comfort zone? Stagnant creatives are individuals who have experienced a prolonged period of mental stagnation or a lack of forward progress in their creative pursuits. Due to creative blocks, they may find themselves stuck in a state of inertia, unable to generate new ideas. Because of this, they are unable to make meaningful progress or experience personal growth in their creative endeavors. Stagnant creatives often feel trapped in a creative rut, where inspiration and motivation have waned, resulting in a sense of frustration and dissatisfaction. These creatives may have once been passionate and driven in their creative pursuits, but over time, they begin to experience a diminished sense of inspiration and productivity. It is important to note that stagnation is a common experience that many creatives encounter at various points in their journey. However, recognizing the signs of stagnation and taking proactive steps to break free from it can help stagnant creatives reignite their passion, continue to evolve and grow.

## The silent killer

Stagnation is a silent killer that can undermine your progress without you even realizing it. It lulls you into a false sense of security, making you believe that staying in your comfort zone is enough. However, while you remain stagnant, the world around you continues to evolve and progress at a rapid pace. Before you know it, you're left behind, wondering how you ended up in such a state. It is a canker that eats deep into your progress until it becomes too late. This is because when you are stagnated, it does not look like you are moving backwards; you just remain in the same spot. However, while you stay in that spot, the world moves on, and when you finally realize it, it is already too late. This phenomenon is not limited to individuals alone; it can also affect companies. Many once powerful and innovative companies have disappeared or become irrelevant today due to their inability to adapt and innovate. They fell victim to the trap of resting on their laurels, relying on past achievements as an excuse to avoid pushing boundaries and exploring new possibilities. As the world moved forward, these companies failed to keep up, losing their competitive edge and ultimately fading away. Similarly, individuals can fall into the trap of stagnation in their personal and professional lives. They may become complacent in their careers, relying solely on their existing skills and knowledge without seeking opportunities for growth and development. This complacency can hinder their progress, limit their potential, and prevent them from seizing new opportunities.

One example of a company that experienced stagnation is Blockbuster. At its peak, Blockbuster was the go-to video rental store, dominating the market with its vast selection of movies and convenient rental options. However, with the rise of digital streaming and on-demand services, Blockbuster failed to adapt to the changing landscape. While Netflix embraced the digital revolution, Blockbuster clung to its traditional brick-and-mortar model. As a result, Blockbuster became stagnant, and its failure to innovate ultimately led to its demise. Maybe you currently run a thriving business. Take a cue from companies that have gone the way of dinosaurs and make sure you don't fail to reinvent your business. Nokia is another prime example of a company that experienced stagnation and faced significant challenges as a result. Once a global leader in the mobile phone industry, Nokia dominated the market with its iconic and durable handsets. However, the company's failure to adapt to the rise of smartphones and the shift towards touchscreen technology led to its downfall. While competitors like Apple and Samsung introduced innovative smartphones, Nokia remained focused on its traditional mobile phone offerings. This lack of agility and failure to embrace the evolving market trends resulted in a sharp decline in Nokia's market share and profitability. The case of Nokia highlights the importance of anticipating and responding to industry disruptions. Stagnation can occur when companies become complacent, relying on past successes and failing to recognize or act upon emerging trends. Nokia's story serves as a cautionary tale, demonstrating the need for companies to continuously innovate, invest in research and development, and stay ahead of the curve to maintain relevance in a rapidly evolving market. It is crucial for you to learn from the examples of stagnant companies and understand the importance of adaptability, innovation, and a growth mindset. By being sensitive to change, continuously seeking new opportunities, and being willing to step out of your comfort zones, you can avoid falling into the trap of stagnation and thrive in dynamic and competitive environments.

Have you ever found yourself clinging to past successes or accomplishments as a reason to avoid taking new creative risks or exploring different creative paths? Have you become complacent in your creative pursuits, relying on familiar techniques or ideas without actively seeking new inspiration or growth? Have you stopped seeking feedback or constructive criticism on your work, choosing to remain within your own bubble and avoiding opportunities for improvement? Some stagnant creatives often become complacent and rest on their past successes or achievements. They may rely on their previous accomplishments as a justification for not pushing themselves further or exploring new avenues of creativity. This kind of complacency can hinder growth and prevent you from reaching your full potential. By clinging to past successes, stagnant creatives may resist taking risks or try to resist inevitable change. This complacency can lead to a lack of innovation as they become resistant to new ideas or approaches that could propel their creative work forward.

## The stagnant auto-mechanic

In a small town, there was an auto-mechanic named John who had gained a reputation for his expertise in repairing vintage cars. He was particularly renowned for his exceptional skills in fixing classic American muscle cars. His workshop was a haven for car enthusiasts, and people from far and wide brought their vintage treasures to him for restoration. For years, John thrived in his niche as the go-to mechanic for classic cars. He took pride in his ability to restore these beautiful vehicles to their former glory. However, as time passed, the automotive industry began evolving rapidly, with the rise of electric cars and advanced technologies. While many other mechanics adapted to the changing times, John stubbornly clung to his love for vintage cars and resisted embracing the new technologies. He became known as the "king of classic cars," but as the demand for vintage car repairs dwindled, so did his business. Customers started looking for mechanics who specialized in electric cars and hybrid vehicles, leaving John with fewer and fewer clients. His workshop, once buzzing with activity, began to feel empty and desolate. Yet, he remained steadfast in his refusal to adapt, convinced that the classic car market would rebound. One day, a young entrepreneur named Emily stumbled upon John's workshop. She had a vision for a business that combined classic car restoration with cutting-edge electric car conversions. Intrigued by the idea, Emily approached John and shared her plans. Initially resistant, John was captivated by Emily's passion and innovative thinking. He realized that he had been clinging to the past, neglecting the potential for growth and reinvention. Inspired by Emily's vision, he agreed to join forces and embark on a new venture together. John began learning about electric car technology, attending workshops, and collaborating with engineers. With Emily's guidance, they transformed their workshop into a hub for sustainable car transformations, combining the timeless beauty of classic cars with modern, eco-friendly technology. Their business flourished as they tapped into a market that bridged the gap between classic car enthusiasts and environmentally conscious consumers. People admired their unique approach and commitment to innovation. John's reputation as a master mechanic expanded beyond vintage cars, and he became a respected figure in the realm of electric vehicle conversions.

This story serves as a powerful reminder that stagnant creatives can find new purpose and success by embracing change and adapting to evolving trends. Just as John discovered the potential for growth by combining classic cars with modern technology, stagnant creatives can overcome their limitations by exploring new avenues, acquiring new skills, and seizing opportunities for reinvention.

To overcome stagnation, it is crucial to embrace a mindset of continuous learning, growth, and adaptability. This involves stepping out of your comfort zone, seeking new challenges, acquiring new skills, and staying updated with industry trends. It also requires being open to feedback, embracing change, and cultivating a proactive attitude towards personal and professional development. By avoiding the trap of stagnation, individuals and companies can position themselves for long-term success and relevance in an ever-evolving world. Have you found yourself caught in a monotonous routine that leaves little room for creative expression? Stagnant creatives are individuals who have reached a plateau in their creative journey. They may feel stuck, uninspired, or lacking motivation to explore new avenues. To reignite their creativity, such individuals need to flip the switches of inspiration. If you find that you have become stagnant and redundant in your creative journey, exposing yourself to new experiences, seeking fresh inspiration from different sources, and setting creative challenges can revitalize your creative spirit and push you beyond your comfort zones.

**SAY THESE WORDS**

I am capable of adapting to evolving trends and technologies in my field. I welcome challenges as opportunities to expand my skills and knowledge. I trust in my ability to reinvent myself and find fresh inspiration in my creative endeavors. I am committed to lifelong learning and staying up to date with industry advancements. I am open to collaboration and learning from others who can inspire and push me forward. I believe in my ability to create meaningful and impactful work that resonates with others.

Remember, affirmations are most effective when repeated regularly and with conviction. They can help shift your mindset and empower you to break free from stagnation, embrace change, and reignite your creative spark.

## FLIP THE SWITCH EXERCISE  #23

    a)  Do you identify as a stagnant creative? ____________________

    b)  If not, what steps can you take to ensure you don't fall into the trap of stagnation in your creative pursuits?

_______________________________________________

_______________________________________________

    c)  If yes, what factors do you believe have contributed to your stagnation? (Take responsibility and avoid blaming external circumstances)

_______________________________________________

_______________________________________________

d) What aspects of stagnant creatives resonate with you the most? What patterns or behaviors have kept you stuck in a state of stagnation?

_______________________________________________

_______________________________________________

e) What actions or mindset shifts can you implement to revitalize your creativity and pursue growth?

_______________________________________________

_______________________________________________

Remember, stagnation is a choice, and it's never too late to make a change. Develop a growth mindset and take intentional steps towards self-improvement and forward progress. Let go of complacency and embrace the journey of continual growth and reinvention as a creative individual.

## 6. Discouraged Creatives

Imagine being an aspiring entrepreneur who has poured your heart and soul into developing a groundbreaking product. You believe it has the potential to solve a common problem and make a significant impact in the market. Excitedly, you invest a significant amount of time and money into marketing this product. However, as the days and weeks go by, you start to notice that the results are far from what you expected. The ads generate little to no conversion, and the sales numbers remain disappointingly low. You begin to question the effectiveness of your marketing strategy and doubt the viability of your product. Each day, you check the ad analytics and sales reports, hoping to see a positive shift, but the numbers continue to tell a disheartening story. Doubts creep into your mind, and discouragement sets in. You start questioning your abilities and your product's value proposition. Despite your initial enthusiasm, the lack of tangible results weighs heavily on your motivation. You feel stuck, unsure of how to improve the situation and whether your creative endeavor will ever gain the recognition and success you envisioned.

Discouragement is something that can crush your spirit if you let it. Whether you're a digital entrepreneur running ads and getting minimal sales, or a graduate facing rejection emails without any interview requests, it is important to stay resilient. Discouraged creatives are individuals who have experienced a significant loss of motivation, confidence, or enthusiasm in their creative pursuits. They may have encountered setbacks, criticism, or personal challenges that have deeply affected their belief in their abilities and potential. Discouragement can manifest as a lack of inspiration, self-doubt, feelings of inadequacy, and a general sense of hopelessness or apathy towards their creative endeavors. These creatives may have faced repeated rejections, failed projects, or negative feedback that has eroded their self-esteem and belief in their talents. They may have compared themselves to others, feeling like they don't measure up or that their work is not valuable or meaningful. Discouraged creatives often struggle to find the motivation to continue pursuing their passions, as they may fear further disappointment or fear being judged by others. These creatives may feel trapped in a cycle of negativity, unable to break free from the discouragement that holds them back from fully expressing themselves creatively. If you are currently in this boat, it's important to recognize that discouragement is a common experience for many creatives, and it's not a reflection of your inherent talent or worth. It's a temporary state that can be overcome with the right mindset and support. By addressing the underlying causes of discouragement, developing resilience, seeking inspiration, and fostering a positive environment, discouraged creatives can reignite their passion, regain confidence in their abilities, and find renewed joy in their creative pursuits. Interestingly, the way out of discouragement still happens to be creativity. Creativity does not back down in the face of disappointments or discouragements. It persists and figures out new and different ways to overcome whatever obstacle that besets it. However, if you do not do this intentionally and you leave it to chance, your creative spark could get extinguished by these external forces.

**SAY THESE WORDS**

I am resilient and can bounce back from discouragement. I find inspiration and motivation in the face of adversity. I trust that my smart work and dedication will pay off in due time. I am open to learning and improving my skills to reach my goals. I acknowledge that setbacks are temporary and opportunities for growth. I choose to focus on the progress I've made and the potential for future success.

Note: Remember, affirmations are most effective when personalized to your specific situation and needs. Feel free to modify or create your own affirmations that resonate with you personally.

## FLIP THE SWITCH EXERCISE  #24

    a)  Do you identify as a discouraged creative? _______________________

    b)  If not, what can you do to avoid ever becoming a discouraged creative if you do not identify as one?

_______________________________________________________

_______________________________________________________

_______________________________________________________

c) If yes, what do you think is responsible for your discouragement? (Try to avoid blaming external factors and focus on internal mindset and beliefs).

_______________________________________________

_______________________________________________

_______________________________________________

d) What aspects of being a discouraged creative stand out to you most?

_______________________________________________

_______________________________________________

_______________________________________________

## 7. Fearful Creatives

Have you ever felt hesitant to share your creative work because of fear of judgment or criticism? Did you ever experience self-doubt that made you question your creative abilities or worth? Are you ever held back from pursuing a creative project or idea due to fear of failure or rejection? Have you ever compared yourself to others in your field and felt inadequate or intimidated? Do you ever feel paralyzed by the fear of not meeting your own or others' expectations? Have you ever avoided taking risks or exploring new creative territories due to fear of stepping out of your comfort zone? Are there past failures or setbacks that discouraged you from fully embracing your creative potential? If you answered yes to any of these questions, then you belong to this category. If so, there is absolutely nothing to worry about because by the time you are done going through this book, you will be transformed into a fearless creative.

Fearful creatives are individuals who possess creative talents and aspirations but are hindered by fear. They long to express their gifts, pursue their artistic passions, and share their work with others. However, various fears hold them back, creating barriers to their creative growth. These fears manifest in different ways. Fear of failure prevents them from taking risks and reaching their potential. Fear of rejection stifles their willingness to share their work and seek feedback. Fear of vulnerability keeps them from expressing their true selves. Fear of inadequacy undermines their confidence and originality. Fear of the unknown deters them from exploring new creative possibilities. However, it's important to recognize that fear is not insurmountable. With determination, you can unlock your creative potential, pursue your passions, and confidently share your unique gifts with the world. If you identify yourself as a fearful creative, you should start unlocking your creativity by learning to take small steps, embracing imperfections, and believing in your unique vision. This can help you overcome your fears and unlock your creative energy.

## Stories of fearful creatives with untapped potential

Fearful creatives often find themselves trapped in a cycle of self-doubt and hesitation, their creative ideas stifled by the overwhelming fear of judgment and the unknown. This fear can manifest in various professional settings, inhibiting them from expressing their innovative thoughts and making a lasting impact.

Let's explore a range of scenarios where people, despite possessing immense creative potential, were held back by fear. In one instance, we have Anthony, an architect with a wealth of groundbreaking ideas for sustainable building designs. However, when it came time to share his concepts in team meetings, a fear of being wrong, ridiculed by his colleagues, or dismissed by his superiors silenced his voice. As a result, his innovative contributions remained untapped, leaving unrealized potential in the realm of environmentally friendly architectural projects.

Similarly, we encounter Lisa, a talented software engineer who carried within her the vision of a revolutionary software application. Unfortunately, her fear of being perceived as inexperienced or irrelevant prevented her from voicing her ideas during brainstorming sessions. Consequently, her breakthrough concept remained buried, depriving her company of a game-changing product. But it's not only in the confines of the corporate world that fear hinders creative expression. In the realm of entrepreneurship, individuals like Jason, an aspiring entrepreneur, find themselves at a crossroads. Despite having a solid business plan and the skills to launch their own company, the fear of the unknown and the risks associated with venturing into the uncharted territory of entrepreneurship keep them anchored in their comfort zones, stunting their personal growth and potential impact. Meanwhile, we meet Anastasia, a talented graphic designer yearning to establish her design agency. She possesses the skills, creativity, and drive necessary to succeed, but the fear of financial uncertainty and the weight of potential failure loom large. These fears hold her back from taking the leap and pursuing her dream of owning a thriving design company, relegating her innovative ideas to the confines of her imagination.

Lastly, we encounter David, a marketing professional who harbors a unique concept for a niche market that holds tremendous business potential. However, his fear of inadequacy and the belief that he lacks the necessary expertise and resources prevent him from embracing his entrepreneurial spirit. As a result, his innovative business idea remains dormant, a missed opportunity to make a mark in the industry. These stories serve as reminders of the grip that fear can have on the creative spirit. Whether it's the fear of judgment, uncertainty, or failure, it is essential for you to confront and overcome these barriers to fully unleash your creative potential. Only by acknowledging and challenging their fears can fearful creatives break free from the constraints that hinder their progress and embark on a journey of self-discovery and creative expression.

## 5 Easy Steps to overcome fear as a Creative

Here are some expert insights to help fearful creatives:

### a) **Recognize your fear:**

Dr. Brené Brown, a renowned researcher and author, suggests acknowledging and naming your fears[1]. Identifying the specific fears that hold you back allows you to better understand and address them. Don't be like Anthony, who had revolutionary architectural designs and suggestions but buried his ideas shamefully for fear of being wrong. Understand that your ideas do not have to be perfect all the time, and it is okay to be wrong sometimes. Most creatives make fantastic discoveries by expressing their ideas, finding out they are wrong, and going back to brainstorm better solutions. That is how you grow as a creative. Your voice deserves to be heard! Just say, "Correct me if I'm wrong, I think we could achieve a better outcome if we explore the XYZ approach based on so-and-so information." I have noticed that speaking up when you have ideas improves your problem-solving skills. If this is something you are dealing with, consciously identify your fear and its impact on your ability to share your innovative ideas in meetings. By acknowledging this challenge, you can begin to work on strategies to overcome it.

### b) **See Fear as Opportunity:**

Psychologist Kelly McGonigal suggests reframing fear as excitement[2]. Instead of viewing fear as a negative emotion, see it as a sign that you're stepping out of your comfort zone and embarking on something meaningful. Perhaps, like Lisa, you fear being perceived as inexperienced or irrelevant, which hinders you from expressing your ideas during brainstorming sessions at work. Reframe your fear of being looked down on or ridiculed. Embrace it as an exciting opportunity to learn and grow, even if you turn out to be sincerely wrong. Remember, if your idea proves to be right, you will have made a difference by contributing your revolutionary idea. Ask yourself, "What is the worst that can happen if I suggest or explore this idea?" Even if the idea fails or gets rejected, the important thing is what you learn in the process of discussing and exploring it. Every experience is an opportunity to learn and improve. Shifting your perspective can help you use fear as a positive motivator and fuel your confidence to speak up. Do not bury your creativity in the mud of fear; you owe your inner genius this much! Embrace the excitement of growth and discovery as you share your unique ideas with the world.

**c) Challenge Your Limiting Beliefs:**

Dr. Carol Dweck, a psychologist known for her work on growth mindset, advises challenging limiting beliefs about your abilities[3]. If, like Anastasia, your mindset is holding you back and causing fears, it is time to question the basis for those beliefs. For example, if you believe that a lack of financial resources is enough reason for you not to unleash your potential, consider this: Creativity knows no bounds when it comes to financial status. It has the power to harness gifts and talents even in the face of limited resources. The first step is to challenge the limiting beliefs that give financial uncertainty and fear of failure the power to hinder you. By doing so, you can actively work on replacing them with a resourceful mindset.

## d) Use Fear as Fuel:

Elizabeth Gilbert, author of "Big Magic," encourages embracing fear as an indicator that you're pursuing something important[4]. Instead of letting fear paralyze you, use it as a catalyst to take action and move forward with your creative endeavors. Embrace your fear of the unknown and use it as fuel to thoroughly research and plan your business venture, if you are like Jason, the fearful entrepreneur. Rather than letting fear paralyze you, you can channel it into motivation and take small steps towards your goals.

## e) Practice Exposure Therapy:

Dr. Albert Bandura, a psychologist, suggests exposure therapy to overcome fear[5]. Gradually expose yourself to the situations that trigger fear, starting with small steps, and gradually increasing the difficulty. This process helps desensitize you to fear and builds confidence. For example, David, the marketing professional, can gradually expose himself to situations that trigger his fear of inadequacy in launching his own company. Start with small steps, such as attending networking events or seeking mentorship. You can gradually build your confidence and desensitize yourself to the fear of not having enough expertise or resources.

These expert insights highlight the importance of understanding and confronting fear, reframing beliefs, and embracing vulnerability as you pursue your aspirations. Incorporating these insights into your journey can help you navigate fear and unlock your full creative potential.

> **SAY THESE WORDS**
>
> I fearlessly and shamelessly release my creative gifts, talents, skills and potential, knowing that my ideas have value and impact. I trust in my creative instincts and follow them without hesitation. I let go of the fear of failure and allow myself to take risks in my creative pursuits. I embrace vulnerability as a strength and share my creative work with courage. I am open to receiving feedback and constructive criticism to grow as a creative individual. I am free from perfectionism and allow myself to explore and experiment with my creativity.

## FLIP THE SWITCH EXERCISE  #25

a)  Do you identify as a fearful creative?

_______________________________________________

_______________________________________________

b)  If not, how can you support and encourage fearful creatives around you, fostering an environment of creativity and growth?

_______________________________________________

_______________________________________________

_______________________________________________

c)  If yes, explore the following aspects to gain insights and self-reflection:

  i.  What specific fears are holding you back from expressing your creativity?

______________________________________________________

______________________________________________________

______________________________________________________

ii.    How have these fears impacted your creative pursuits and self-belief?

______________________________________________________

______________________________________________________

______________________________________________________

iii.    What patterns or habits have you developed to cope with or avoid facing your fears?

______________________________________________________

______________________________________________________

______________________________________________________

d) Take Action and Embrace Risk:

i.    What small steps can you take now in order to overcome your fears as a creative?

______________________________________________________

______________________________________________________

______________________________________________________

ii.    What mistakes have you made in the past when you tried to express or explore your creative ideas?

______________________________________________________

______________________________________________________

______________________________________________________

iii.   What key takeaways or learning did you get from those failed attempts, rejections or mistakes made in time past?

___________________________________________

___________________________________________

___________________________________________

iv.   What is your resolve and decision on how you will deal with your fears from now onward?

___________________________________________

___________________________________________

___________________________________________

Remember, flipping the switch from being a fearful creative to an empowered one takes time and effort. Embrace these principles, trust in your abilities, and take bold steps towards unlocking your creative potential.

**SAY THESE WORDS**

I arise, I shine because my light has come, and the creativity that God displayed in the beginning radiates in and through me. The brilliance of my creative ideas, gifts, talent, and potential produces solutions to problems around me. I refuse to cower at the sight of problems, but I see obstacles as opportunities for inspiration and innovation. I will not miss out on any lightbulb moment that will catapult me into greatness as I read this book. My refined gifts attract people from all walks of life to experience my unique expression. I open my eyes to the endless possibilities and creative opportunities that surround me. The abundance of creative resources and opportunities flow effortlessly into my life. And even in the face of a lack of resources, I am abundantly resourceful.

# CREATIVITY WORKSHEET #3

**Instructions:**

Use this worksheet to reflect on your creative journey and discover which type of creative you resonate with the most. Answer the questions and prompts below to gain insights into your creative strengths, passions, and areas for growth. This worksheet will help you understand where you belong in the world of creativity and guide you in developing your creative potential.

1.  Identify Where You Belong:

    Based on your self-reflection, understanding of the 7 types of creatives, and insights from the "Flip the Switch" exercises, identify which type(s) of creative you believe you belong to the most. Explain your choice and provide examples or reasons that support your decision.

    _______________________________________________

    _______________________________________________

    _______________________________________________

    _______________________________________________

2.  Goal Setting:

a)  What are your short-term creative goals? These can be specific projects, skills you want to develop, or creative challenges you want to undertake.

    _______________________________________________

    _______________________________________________

    _______________________________________________

    _______________________________________________

b) What are your long-term creative aspirations? Where do you envision yourself and your creativity in the future?

_______________________________________________

_______________________________________________

_______________________________________________

_______________________________________________

c) List three actionable steps you can take to move closer to your creative goals.

_______________________________________________

_______________________________________________

_______________________________________________

_______________________________________________

3. Personal Action Plan:

Create an action plan to nurture and develop your creative potential:

a) Identify potential obstacles or challenges that may hinder your creative growth.

_______________________________________________

_______________________________________________

_______________________________________________

_______________________________________________

b) Outline strategies to overcome these obstacles and stay motivated.

_______________________________________________

_______________________________________________

_______________________________________________

_______________________________________________

c) Set a timeline and deadlines for your creative projects and milestones.

_______________________________________________

_______________________________________________

_______________________________________________

_______________________________________________

Remember, this worksheet is meant to guide your self-reflection and provide a framework for understanding your creative journey. Feel free to add any additional thoughts or insights as you work through the questions. Leverage the process and use this worksheet as a tool to unlock your creative potential and release your gift, talent, and skills.

# CHAPTER FOUR

## SWITCHES OF CREATIVITY

$\mathcal{M}$ost people have either never ignited their creativity or have lost the creative spark they once had. Some do not even know that they have what it takes to be creative. The good news is that while losing your creative spark may be disheartening, it is not a permanent state. There are ways to reignite the flames and reconnect with your innate creative abilities. Creativity is not just about having an innate talent for thinking outside the box; it is a process that can be triggered by a series of mental, behavioral, and attitudinal switches. Each switch facilitates a different aspect of creativity, from critical thinking to ruthless execution, entrepreneurial spirit, and more. Creativity is a process that can be cultivated and activated through deliberate actions and mindsets. By recognizing and understanding these switches, anyone can enhance their creative abilities and approach problem-solving and innovation with a more intentional and effective mindset.

## A cursory look at ignition switches

The car's ignition switch, operated by a key or button, regulates the flow of electrical power to various vehicle components, including the engine. It is called the 'ignition switch' because it's responsible for starting the car engine by creating a spark. When you flip the ignition switch with a key or button, it sends power from the car's battery to the ignition coil, which produces a spark. This spark ignites the fuel mixture in the engine, allowing it to start and run. Airplanes also have ignition switches, which serve a similar purpose to those in cars. They control the power to the engine's ignition system, starting the combustion process in the plane's engines. However, commercial planes have multiple ignition switches, one for each engine. Each engine has its own ignition system, and the switches are usually located in the plane's cockpit. Pilots can control the ignition systems of each engine independently. This helps with starting, operating, and fixing the engines.

To start a car's engine, you just need to use the single ignition switch available. But to fly a plane, you need to turn on several switches, knobs, and buttons because planes have more parts that need to be activated for a successful flight. Similarly, there are 'switches of creativity' that can ignite or reactivate your creativity. Depending on what you want to achieve, you can use these switches to spark your creativity and reach new heights or solve tough problems. Prepare to be astonished as you activate these switches! Most people are like an airplane that is about to pack up, running with just one engine. They are running below their full capacity because they have not flipped on the switch of their creative mind. By igniting your creativity, you can unlock your full potential and achieve remarkable outcomes. This chapter will provide an overview of these switches, equipping you with a better understanding of how to use creativity in all your endeavors. Below are the switches of creativity that we will delve into in this chapter:

- Troubleshooting
- Critical Thinking
- Ardent Research
- Entrepreneurial Spirit
- Initiative
- Ruthless Execution
- Vocational Aptitude
- Intuition
- Tipping Point
- Yearning

## Troubleshooting

In the realm of creativity, troubleshooting can indeed be considered one of the essential switches that fuel innovative thinking and problem-solving. By understanding and leveraging the concept of troubleshooting, you can tap into your creative potential and apply it to various aspects of everyday life. Troubleshooting involves a systematic approach to identifying and resolving problems, which requires analytical thinking, attention to detail, and the ability to break down complex issues into manageable components. This process of finding the underlying causes of a problem forms the foundation for leveraging this switch of creativity. In the realm of creativity, problem-solving lies at its very core. When we think of +9-creativity, we often envision artists, writers, or inventors bringing novel ideas to life. However, behind every stroke of genius or breakthrough innovation, there is a significant problem to be solved. This is where the art of troubleshooting enters the scene, bridging the gap between having ideas and the practical implementation of the same. So, who is a troubleshooter? A troubleshooter is a person who is skilled at discovering or locating existing problems and rectifying them. Troubleshooting is a skill, and when you turn on the switch for troubleshooting problems and come up with optimal solutions, you can literally unlock your creativity.

> *In the second year of his reign, Nebuchadnezzar had dreams; **his mind was troubled**, and he could not sleep. So, the king summoned the magicians, enchanters,*

*sorcerers, and astrologers to tell him what he had dreamed.*

*Dan 2:1-2 NIV*

In the above verse, the powerful king faced a problem, but he couldn't find a solution, which troubled him greatly. What's even more concerning is that he couldn't even remember the dream or puzzle that disturbed him in the first place. He had a disturbing dream, but the details eluded him. As a professional software engineer, I can relate to such a situation. In a global tech company, one of the most challenging days at work is when you attempt to fix an elusive "bug" that engineers cannot replicate or identify the cause of. However, the situation in Daniel's time was far more challenging because not only jobs were at stake, but people's lives were on the line (Daniel 2:6). The king had demanded that all the smart people in the land be killed if they were unable to figure out the problem, identify its root cause, and solve it. These wise men, sorcerers, astrologers, and magicians—people we can consider the smartest in the country—were facing the threat of losing their lives simply because they couldn't troubleshoot the king's problem.

*The king replied to the astrologers, "This is what I have firmly decided: If you do not tell me what my dream was and interpret it, I will have you cut into pieces and your houses turned into piles of rubble. But if you tell me the dream and explain it, you will receive from me gifts and rewards and great honor. So, tell me the dream and interpret it for me."*

*Dan 2:5-6 NIV*

When Daniel told the king to give him time to deliver both the dream (puzzle) and its interpretation (solution), he knew he needed to activate the switch of troubleshooting. That's exactly what he did in the unfolding story. It's one thing to find a solution to a problem you already know, but an entirely different challenge to find a solution to a problem you have little or no knowledge about. Discovering solutions to such non-obvious problems represents one of the greatest challenges of creativity, especially when dealing with complex systems. Therefore, troubleshooting and investigative skills are essential requirements if you wish to identify such issues. A problem that goes undetected cannot be adequately solved. That's why troubleshooting, in the pursuit of identifying problems and their root causes, becomes an essential initial step for creating effective solutions. When you ignite your creativity by activating this switch, you gain the uncanny ability to spot and detect problems before they even arise. Not only can you prevent existing problems from festering, but you can also proactively create solutions for potential issues that others have yet to encounter. When the opportunity arises to showcase your solutions, your creativity will captivate and mesmerize those around you.

> *Now all the king's wise men came, but they could not read the writing, or make known to the king its interpretation. Then King Belshazzar was greatly troubled, his countenance was changed, and his lords were astonished. The queen, because of the words of the king and his lords, came to the banquet hall. The queen spoke, saying, "O king, live forever! Do not let your thoughts trouble you, nor let your countenance change. There is a man in your kingdom in whom is the Spirit of the Holy God. And in the days of your father,* **light** *and* **understanding** *and* **wisdom, like the wisdom***

> *of the gods, were found in him; and King Nebuchadnezzar your father — your father the king — made him chief of the magicians, astrologers, Chaldeans, and soothsayers. Inasmuch as an excellent spirit, **knowledge, understanding, interpreting dreams, solving riddles, and explaining enigmas** were found in this Daniel, whom the king named Belteshazzar, now let Daniel be called, and he will give the interpretation."*

> *Dan 5:8-12 NKJV*

## Benefits of Being a Troubleshooter

The troubleshooting switch is important for several reasons:

1. Problem-Solving: Troubleshooting is essentially a problem-solving approach. It equips you with the skills and mindset to identify, analyze, and resolve issues effectively. It allows for the systematic exploration of challenges and the development of practical solutions. Without troubleshooting, problems may persist or escalate, hindering progress and productivity.

2. Adaptability: The troubleshooting switch promotes adaptability and flexibility in dealing with unexpected situations. It makes you think critically, consider alternative approaches, and adjust your strategies accordingly. Troubleshooting helps you navigate through uncertainties and change, allowing you to adapt and find innovative solutions.

3. Efficiency and Productivity: Troubleshooting improves your efficiency and productivity by minimizing downtime and obstacles. When problems arise, you can quickly diagnose and address the

root causes, reducing the impact on workflow and enabling a swift return to normal operations. Troubleshooting also helps streamline processes, identify bottlenecks, and optimize systems, leading to improved productivity.

4. Creativity and Innovation: Troubleshooting often demands creative thinking to generate unique solutions. It challenges you to think beyond conventional approaches and consider alternative possibilities. By leveraging the troubleshooting switch, you can tap into your creative potential, exploring innovative ideas and methods to solve problems.

5. Pattern Recognition: By analyzing problems and their resolutions, you can identify patterns, root causes, and opportunities for improvement. This iterative process contributes to your creativity as a problem solver.

6. Personal Development: It builds valuable skills within you that extend beyond problem-solving. It cultivates critical thinking, analytical abilities, decision-making, and resilience. You develop a problem-solving mindset that can be applied to various aspects of life, enhancing personal and professional development.

7. Enhances Relationships and Collaboration: Troubleshooting often involves working with others to identify and resolve problems. It fosters collaboration, communication, and teamwork as you pool your knowledge, skills, and perspectives with others to troubleshoot problems.

## How to Troubleshoot

To apply troubleshooting for creativity in everyday life, consider the following steps:

- **Recognize the Problem:**

Begin by acknowledging the presence of a problem or challenge. Whether it's a personal obstacle, a creative block, or a practical issue, clearly defining the problem is crucial for effective troubleshooting.

- **Analyze the Situation:**

Take a step back and examine the problem from different angles. Break it down into smaller components and identify any patterns or recurring issues. This analysis helps in understanding the root causes and potential interconnections.

- **Generate Alternative Perspectives:**

Encourage yourself to think beyond conventional solutions. Challenge assumptions and explore multiple viewpoints. This step involves shifting your mindset, allowing yourself to consider unexplored possibilities, and embracing a more expansive way of thinking.

- **Brainstorm and Ideate:**

Engage in brainstorming sessions to generate a wide range of ideas and potential solutions. Embrace quantity over quality during this stage, as it allows for a broader exploration of possibilities. Encourage wild ideas, unconventional approaches, and combinations of different concepts.

- **Experiment and Iterate:**

Put your ideas into action through small-scale experiments or prototypes. Embrace a trial-and-error approach, as this enables you to learn from the outcomes and refine your ideas. Iteration helps in refining and improving your creative solutions over time.

- **Embrace Flexibility and Adaptability:**

Be prepared to adapt your troubleshooting process and creative solutions as new information emerges. Flexibility allows for the incorporation of unexpected insights and the ability to adjust your approach based on feedback and results.

- **Learn from Failures:**

View failures as learning opportunities. Troubleshooting often involves encountering setbacks, but it can provide valuable insights and lessons for future endeavors. Embrace a growth mindset that sees failures as steppingstones toward creative success.

You can apply this approach to a wide range of everyday scenarios. The troubleshooting mindset helps you solve problems at work, find innovative solutions to personal challenges, and enhance your creative pursuits. It enables you to think critically, devise unconventional approaches, and unlock your creative potential.

---

**SAY THESE WORDS**

I am sought after for my problem-solving skills around the world, just like Daniel was called upon for his expertise. I have the ability to interpret and solve complex problems, because the wisdom of God is at work in me. When faced with difficult challenges, I remain calm and confident, knowing that I have the spirit of excellence within me. I am skilled at interpreting dreams, solving riddles, and explaining enigmas, just like Daniel. My ability to troubleshoot and provide accurate interpretations brings honor and recognition. I am confident in my ability to uncover hidden meanings and provide clarity in complex situations. I use my gift of interpreting and solving problems to bring value and insight to others. Thank you Lord!

## FLIP THE SWITCH EXERCISE #26 - Troubleshooting

Instructions: Grab a pen and notepad, think through the exercises and write down your responses. You can repeat this exercise anytime you want to troubleshoot.

1. Identify Your Personal Challenge: Think about a specific challenge you're currently facing in your life, whether it's related to work, relationships, personal growth, or a creative pursuit.

2. Break it Down: Take a moment to break down your challenge into smaller components or sub-problems. This will help you analyze the situation and understand the various aspects that need troubleshooting.

3. Generate Alternative Perspectives: Now, let's approach your challenge from different perspectives or viewpoints. Think outside the box and consider unconventional approaches. Challenge your assumptions and imagine new possibilities.

4. Reverse Your Assumptions: Flip your assumptions about the challenge. Imagine a scenario where the problem is reversed or non-existent. This shift in perspective can unlock new insights and potential solutions.

5. Brainstorm Solutions: It's time to brainstorm! Write down as many potential solutions to your challenge as possible. Don't worry about judgment or self-editing at this stage. Let your creativity flow freely.

6. Prototype and Experiment: Select one or more ideas from your brainstorming session and create small-scale prototypes or

experiments to test their viability. This hands-on approach allows for iterative learning and refinement.

7. Seek External Input: Share your challenge and potential solutions with trusted friends, colleagues, or mentors. Seek their feedback and input. Sometimes, fresh perspectives can provide valuable insights and spark new ideas.

8. Embrace Constraints: Consider any constraints or limitations associated with your challenge. View these constraints as creative opportunities. They can push you to think innovatively within the given boundaries.

9. Learn from Failure: Embrace failures and setbacks as valuable learning experiences. Extract lessons and insights from any unsuccessful attempts. Write them down. Remember, failure is a steppingstone to success.

10. Reflect and Iterate: Take time to reflect on your progress, the lessons you've learned, and the outcomes of your troubleshooting efforts. Use this reflection to iterate and refine your solutions based on feedback and insights gained.

## Critical Thinking:

In a world inundated with clickbait headlines, manipulated images, and viral rumors, critical thinking acts as a shield, equipping us with the tools to distinguish fact from fiction. It prompts us to ask critical questions such as: What evidence supports this claim? Who is the source of this information, and what are their credentials? Are there alternative perspectives or counterarguments? By making these critical inquiries, we become active participants in the information ecosystem rather than passive recipients who swallow anything and everything, hook, line, and sinker. **In the context of creativity, critical thinking refers to the ability to analyze and evaluate information to form reasoned judgments and make decisions that foster creative outcomes.** Critical thinking involves questioning assumptions, considering alternative perspectives, and evaluating the strengths and weaknesses of different ideas.

> *Only simpletons believe everything they're told!* ***The prudent carefully consider*** *their steps.*

> *Prov 14:15 NLT*

Critical thinking is essential for creativity because it allows individuals to identify and challenge common assumptions, as well as conventions. By evaluating information critically, you can identify gaps in knowledge or opportunities for improvement and use this information to generate creative solutions. Furthermore, the complex challenges facing our world require us to think creatively and come up with innovative solutions. By turning on the switch of critical thinking, you can become a more effective problem-solver who generates creative solutions. Whether you are an artist, an entrepreneur, or a scientist, critical thinking is an essential skill that can help you unlock your full creative potential. It enables you to evaluate the feasibility and potential impact of your creative ideas. Additionally, critical thinking allows you to consider different options and weigh the pros and cons of each, which can ultimately lead to more effective and successful outcomes for you. Overall, critical thinking is a vital switch for creativity because it helps you approach problems and challenges from multiple angles and identify opportunities for improvement. It enables you to think outside the box and generate creative solutions that have a significant impact.

*But the people of Berea were more **open-minded** than those in Thessalonica, and gladly listened to the message. **They searched** the scriptures day by day **to check up on Paul and Silas' statements to see if they were really so.***

*Acts 17:11 TLB*

According to the scripture above, the people of Berea were known for their open-mindedness, as they were not fixed in their own established knowledge or understanding. Instead, they had the ability to scrutinize information, verify its sources, and fact-check before drawing any conclusions or accepting it as true. This approach is akin to that of a just judge who considers both sides of a case before arriving at a decision. It is important to recognize that being open-minded is a vital aspect of critical thinking, but it is not the same thing as being a critical thinker. Open-mindedness involves being receptive to new ideas and perspectives, and being willing to consider and evaluate evidence and arguments that may challenge one's own beliefs or assumptions. This is an essential component of critical thinking as it allows you to approach a problem or situation with an unbiased mindset and consider a range of possible solutions. However, critical thinking involves more than just being open-minded. It also includes analyzing and evaluating information, identifying biases and assumptions, and making reasoned judgments based on evidence and sound logic. So, while being open-minded is an important component of critical thinking, it is only one part of a broader set of skills and abilities required to think critically. Critical thinkers identify flaws in arguments and evidence, evaluate the credibility of sources, and make informed decisions based on a careful analysis of available information. This is what the Bereans were reputed for, as stated in the above scripture.

## Solomon's critical thinking

To be creative, your thought process plays a vital role. The ability to think critically is the foundation of creativity, and it is essential to unleash your full creative potential. Imagine you are faced with a problem that requires a creative solution. Your initial response may be to approach the problem from a conventional perspective, relying on familiar assumptions and routines. However, critical thinking allows you to break free from these constraints and consider alternative perspectives and ideas. By challenging assumptions, exploring various viewpoints, and assessing the merits and drawbacks of different choices, you can uncover innovative solutions that would have otherwise gone unnoticed. This was precisely what Solomon did when he was faced with a very difficult situation that required him to make a decision. After hearing two women argue about their ownership of a child, he used critical thinking to determine the true mother of the disputed child. Solomon suggested cutting the child in half and giving each mother one half of the child. The true mother, on hearing this, immediately offered to give up her claims just to save the child's life, while the false mother was willing to go along with the plan. Solomon was then able to identify the true mother and gave the child to her. After Solomon's astute display of critical thinking, the people made a profound statement that sheds further light on what critical thinking is about.

> *When all Israel heard the verdict the king had given,*
> *they held the king in awe, because they saw that **he had***
> ***wisdom** from God to **administer justice.***

> *1 Kings 3:28 NIV*

## Joseph's critical thinking

Critical thinking is what helps you demystify a problem and dissect its different aspects while offering a solution. In Genesis 41, we see how Joseph was imprisoned in Egypt and had the ability to interpret dreams. Pharaoh encountered a significant challenge when he had a dream that nobody could decipher. Eventually, Joseph was summoned to interpret the dream, and he unraveled its meaning and message. The dream served as an indication to Pharaoh that a problem existed, but he couldn't identify it or determine a solution because he didn't understand the dream. Have you ever found yourself in a comparable situation where you sense a problem but can't pinpoint its cause or symptoms due to a lack of understanding? That was Pharaoh's dilemma. So, instead of only interpreting the dream, Joseph went a step further and turned on the switch of critical thinking. He used critical thinking and creativity to offer a solution to the problem that the dream presented, after interpreting it. You see, critical thinking does not only analyze problems or do root cause analysis; it goes further to devise a creative solution to the problem after careful consideration and cross-examination. Joseph suggested that Pharaoh appoint a wise and discerning man to oversee the collection and storage of grain during the seven years of plenty, to prepare for the seven years of famine that were to come. Critical thinking was what turned Joseph the prisoner into a prime minister overnight. It was not just his gift for interpreting dreams. If he had interpreted the dream without proffering a critical solution to the problem he uncovered, that wouldn't have been of much effect.

> ***[Here is the problem analyzed]*** *The reason the dream was given to Pharaoh in two forms is that the matter has been firmly decided by God, and God will do it soon.*

> ***[The recommended critical solution]*** *And now let Pharaoh look for a discerning and wise man and put him in charge of the land of Egypt.*
>
> *Gen 41:32-33 NIV (Emphasis added).*

The verse mentioned above depicts Joseph's analytical approach as he explains the reason behind the dream coming in two forms, which, in turn, clarifies why the problem was recurring at its current rate. Joseph then goes on to provide a well-thought-out solution in the verses that follow. Due to his critical thinking, the king saw him as the best person to implement the solutions and ideas Joseph had recommended. Joseph's critical thinking and creative solutions not only saved Egypt from famine but also elevated him to a high position in Pharaoh's court. This story shows that critical thinking is not just about solving problems, but also about coming up with unique and effective solutions. By engaging the switch of critical thinking, you can find innovative solutions to complex problems and demonstrate effective leadership wherever you find yourself. This switch of critical thinking can help you succeed in your personal and professional life, just as it helped Joseph in the story.

## Ben Carson's critical thinking

Ben Carson, a renowned neurosurgeon, is known for deploying his critical thinking skills throughout his career. One notable example is his successful separation of conjoined twins in 1987. Before attempting the surgery, Carson and his team carefully analyzed the medical scans to determine the best approach for separating the twins. They spent months practicing and preparing for the surgery, considering all possible risks and complications. During the surgery, Carson had to make several critical decisions, such as which blood vessels to divide and which tissues to preserve, based on his extensive medical knowledge and experience. Carson's critical thinking skills were also evident in his work as Director of Pediatric Neurosurgery at Johns Hopkins Hospital. He was known for taking on challenging cases that other surgeons deemed too risky or impossible, and he would carefully evaluate each case to determine the best course of action. He was not afraid to challenge conventional medical wisdom and was always seeking new ways to improve patient outcomes.[1] Overall, Carson's critical thinking skills were demonstrated through his ability to analyze complex situations, evaluate risks and benefits, make sound decisions, and continually seek innovative solutions to challenging problems in his field.

**SAY THESE WORDS**

I affirm that I am capable of identifying logical fallacies and biases, allowing me to make sound judgments. I continuously develop my critical thinking skills through practice. I trust my intuition while also relying on evidence and rational analysis in my critical thinking process. I embrace challenges as opportunities to exercise my critical thinking abilities and find innovative solutions. I am a skilled critical thinker, capable of finding creative solutions and making informed decisions. Glory to God!

## FLIP THE SWITCH EXERCISE #27 – Critical Thinking

1. How can you apply critical thinking to question the assumptions, difficulties, or situations you encounter as you journey from ideas, skills or talent to creative solutions?

   _______________________________________________

   _______________________________________________

   _______________________________________________

2. How can critical thinking help you evaluate the credibility and value of the different ideas you have?

_______________________________________________

_______________________________________________

_______________________________________________

3. How can critical thinking help you determine the reliability and accuracy of the information or data you base your ideas on?

_______________________________________________

_______________________________________________

_______________________________________________

4. How can critical thinking help you break down and analyze a complex problem you are currently dealing with?

_______________________________________________

_______________________________________________

_______________________________________________

5. How can critical thinking help you evaluate and compare different options between different possible alternatives to deliver on a project you are working on?

_______________________________________________

_______________________________________________

_______________________________________________

6. How can critical thinking help you challenge assumptions and find new solutions?

_______________________________________________

_______________________________________________

_______________________________________________

7.  How can critical thinking help you evaluate feedback and use it to improve your ideas?

______________________________________________

______________________________________________

______________________________________________

8.  How can critical thinking help you develop your own perspective and contribute to a conversation with your colleagues, friends or clients about a work-related issue?

______________________________________________

______________________________________________

______________________________________________

## Ruthless Execution

Many brilliant minds with billion-dollar ideas have failed to bring forth their gifts to the world. Some have gone to the grave with their unsung songs, unwritten ideas, unexecuted business plans, unpublished books, unrendered services, or unpackaged product ideas. This is due to a lack of mental fortitude and determination to turn their dreams into reality. They often lacked the persistence and relentless effort needed to execute their plans. However, history shows that all the great men and women who have made an impact shared a common trait: they were unwavering and uncompromising in their execution.

> ***Lazy people don't even cook the game they catch,*** *but the diligent make use of everything they find.*
>
> *Prov 12:27 NLT*

Many people with great ideas fail to turn them into tangible, valuable, or profitable creations because they lack the drive to follow through with their plans, ideas, and visions. They are comparable to a hunter who catches an animal but never bothers to prepare and cook it for consumption. For example, hunters usually roast their meat after a successful hunt in the bush. The effort spent capturing the rabbit or the deer in the bush is wasted if it is allowed to spoil without being cooked and served for all who are hungry to eat. Similarly, having a brilliant idea but failing to make it a reality is like hunting for a game but letting it go to waste. It's no surprise that many creatives never see their ideas come to life. I have several brainchildren today because whenever I capture an idea, I go straight to the kitchen and begin to cook. Then I come out with a well-prepared delicious soup and serve it hot to the world! The fact that you are reading this book today is living proof of this reality! I can be ruthless when it comes to execution, and you should be too.

## The Calendly story

Tope Awotona, the founder of Calendly, faced several obstacles on his path to creating and launching the popular scheduling platform. He witnessed the murder of his dad at the age of twelve. Seeking a fresh beginning, his mother moved him and his siblings from their home country to the United States. Before he went on to create Calendly, he had failed 3 times when he tried to start a business. Despite previous failures in business endeavors, he possessed an unwavering resolve to execute his ideas. He firmly believed that learning from an attempt that failed was preferable to the regret of not trying. During his time as a salesman, Awotona experienced the frustrations of scheduling meetings, which ultimately sparked the conception of Calendly. He discovered that coordinating meeting times and finding availability among multiple individuals was both time-consuming and typically resulted in cumbersome email and phone exchanges. The current tools available to him also proved to be less than ideal. Recognizing a need for a simpler and more streamlined solution, Awotona took it upon himself to establish Calendly in 2013. One of the major challenges Tope Awotona faced was the fact that he was working a full-time job while working on Calendly in his spare time. This is the same reason why many creatives never execute nor ignite their creativity with this switch. They keep telling themselves that they are too busy with their full-time job to work on their ideas and turn them into a reality. However, for Tope, this meant he had to be extremely disciplined and efficient with his time, often working long hours into the night and on weekends[2].

## Money problems

One predominant obstacle that many people struggle with is the "lack of funding." Numerous potential creatives often claim that they lack funds, stating, "If I had money, I would do XYZ because I am full of ideas on how to make it work." As mentioned in previous chapters, I firmly believe that true creativity and a wealth of ideas should not be deterred by a lack of money. Instead, creativity should drive individuals to find innovative ways to overcome financial constraints and bring their ideas to life. Notably, Tope Awotona also faced challenges securing funding for the Calendly project. Despite investing his life savings into the project and making considerable efforts to attract investors, he struggled to gain their interest. Nevertheless, Tope's determination led him to bootstrap the project with his own savings, continuously improving Calendly and gaining traction on his own. If a creator lacks the faith in their concept to make personal sacrifices towards its realization, why would an investor be willing to risk their own hard-earned capital? Therefore, it is essential to introspect and invest one's own resources into the idea when seeking external funding, as many investors are put off by potential creatives who expect funding without demonstrating their commitment.

Another obstacle Tope faced was the competition in the scheduling software market. Despite several established players, Tope firmly believed that Calendly was unique and offered distinctive features that set it apart from the competition. He pursued his goal of making Calendly the best scheduling tool relentlessly, continuously working to enhance it and attract users. He displayed tremendous discipline and focus in overcoming these challenges.

To overcome these obstacles, Tope was extremely disciplined and focused on his goal. He was dogged in his execution, working tirelessly to improve the platform and gain traction. He also used his creativity to find new and innovative ways to market Calendly and attract users. Despite the challenges, Tope's hard work and determination paid off. At this writing, Calendly is one of the most popular scheduling platforms in the world, with over 10 million users. According to the company's report, Calendly has over 10 million individuals and 50,000 businesses globally. With monthly active users spanning across 155 countries, the company has established a notable global presence. As of 2022, Calendly has been instrumental in scheduling over 200 million meetings[3]. Tope's story is a great example of how being determined to pursue your goals and overcome obstacles through resourcefulness can lead to great success.

**Analysis paralysis**

Hear this: it is better to execute an idea than to sit around and do nothing with it because you are afraid of failing. It is better to fail while trying to create than to not attempt anything for fear of failure because you will learn a valuable lesson from that failed attempt. That lesson would eventually come in handy in your next try, or at the very least, you would have gained some experience that will provide insight for your next endeavor. Do not become a victim of analysis paralysis just because you fear failure. This is the major reason why many potential creators, brimming with brilliant ideas, end up failing to act, and eventually, they either abandon those brilliant ideas or lose the ability to generate fresh ones.

> *Then the man who had received the one talent came. 'Master,' he said, 'I knew that you are a hard man, harvesting where you have not sown and gathering where you have not scattered seed. So,* **I was AFRAID and went out and hid your talent in the ground.** *See, here is what belongs to you.'*

> *Matt 25:24-25 NIV*

In the story above, a master entrusts his servants with different amounts of money, or talents, before going on a journey. To one servant, he gives five talents, to another he gives two talents, and to the third, he gives one talent, according to their abilities. When the master returns, he calls his servants to account for what they have done with the talents. The servant who received five talents promptly swung into action, putting them to work and gaining five more talents. The servant who received two talents also acted, invested, and gained two more talents. However, the servant who received one talent buried it in the ground out of fear and returned it unchanged. Many potential creatives are like the third servant who possessed a talent, gift, or idea to create but never acted on it due to fear of failure. In the story, the master commends the first two servants for their faithful execution and rewards them by giving them more responsibilities. He says to them, "Well done, good and faithful servant! You have been faithful with a few things; I will put you in charge of many things. Come and share your master's happiness." This illustrates that when you become creative with whatever knowledge, gift, idea, or talent you have, you gain more opportunities and an enlarged capacity.

On the other hand, the master rebukes the third servant for his lack of action and says, "You wicked, lazy servant! You knew that I harvest where I have not sown and gather where I have not scattered seed? Well then, you should have put my money on deposit with the bankers, so that when I returned, I would have received it back with interest." This story highlights the significance of consistent execution and responsible stewardship of the ideas, gifts, talents, knowledge, experience, resources, and abilities we have been given. The first two servants demonstrated creativity, diligence, and a willingness to take risks by investing and multiplying the talents entrusted to them. As a result, they were rewarded with even greater responsibilities. Conversely, the third servant's lack of execution resulted in reprimand, and the talent was taken away from him. This story underscores why producers, inventors, and creators continue to innovate and expand, while consumers and non-creators often languish in cluelessness despite the opportunities that surround them. It also emphasizes the importance of taking action, being creative, and embracing responsible stewardship to unlock greater potential and opportunities in life.

> *Take the talent from him and give it to the one who has the ten talents. For everyone who has will be given more, and he will have an abundance.*
>
> *Matt 25:28-29 NIV*

This parable provides a compelling illustration of why you must start executing your ideas with immediate alacrity. The importance of taking action, using our abilities creatively, and maximizing the potential of what we've been entrusted with cannot be overstated. Through ruthless execution, you can foster growth, make a positive impact, and ultimately be rewarded for your creativity. Do not let your creative engine remain stagnant without stimulation or ignition. Just like a car engine that sits idle for too long without being ignited, various problems start to surface, eventually impacting the car's ability to run smoothly as it should. In some cases, an engine left unused for an extended period may even get knocked. Similarly, not igniting your creativity can have damaging implications for your creative potential. So, what is holding you back from executing the ideas you've pondered for so long? It's time to take action, wake up, unblock yourself, and ignite your creativity.

---

**SAY THESE WORDS**

I embrace ruthless execution as a vital switch that propels my creative ideas into tangible results. I am determined and persistent in bringing my creative visions to life, no matter the challenges I encounter. I take decisive action and follow through with unwavering commitment to turn my dreams into reality. I overcome obstacles and setbacks with resilience, using them as steppingstones on my path to success. I prioritize discipline and focus, channeling my energy into productive actions that bring my creative ideas to fruition.

---

## FLIP THE SWITCH EXERCISE #28 – Ruthless Execution

Instructions: Grab a pen and a personal notepad.

1. Set Clear Goals and Prioritize Them:

- List your current creative goals.

- Identify the most important goal that you want to focus on.

- Write down three actionable steps you can take to achieve that goal.

2. Embrace Failure as a Learning Opportunity:

- Recall a past failure or setback in your creative journey.

- Write down three lessons or insights you gained from that experience.

- Identify one specific action you can take to apply those lessons in your current endeavors.

3. Stay Focused and Disciplined:

- Identify potential distractions or obstacles that hinder your execution.

- Write down three strategies or techniques you can use to maintain focus and discipline.

- Commit to implementing these strategies in your creative process.

4. Collaborate with Others:

- Identify individuals or groups who can contribute to your creative projects.

- Write down three ways you can actively seek collaboration and leverage collective skills and knowledge.

- Reach out to at least one person or group to initiate a collaborative effort.

5. Celebrate Your Progress:

- Reflect on recent achievements or milestones in your creative journey.

- Write down three ways you can acknowledge and celebrate your progress.

- Schedule specific moments to recognize and appreciate your achievements.

6. Break Down Barriers:

- Identify any limiting beliefs or fears that hold you back from executing your ideas.

- Write down three strategies to overcome these barriers.

- Choose one strategy and commit to taking action to overcome a specific limitation.

7. Stay Adaptable:

- Reflect on a time when you had to adapt to unexpected circumstances in your creative pursuits.

- Write down three ways you can cultivate adaptability in your approach.

- Embrace flexibility and be open to adjusting your plans as needed.

8. Take Calculated Risks:

- Identify a creative opportunity or idea that involves some level of risk.

- Assess the potential rewards and challenges associated with that opportunity.

- Write down three reasons why it's worth taking the calculated risk and outline a plan to minimize potential setbacks.

9. Prioritize Action Over Perfection:

- Reflect on any tendencies to overthink or seek perfection in your creative process.

- Write down three ways you can shift your focus towards acting rather than seeking perfection.

- Commit to embracing imperfections and allowing your work to evolve through action.

10. Maintain a Growth Mindset:

- Reflect on your attitude towards challenges and setbacks in your creative journey.

- Write down three affirmations or positive statements that encourage a growth mindset.

- Repeat these affirmations regularly and remind yourself of the value of continuous growth and improvement.

Remember, flipping the switch of ruthless execution takes time and effort. Use this exercise as a guide to ignite your creativity and turn your ideas into reality. Stay committed to executing your ideas with determination and see the impact they can have on your creative journey.

## Entrepreneurial spirit

To be entrepreneurial means to be daring and enterprising. It also involves being ingenious in business dealings. Every true entrepreneur is a creative person, and every genuinely creative individual possesses that enterprising spirit and attitude. The reason behind this is that most entrepreneurs venture into uncharted territory, taking risks that others shy away from due to fear of the unknown. They are willing to invest their time, money, luxury, and even their lives to pursue their ambitions. When you ignite your creativity, you become an astute problem solver, becoming more daring and enterprising in your pursuits.

## A man named Strive thrives

In the late 1990s, a man from Zimbabwe named Strive Masiyiwa recognized the potential of mobile technology to revolutionize communication in Africa. However, at that time, Zimbabwe's telecommunications sector was dominated by a state-owned monopoly, making it difficult for private players to enter the market. Rather than accepting the existing barriers, Strive Masiyiwa used his creative thinking and entrepreneurial spirit to find a solution. He leveraged legal expertise and innovative business strategies to challenge the monopoly and pave the way for competition. His breakthrough came in 1998 when he launched Econet Wireless, the first privately owned mobile telecommunications company in Zimbabwe. He navigated legal battles and regulatory hurdles to secure the necessary licenses, demonstrating his resilience and determination. Through his entrepreneurial creativity, Masiyiwa introduced new services and pricing models that catered to the needs of Zimbabweans. His approach transformed the telecommunications landscape in Zimbabwe, bringing mobile services to a wider population and stimulating economic growth. Masiyiwa's entrepreneurial spirit and creative thinking allowed him to disrupt the established industry and provide innovative solutions where others saw obstacles. Masiyiwa's ability to think outside the box, challenge the status quo, and find creative solutions to overcome barriers were driven by his entrepreneurial spirit. This exemplifies how entrepreneurial spirit and creativity go hand in hand to drive innovation and create opportunities in the business world[4].

Creativity is a powerful force that fuels innovation and drives progress in various domains. When it comes to igniting creativity, people often overlook the crucial role of the entrepreneurial spirit. The entrepreneurial mindset, with its unique blend of vision, risk-taking, and resourcefulness, serves as a switch that unlocks the full potential of creative thinking. The entrepreneurial spirit refers to a mindset and set of characteristics commonly associated with entrepreneurs. It encompasses traits such as innovation, creativity, risk-taking, adaptability, resilience, and a proactive approach to identifying and pursuing opportunities. Individuals with an entrepreneurial spirit possess a strong drive to create something new, whether it be a business, product, or service. They exhibit a willingness to take calculated risks, embrace challenges, and persevere in the face of obstacles. The entrepreneurial spirit is characterized by a proactive and forward-thinking mindset, an ability to think outside the box, and a relentless pursuit of goals. It involves a combination of visionary thinking, resourcefulness, and the ability to effectively manage and leverage available resources. Those with an entrepreneurial spirit often exhibit a passion for problem-solving, a desire for continuous learning and improvement, and an openness to collaboration and networking. Overall, the entrepreneurial spirit represents a mindset and set of qualities that drive individuals to pursue innovation, create value, and make a meaningful impact in their chosen endeavors.

## Elisha the business coach

> *The wife of a man from the company of the prophets cried out to Elisha, "Your servant my husband is dead, and you know that he revered the Lord. But now his creditor is coming to take my two boys as his slaves." Elisha replied to her, "How can I help you? Tell me,* **what do you have in your house? Your servant has nothing there at all,"** *she said,* **"except a little oil."** *Elisha said, "Go around and ask all your neighbors for empty jars. Don't ask for just a few. Then go inside and shut the door behind you and your sons. Pour oil into*

*all the jars, and as each is filled, put it to one side." She left him and afterward shut the door behind her and her sons. They brought the jars to her and she kept pouring. When all the jars were full, she said to her son, "Bring me another one." But he replied, "There is not a jar left." Then the oil stopped flowing. She went and told the man of God, and he said, "Go, sell the oil and pay your debts. You and your sons can live on what is left."*

*2 Kings 4:1-7 NIV*

The story of the widow's oil above illustrates how Elisha helped the widow embrace the entrepreneurial spirit and become resourceful in the face of a dire situation. While there is a supernatural and miraculous aspect to the story, we can also draw several entrepreneurship principles from it. In the story, the widow finds herself in deep financial distress following the death of her husband, who was a prophet. Left with mounting debts and no means to repay them, she faced the risk of losing her two sons to slavery as payment. A desperate situation indeed. In her desperation, she turns to the prophet Elisha for help. Let us view Elisha as a mentor attempting to guide the widow through a tough situation, even though we know from the story that he was a prophet.

Elisha, recognizing her dire circumstances, asks her what resources she has available. Initially, the widow replies that she has nothing at all, overlooking the value in the little jar of oil she possesses. This mindset of despising little beginnings is common among those lacking an entrepreneurial spirit. However, Elisha helps her see with the eyes of an entrepreneur, and she admits to having a small jar of oil. He then instructs her to borrow empty jars from her neighbors and pour the oil she has into those jars. As she obeys his instructions, a miraculous event unfolds: the small jar of oil keeps pouring until all the borrowed jars are filled to the brim. Despite her state of despair, the right mentoring and guidance from Elisha led her to explore unconventional solutions and take calculated risks. Instead of succumbing to hopelessness, she seizes the opportunity presented by the small jar of oil and follows Elisha's guidance. Her resourcefulness and willingness to seek mentoring when she knew she needed help are commendable traits. Not only does she seek Elisha's business coaching advice, but she also takes action when shown how to transform the little jar of oil into a business through resourcefulness. She demonstrates an entrepreneurial mindset by recognizing the value of collaboration and leveraging her community. By reaching out to her neighbors to borrow empty jars, she taps into the resources available to her. Her story serves as a powerful reminder that even in the face of adversity, entrepreneurial thinking and resourcefulness can lead to transformative outcomes. It highlights the importance of seeing the potential in what may seem insignificant, seeking guidance and mentoring, and embracing creative solutions to overcome challenges.

Below are some essential attributes that come with the entrepreneurial spirit when that switch is flipped on:

- **Seize Opportunity:**

  At the heart of the entrepreneurial spirit lies the ability to identify and seize opportunities. Entrepreneurs possess a keen eye for recognizing unmet needs, gaps in the market, and emerging trends. When you activate this mindset, your thinking shifts from playing the victim card to an ingenious one, leading you to devise novel ways to take advantage of opportunities. Nathan Blecharczyk, Brian Chesky, and Joe Gebbia, the co-founders of Airbnb, provide an excellent example of this entrepreneurial mindset. They recognized an unmet need for affordable accommodations during a design conference in San Francisco when all the hotels were fully booked[5]. In that situation, they saw an opportunity to transform spare rooms and vacant apartments into temporary accommodations for travelers. By thinking creatively and seizing the opportunity, they started Airbnb, which has since disrupted the hospitality industry and revolutionized the way people travel and find accommodations. What opportunities surround you that are yet to be taken advantage of? What is stopping you from seizing that opportunity?

- **Take Calculated Risks:**

Entrepreneurs understand that taking calculated risks is an inherent part of the creative process. They embrace uncertainty and navigate through setbacks, failures, and adversity with resilience. Elon Musk, the CEO of Tesla and SpaceX, exemplifies the entrepreneurial spirit of taking risks and displaying resilience. Musk has embarked on ambitious ventures that have faced numerous challenges and setbacks, from electric vehicles to space exploration. He has taken calculated risks, embraced uncertainty, and persisted through failures[6]. His unwavering determination and resilience have enabled him to overcome obstacles and achieve groundbreaking innovations, such as the successful launch and landing of reusable rockets. The entrepreneurial spirit drives individuals to push beyond their comfort zones, experiment with unconventional ideas, and learn from both successes and failures. This explains why entrepreneurs are reputed for their ability to turn setbacks into steppingstones for creative breakthroughs. Despite the risk of failing, they end up driving innovation through their doggedness.

- **Resourcefulness:**

Entrepreneurs are known for their resourcefulness, finding innovative ways to leverage limited resources and maximize their impact. The entrepreneurial spirit nurtures resourcefulness, and this quality is closely intertwined with creativity. Often, entrepreneurs creatively utilize their available resources to disrupt industries and bring their ideas to life by first displaying resourcefulness with what they already have before seeking external resources.

Back in 2008, Brian Chesky, Joe Gebbia, and Nathan Blecharczyk, the co-founders of Airbnb, were struggling to pay their rent in San Francisco. They noticed that a design conference was happening in the city, and all hotels were fully booked. Recognizing an opportunity, they decided to turn their living space into a makeshift bed and breakfast. They provided air mattresses and offered breakfast to the conference attendees in their room. Instead of worrying about their apparent lack of resources, they became resourceful with what they had. To make their idea more appealing, Chesky, Gebbia, and Nathan took creative photos of their space and created a website called "Air Bed and Breakfast." They managed to attract three guests who were willing to pay for a place to stay as they were stranded. This experience sparked the idea for Airbnb, a platform that allows people to rent out their homes or spare rooms to travelers5. Having money is great, but it is not a guarantee that a business idea will succeed when executed. There are startups that had substantial funding but did not achieve the expected success. For instance, Jawbone, despite raising over $900 million in funding for its wearable devices and audio products, faced financial challenges. Similarly, Quibi, which secured approximately $1.75 billion in funding for its short-form mobile video streaming platform, struggled to gain traction and ultimately closed down[7]. In the early days of Airbnb, the founders faced numerous challenges, with convincing people to trust strangers and stay in their homes being one significant obstacle. To address this, they implemented various resourceful strategies. They personally reached out to hosts and guests, building a sense of community and establishing trust. They also utilized professional photography to enhance the quality of listings, making them more visually appealing and trustworthy. Another resourceful move was utilizing existing online platforms to spread the word about Airbnb. The founders took advantage of the power of Craigslist to cross-post their listings, gaining initial traction and attracting more users to their platform[8]. This approach allowed them to leverage an existing user base and effectively expand their reach with minimal marketing costs.

Over time, as Airbnb grew, the founders continued to demonstrate resourcefulness. They faced legal challenges and regulatory hurdles in different cities. To address this, they adapted their strategies to comply with local laws and build relationships with governments and communities. The resourcefulness displayed by Nathan, Chesky, and Gebbia throughout their entrepreneurial journey played a pivotal role in the success of Airbnb. They turned their own financial challenges into an opportunity, leveraged existing resources and platforms, and creatively addressed obstacles they encountered along the way. This exemplifies how resourcefulness is a key trait of successful entrepreneurs. It involves thinking outside the box, making the most of available resources, finding innovative solutions to problems, and adapting to changing circumstances. By being resourceful, you can navigate challenges, seize opportunities, and bring your creative ideas to fruition. It is not what you do not have that hinders your creativity. It is what you already have but do not know how to use.

- **Collaboration:**

The entrepreneurial attitude recognizes the power of collaboration and the value of building strong networks. It actively seeks diverse perspectives, forges strategic partnerships, and taps into collective intelligence. This fosters an environment where diverse ideas can intersect, blend, and spark creative innovation. A prime example of collaboration and networking in entrepreneurship is the partnership between Steve Jobs and Steve Wozniak, the co-founders of Apple Inc. Jobs and Wozniak brought together their different skills and perspectives to create groundbreaking products[9]. Jobs was a visionary marketer, while Wozniak was a technical genius. Their collaboration and networking extended beyond their partnership, as they also collaborated with other talented individuals, including designers and engineers, to build a strong team that fueled Apple's success. The problem with most potential creators is that they are in the wrong circle of people who always project impossibility when they speak of their ideas. When you surround yourself with people who are uninspired by your enthusiasm and vision to create, you would end up becoming unimaginative. You have no business being around such individuals. You must handpick the people you associate yourself with and make sure they align with your creative goals and even push you out of your comfort zone.

- **Adaptability:**

The entrepreneurial spirit embraces adaptability and continuous learning as essential components of creative thinking. Entrepreneurs embrace change, pivot when needed, and constantly acquire new knowledge and skills. The inspirational story of Amazon's evolution from being a platform for selling books to becoming a Global Marketplace is worthy of note. Originally starting as an online bookstore, Amazon recognized the need to adapt and expand its offerings to stay relevant in the rapidly changing marketplace[10]. Embracing the entrepreneurial mindset, Amazon ventured into new territories, diversifying its product range to include electronics, clothing, household goods, and more. This strategic pivot allowed Amazon to tap into emerging markets and capitalize on evolving consumer needs, propelling it to become a global e-commerce powerhouse. Amazon's remarkable adaptability showcases how the entrepreneurial spirit fosters innovation and success through the ability to embrace change and proactively respond to market demands. The entrepreneurial spirit serves as a powerful switch that ignites and amplifies creativity. Understanding the role of the entrepreneurial spirit as a catalyst for creativity empowers you to embrace an innovative mindset, tackle challenges with resilience, and make a lasting impact in your chosen field.

## SAY THESE WORDS

I embody the entrepreneurial spirit, embracing innovation, risk-taking, and a relentless drive to create and succeed. I see opportunities where others see challenges, and I fearlessly pursue new ventures with confidence and determination. I am fueled by passion and a strong belief in my creative ideas, allowing me to overcome obstacles and persevere in the face of adversity. I continuously seek out new ways to improve and grow, adapting to changing circumstances and seizing emerging trends. I cultivate a mindset of abundance, recognizing that

> there are endless possibilities to explore and capitalize on with my creative endeavors. Thank you Spirit of God!

## FLIP THE SWITCH EXERCISE #29 - Entrepreneurial Spirit

Instructions: Please grab a pen and notepad.

1. Reflect on Your Entrepreneurial Mindset:
- What does the term "entrepreneurial spirit" mean to you?
- Write down three characteristics or qualities you associate with an entrepreneurial mindset.
- Reflect on how you currently embody these characteristics and note areas for improvement.
2. Identify Opportunities for Innovation:
- Think about your current work or personal projects.
- Identify three areas or aspects where you see opportunities for innovation or improvement.
- Write down specific ideas or solutions you could explore to bring innovation to those areas.
3. Embrace Risk and Overcome Fear:
- Consider a situation where fear of failure or risk has held you back.
- Reflect on the potential rewards of taking calculated risks.
- Write down three ways you can overcome fear and embrace risk in your creative pursuits.
4. Cultivate a Growth Mindset:
- Reflect on your beliefs about personal growth and development.
- Write down three affirmations or statements that promote a growth mindset.
- Repeat these affirmations regularly to reinforce your entrepreneurial spirit.

5. Develop a Bias for Action:
- Consider a project or idea that you have been hesitant to act upon.
- Write down three specific actions you can take to move forward with that project or idea.
- Commit to a timeline and hold yourself accountable for taking consistent action.

6. Nurture a Learning Mentality:
- Reflect on how you currently approach learning and acquiring new skills.
- Identify three areas where you can expand your knowledge or develop new skills relevant to your entrepreneurial goals.
- Write down a plan of action to acquire or enhance those skills.

7. Seek Feedback and Collaboration:
- Consider the value of seeking feedback and collaborating with others.
- Identify three individuals or groups who can provide valuable insights or contribute to your projects.
- Reach out to at least one person or group to seek feedback or initiate a collaborative effort.

8. Foster Resilience and Adaptability:
- Reflect on a past challenge or setback you faced in your creative pursuits.
- Write down three ways you can foster resilience and adaptability in the face of obstacles.
- Commit to implementing these strategies when faced with future challenges.

9. Develop a Vision and Set Goals:
- Reflect on your long-term vision and entrepreneurial goals.
- Write down three specific goals that align with your vision.

- Break down each goal into actionable steps and create a timeline for achieving them.

10. Celebrate Your Entrepreneurial Journey:

- Reflect on your accomplishments and milestones as an entrepreneur.
- Write down three ways you can acknowledge and celebrate your progress.
- Schedule moments of celebration to recognize your achievements and fuel your entrepreneurial spirit.

Remember, developing and nurturing your entrepreneurial spirit is a continuous process. Use this worksheet as a tool to ignite your creativity, build an entrepreneurial mindset, and take purposeful actions towards your goals. Keep exploring and evolving your entrepreneurial spirit as you embark on your creative journey.

## Ardent Research:

Those who unleash their creative genius possess an insatiable passion for seeking answers to unanswered questions and unresolved problems. Their curiosity drives them to engage in continuous research and development, even when not obligated to do so. They defy the odds and follow their quest for answers until they get the desired solutions. Research refers to the systematic investigation and study of a particular topic or subject. It is usually done with the goal of gaining knowledge, understanding, and generating new insights. Research involves a structured and methodical approach to collecting, analyzing, and interpreting information to answer questions, test hypotheses, or address specific problems. The primary objective of research is to contribute to the existing body of knowledge, expand understanding, and make meaningful advancements in various fields. It is conducted across disciplines, including science, social sciences, humanities, technology, and more. While research is often associated with the systematic investigation and analysis of existing knowledge, it also involves the generation of new ideas, approaches, and solutions. When you become an ardent researcher, you fan the flames of your creativity in ways words may not be able to describe. In case you're wondering, 'How does research have anything to do with creativity?' The scripture below puts it succinctly.

> *Wisdom and good judgment live together, for wisdom knows where to discover knowledge and understanding.*

> *Prov 8:12 TLB*

Solomon's writings exemplify the power of research, knowledge, and creativity. His wisdom and understanding were renowned, and his writings reflect a deep knowledge of various subjects. His own research likely involved studying historical records, observing nature, and engaging in philosophical and theological inquiries (1 Kings 4:22-23 TLB). Through diligent study and contemplation, he sought to gain insights into human nature, relationships, wisdom, and the meaning of life. Now you can understand why he said what he said in the scripture above.

## The Concept of R&D

R&D stands for Research and Development. It refers to the systematic and purposeful activities undertaken by organizations or individuals to expand knowledge, explore new possibilities, and develop innovative solutions or technologies. R&D serves as a vital catalyst for pushing the boundaries of creativity and paving the way for discoveries. It serves as a testament to the belief that investing in research can foster innovation, propel advancements, and drive revolutionary changes in various industries. The substantial financial commitments made by big companies known for their innovation underscore the significance of R&D in fueling creativity. Companies like Apple, Google, and Microsoft have built their reputation on groundbreaking innovation. These tech giants invest heavily in R&D to drive their continuous growth and maintain a competitive edge. The pharmaceutical industry heavily relies on research and development to discover new drugs, treatments, and therapies. In recent years, the automotive industry has witnessed a significant shift towards sustainable and electric mobility. Companies like Tesla, Toyota, and BMW have invested heavily in R&D to drive the development of electric vehicles and renewable energy solutions. Research has shown that companies actively engaged in collaborative R&D initiatives tend to generate more innovative ideas and accelerate technological advancements[11]. The truth is that not every researcher is creative, but every creative must flip the switch of creativity known as research. The creative aspects of research can manifest in several ways:

a) **Problem formulation:** Research begins with identifying a problem or question to investigate. This process requires creativity to identify gaps in knowledge, envision new possibilities, and frame the research problem in a meaningful and original way.

b) **Designing methodologies:** Researchers often devise methodologies to gather data, conduct experiments, or analyze existing information. Developing innovative methodologies often requires creative thinking to design effective and efficient approaches.

c) **Data analysis and interpretation:** Analyzing research data requires creativity to identify patterns, relationships, and insights that may not be immediately apparent. Researchers often need to think critically and imaginatively to make connections and draw meaningful conclusions from the data.

d) **New knowledge:** Research can lead to the discovery of new information, theories, or insights. This process involves creativity in generating new ideas, theories, or conceptual frameworks that contribute to the existing body of knowledge.

e) **Communication and dissemination:** Researchers also need creativity when presenting their findings to others. They must effectively communicate complex ideas and concepts in a clear and engaging manner, using various media such as research papers, presentations, or visualizations.

**Reflection**: Pause for a moment and ponder on this. What research-driven, solution-finding project are you currently on? Need a push, a lift, or a boost?

Daniel exemplifies the importance of research, knowledge, and understanding gained through books and study. Daniel, a young Israelite captive in Babylon, demonstrated exceptional wisdom and understanding, which he acquired through his diligent study of books and the teachings of his faith. In the Book of Daniel, it is mentioned that Daniel and his companions were selected to be trained in the language and literature of the Babylonians. They dedicated themselves to researching, learning, and understanding the wisdom contained in these books. Daniel became renowned for his ability to interpret dreams, understand visions, and provide wise counsel to the Babylonian kings. This is attributable to the fact that he understood by research, the culture, and systems of Babylon even though he was born and raised in Israel.

*Then he [the King] ordered Ashpenaz, who was in charge of his palace personnel, to select some of the Jewish youths brought back as captives-young men of the royal family and nobility of Judah-and to teach them the Chaldean language and literature. "Pick strong, healthy, good-looking lads," he said; **"those who have read widely in many fields, are well informed**, alert and sensible, and have enough poise to look good around the palace."*

*Dan 1:3-4 TLB (emphasis added)*

The statement above was the criterion given to the king's official, tasked with the responsibility of selecting those who would eventually work within the ranks of the king's government. Notice how they wanted "men who had read widely." Now you see that Daniel's selection was not predicated on luck or "unmerited favor," but on the merit of the fact that he was an ardent researcher. This highlights the significance of studying and researching existing knowledge to gain understanding and wisdom. Through his dedication to studying books, Daniel was able to develop his intellectual abilities, acquire specialized knowledge, and apply it in practical and meaningful ways. This story emphasizes the importance of research as a foundation for informed decision-making, problem-solving, and offering innovative solutions. Additionally, the story of Daniel also demonstrates the connection between faith, divine revelation, and intellectual pursuits. It is through this combination of faith and intellectual curiosity that Daniel was able to excel in his role and make significant contributions to the Babylonian court. I believe that the same spirit that propelled Daniel into significance through research will rest upon you as you read this book in Jesus' name! Most people have never looked at research in the context of creativity. However, the relationship between research and creativity is more intertwined than it may appear. Research can act as a switch, triggering and enhancing creativity in various ways. By exploring existing knowledge, generating new ideas, fostering critical thinking, and promoting interdisciplinary connections, research fans the flame of creativity. The switch of research can ignite your innovative mind in the following ways:

### a)  Exposure to New Ideas:

Engaging in research exposes you to a vast array of existing knowledge, theories, and perspectives. Exploring literature, scholarly articles, and previous studies can broaden your understanding and provide a foundation for generating new ideas. By immersing yourself in a wealth of information, researchers can gain insights into the current state of knowledge, identify gaps, and envision novel possibilities. This exposure to diverse concepts and viewpoints serves as fertile ground for the germination of creative ideas, inspiring fresh approaches to existing problems or the discovery of entirely new avenues of inquiry.

### b)  Connecting the Dots:

Research often involves connecting disparate pieces of information to uncover patterns, relationships, and insights. This process of integrating and synthesizing various concepts and perspectives nurtures creativity. As you delve deeper into a subject during research, you may identify unexpected connections or analogies between seemingly unrelated fields. These interdisciplinary connections can spark creative thinking by providing new frameworks, alternative viewpoints, and innovative solutions. Research acts as a switch, enabling you to bridge disciplines and tap into the collective wisdom of diverse knowledge domains.

### c) Questioning Assumptions:

By investigating prevailing beliefs and methodologies, you open the door to fresh perspectives and novel possibilities. This critical inquiry stimulates creativity by encouraging you to think outside the box, challenge conventional wisdom, and consider alternative hypotheses. Research serves as a switch that empowers you to question the status quo and embark on creative journeys fueled by intellectual curiosity and a desire to explore uncharted territories.

### d) Iterative and Reflective Thinking:

Research is hardly a linear process. It involves cycles of exploration, experimentation, analysis, and reflection. This iterative nature of research fosters creativity by promoting continuous refinement, adaptation, and improvement. As you encounter setbacks or unexpected results, you engage in reflective thinking, which stimulates creative problem-solving. This switch-like process of alternating between analysis and reflection allows you to reframe challenges, generate new ideas, and uncover innovative solutions. The iterative nature of research nurtures a mindset of adaptability and resilience, key ingredients for fostering creativity.

### e) Discovery:

Research often leads to unexpected discoveries and serendipitous findings. These unforeseen outcomes can open new avenues for exploration and ignite creative insights. Researchers who maintain an open mind and embrace the unexpected are more likely to seize these moments and leverage them for creative breakthroughs. Research acts as a switch by creating an environment that encourages openness to new possibilities. It allows you to perceive and capitalize on unplanned discoveries, while leveraging them to fuel creativity.

## SAY THESE WORDS

I am driven to conduct thorough research, knowing that it is the key to unlocking my creative brilliance.

Every research endeavor I undertake enhances my creative thinking and propels me towards greater achievements.

I approach research with curiosity and enthusiasm, knowing that it is a powerful switch that sparks my creativity.

I am a relentless researcher, constantly seeking to deepen my understanding and uncover new possibilities.

The more I engage in ardent research, the more my creative faculties expand, allowing me to innovate and create with greater depth.

I honor the role of research in fueling my creative pursuits and recognize its immense value in my journey of self-expression.

## FLIP THE SWITCH EXERCISE #30 - Ardent Research

Instruction: Take some time to reflect on the questions and prompts provided and write your responses in the space provided.

Understanding Research:

    a) Define research in your own words.

       Research is_______________________________________________

    b) Research and Creativity:

1. How do you think research can stimulate creativity? Share your thoughts.

   _______________________________________________

   _______________________________________________

2. Can you think of any examples where research has led to innovative and creative solutions or breakthroughs? Describe them briefly.

   _______________________________________________

   _______________________________________________

Personal Reflection:

a) Reflect on a time when you engaged in research for a specific purpose. What was the topic or subject? How did it impact your understanding or perspective?

   _______________________________________________

   _______________________________________________

Research in Action:

a) Choose a topic or area of interest that you would like to explore further through research. Write it down.

   _______________________________________________

   _______________________________________________

b) Identify three specific research questions related to your chosen topic that you would like to investigate.

   Research question 1: _______________________________

   Research question 2: _______________________________

   Research question 3: _______________________________

Research Plan:

- Outline a basic plan for conducting research on your chosen topic. Consider the following:

   What sources or references will you consult?

   _________________________________________________
   _________________________________________________
   _________________________________________________

   What research methods or tools will you use?

   _________________________________________________
   _________________________________________________
   _________________________________________________

   What steps will you take to gather and analyze information?

   _________________________________________________
   _________________________________________________
   _________________________________________________

Applying Research Findings:

- Can you brainstorm any potential creative ideas, solutions, or projects that could arise from your research findings? Write them down.

   _________________________________________________
   _________________________________________________
   _________________________________________________

Potential Challenges:

- What are some potential challenges or obstacles you may encounter during your research process? How can you overcome them?

  _______________________________________________

  _______________________________________________

  _______________________________________________

Collaboration and Feedback:

- Consider seeking input or collaborating with others during your research process. Who could provide valuable insights or perspectives? Write down their names and roles.

  Collaborator 1: _______________________________

  Collaborator 2: _______________________________

  Collaborator 3: _______________________________

Reflection and Action:

- Identify one specific action step you can take to incorporate research into your creative pursuits or problem-solving endeavors. Write down your action step.

Future Research Goals:

- What are some potential research goals or topics you would like to explore in the future? Write them down.

## Initiative

Initiative can be seen as the ability and willingness to take independent action, be proactive, and seize opportunities. It involves identifying areas for improvement, suggesting new ideas, and taking the lead in initiating projects or actions. Initiative is characterized by being self-motivated, proactive, and creative in finding solutions. As of this writing, WhatsApp has more than 2.78 billion users in 180 countries[12]. WhatsApp Inc. was founded by Jan Koum and Brian Acton before it was acquired by Facebook (now Meta) for 19 billion dollars due to its success. Interestingly, the founders of WhatsApp once sought jobs at Facebook but were rejected. Despite this setback, they went on to sell WhatsApp for $12 billion in cash and $4 billion in shares.[13] This remarkable success exemplifies what can happen when you take the initiative to solve a problem. Sometimes, facing rejection or being laid off from a job can be disheartening. However, it can also present an opportunity to take initiative. If you find yourself encountering job rejections despite your prayers and diligent preparation for interviews, consider it a chance to flip the switch on your initiative and address a genuine problem. The experience of rejection could serve as a catalyst for you to take proactive steps towards making a positive impact and finding solutions. Overall, initiative is a powerful quality that can lead to extraordinary achievements, just like the founders of WhatsApp demonstrated. Embrace the spirit of initiative, and let it guide you in your journey towards making a difference and finding success. Remember, it's not just about the obstacles you encounter but also about how you respond to them with creativity and proactive action.

One reason why most people do not express their creativity is a lack of initiative. They want to be told what to do all the time. Many people fail in their careers and businesses because they only do what they are told, and they refuse to initiate things that can make a difference, even when they know that something needs to be done. Refuse to be a person who lacks the mental fortitude to initiate change, forge new visions, venture unexplored paths, and establish the rhythm that others may follow. Everyone possesses the capacity to lead in their own unique way if they cultivate a mindset that consistently embraces initiative. You see, when you possess initiative, you are often proactive and self-motivated, and this can drive you to explore new possibilities and take creative risks. Initiative can manifest in various ways, such as initiating projects, suggesting innovative approaches, or taking the lead in problem-solving. By actively seeking out opportunities and taking action, you are more likely to engage in creative thinking and come up with novel ideas.

An initiative is also known as a new development; a fresh approach to something; a new way of dealing with a problem. It can be seen as the ability to act first or on one's own. When you unlock your creativity, you become an initiator. You do things that no textbook has written down. You dare to pursue projects that no one in your industry would even imagine, and you accomplish them. You do not seek the approval of anyone before you pursue and live your dreams. Being an initiator is a great way to ignite your creativity. You may not own a business, but you can be an initiator of positive change as a staff member or in any other capacity. Being an initiator goes beyond simply being proactive or taking the first step. It embodies a mindset of self-empowerment, innovation, and leadership. As an initiator, you become a catalyst for change, driving progress and shaping the world around you. Initiators have a unique ability to see possibilities where others may see obstacles. They have the courage to challenge the status quo, question norms, and break free from limitations. They are not content with passively accepting the way things are. Instead, they actively seek opportunities to make a difference. Initiators are driven by a deep sense of purpose and a burning desire to leave a lasting impact. They understand that their actions can inspire others and create a ripple effect of positive change. By taking the initiative, they become agents of transformation, whether in their personal lives, professional endeavors, or within their communities. Initiators are not bound by the fear of failure or the need for external validation. They understand that setbacks and challenges are an inherent part of the journey. They embrace these obstacles as learning opportunities, using them to grow, adapt, and evolve. Initiators are resilient and persevere, even in the face of adversity because they are fueled by their passion and unwavering belief in their vision.

Furthermore, being an initiator is not limited to grand gestures or large-scale endeavors. It can manifest in little actions, such as initiating a conversation, sharing a new idea, or offering support to someone in need. Initiators understand that even the minutest acts can have significant impacts and contribute to a greater collective change. Ultimately, being an initiator is about giving expression to your creative ideas and gifts. It embraces the responsibility to make a positive difference in your personal and professional life, at home, and in the office. It is about recognizing that you can shape the world around you, leaving a legacy that extends far beyond your immediate sphere of influence. By turning on this switch, you become an inspiration to others, igniting their own creative spark, and empowering them to embrace their unique potential. So, assume your role as an initiator and let your creativity guide you on a path of purpose, impact, and fulfillment. Your ideas, actions, and unwavering commitment to making a difference can truly transform the world.

**Benefits of Initiative**

### a) **Catalyst for Exploration:**

Initiative serves as the catalyst that propels you beyond the realm of mere imagination. It encourages you to venture into uncharted territories, explore unconventional paths, and challenge the status quo. By taking the initiative, you break free from routines and comfort zones, opening doors to fresh perspectives and novel ideas. It is through this courageous leap that creativity finds fertile ground to flourish.

## b) It Turns Your Ideas into Reality:

The mind often gives birth to a multitude of ideas, but without initiative, those ideas remain dormant. Initiative empowers individuals to take the necessary steps to transform abstract concepts into tangible reality. Whether it's initiating a project, assembling a team, or simply taking the first small action, initiative bridges the gap between imagination and realization. It infuses your creative visions with purpose, propelling you towards their manifestation.

## c) Embraces Risk and Learning:

Initiative fuels a willingness to embrace risks and navigate the uncertainties that accompany creative pursuits. It encourages you to experiment with new approaches and learn from both successes and failures. By taking the initiative, you embrace a growth mindset, recognizing that every endeavor, regardless of the outcome, offers valuable insights and lessons. This iterative process enhances your creative abilities and broadens your horizon.

## d) Fosters Collaboration:

Initiative not only drives individual creativity but also cultivates collaborative environments that amplify the collective creative power. When you take the initiative, you inspire and motivate others, igniting a chain reaction of innovative thinking and action. By fostering a culture of initiative, teams and organizations can tap into the diverse perspectives and talents of their members, leading to the emergence of groundbreaking ideas and solutions.

People who succeed at igniting their creativity are never satisfied with the status quo. They have an innate hunger for change in a positive direction. They always want to improve systems, processes, and methods to make them better and this causes them to initiate change. It is time to stop waiting for a method to stop working before creating a new and better one. Be a diehard change agent who always takes initiative to improve processes and systems. Do not go with the flow when you could be a reference point for greatness.

Question: what methods, systems and processes in your life, career or business are you currently taking initiative to improve and change?

**SAY THESE WORDS**

I affirm that my initiative fuels my creativity and propels me to take bold and innovative actions. I am proactive in seeking opportunities to express my creativity and bring my ideas to life. Taking initiative is the key to unlocking my creative potential and making a meaningful impact. By taking the initiative, I unleash my creativity and pave the way for new discoveries and breakthroughs. I am an initiator of creative ideas, constantly seeking ways to bring my visions into reality. Initiative is the driving force behind my creative pursuits, empowering me to turn my dreams into tangible outcomes.

## FLIP THE SWITCH EXERCISE #31 - Initiative

Section 1: Self-examine your initiative

a)  On a scale of 1 to 10, rate your level of initiative in different areas of your life (e.g., personal projects, work, relationships).

Personal projects: _____________

Work: _________________________

Relationships: _______________

b) Identify one specific situation where you felt you demonstrated strong initiative. Describe the situation and explain why you consider it a display of initiative.

Situation:

_________________________________________________

Explanation:

_________________________________________________

c) Identify one specific situation where you believe you could have shown more initiative. Describe the situation and reflect on why you feel you lacked initiative.

Situation:

_________________________________________________

Reflection:

_________________________________________________

Section 2: Strategies for Increasing Initiative

a) List three potential barriers or obstacles that have hindered your initiative in the past. How might you overcome or navigate these challenges in the future?

Barrier 1:

_________________________________________________

Overcoming Strategy:

_________________________________________________

Barrier 2:

_________________________________________________

Overcoming Strategy:

_________________________________________________

Barrier 3:

_________________________________________________

Overcoming Strategy:

_________________________________________________

b) Brainstorm a list of five proactive actions you can take to demonstrate more initiative in your personal and professional life. Be specific and consider both short-term and long-term goals.

Action 1:

_________________________________________________

Action 2:

_________________________________________________

Action 3:

_________________________________________________

Action 4:

_________________________________________________

Action 5:

_________________________________________________

c) Reflect on the potential risks or challenges associated with taking initiative. How can you embrace these risks and overcome any fear or hesitation?

Reflection:

___________________________________________

Strategies for Overcoming:

___________________________________________

Section 3: Leveraging Initiative

a) Identify one specific project or goal where you believe your initiative can make a significant impact. Describe the project and outline specific steps you can take to initiate and drive its success.

Project:

___________________________________________

Steps to Initiate and Drive Success:

Step 1:

___________________________________________

Step 2:

___________________________________________

Step 3:

___________________________________________

b) Explore ways in which you can collaborate with others to amplify your initiative and create collective impact. Identify potential individuals, groups, or communities that you can engage with to enhance your initiatives.

Collaboration Opportunities:

---

Section 4: Recognizing and Celebrating Initiative

a)  Reflect on a time when you witnessed someone else's initiative in action. Describe the situation and explain why you found it inspiring or impactful.

Situation:

---

Explanation:

---

b)  Identify one specific way you can recognize and celebrate your own initiative. How will you acknowledge and reward yourself for taking proactive steps and demonstrating initiative?

Recognition and Celebration Method:

---

Conclusion: Reflect on your insights and action steps from this worksheet. Summarize one key strategy or commitment you are making to cultivate and leverage your initiative moving forward.

Key Strategy/Commitment:

---

Remember, developing and harnessing your initiative is an ongoing process. Revisit this worksheet periodically to assess your progress and adapt your strategies as needed. Taking initiative is a powerful switch that can open doors to new opportunities and drive your creative endeavors forward.

## Vocational aptitude:

Vocational aptitude refers to the inherent or acquired ability to excel in a particular occupation or field of work. It involves understanding one's skills, interests, and values and aligning them with a suitable vocation or career path. Vocational aptitude can help you identify the areas where your creative abilities can be most effectively applied. In the context of creativity, the term "aptitude" in "vocational aptitude" refers to your inherent or acquired ability, innate talent, or potential to perform well in a specific vocation, endeavor, field of study, or occupation. It represents your natural inclination, skill set, or suitability for a particular field of work. Aptitude encompasses a combination of innate abilities, such as cognitive, physical, or creative talents, as well as learned skills and knowledge that are relevant to a specific vocation. It goes beyond mere interest or preference and implies a level of inherent capability or potential for success in each area.

Your vocational aptitude is typically driven by your cognitive abilities, personality traits, interests, and values, which determine an individual's compatibility and suitability for specific vocations. You were created to create, and that means everything about the way you were built up, the way you look, and your entire persona is a pointer to your vocation.

> *For we are God's **masterpiece**. He has created us anew in Christ Jesus, so we can do the good things he planned for us long ago.*
>
> *Eph 2:10 NLT*

Understanding your vocational aptitude can help you make informed career choices, pursue paths that align with your strengths and interests, and enhance your chances of success and fulfillment in your chosen vocation. Over the past few years, I have known many people who hear about the potential for high earnings in the information technology (IT) industry and decide to switch careers, thinking they can quickly make good money. However, after three months of trying to learn the necessary skills for entry-level tech opportunities, they lose momentum and conclude, "It's too hard; it's not for me."

Do not jump into businesses and careers you have no business getting involved with. Always align your vocation with your inherent interests, gifts, and abilities, so that you can easily glide on the waves of creativity that flow when you are in your "zone."

## The cook who finally found his vocation

Before founding Kentucky Fried Chicken (KFC), Colonel Sanders held various jobs, including working as a railroad fireman, a farmer, and an insurance salesman where he struggled with rejection. He got fired multiple times, ruined his legal career, and lost money in failed business ventures. It wasn't until his 40s when he started serving his fried chicken recipe at a service station he owned, eventually leading to the creation of KFC and his success as a restaurateur. **Nothing limits your creativity and potential like failing to matchmake your skills with the right vocation**. When you fail to align or match your skills with the appropriate vocation or occupation, it can hinder your creativity and limit your potential. The problem with many born creatives is they are doing what they have no business doing in the first place. They are striving hard to become an average performer in a vocation that appears popular, or a job guarantees a paycheck while sitting on a goldmine and not knowing it. They have what it takes to build an empire that will serve generations to come but cannot afford to see the light because their creativity switch is off.

*Do you see a man skilled **in his work**? He will serve before kings; he will not serve before obscure men.*

*Prov 22:29 NIV*

By recognizing your vocational aptitude and flipping on the switch, you can focus your creative energies in a way that is aligned with your strengths and interests. This can lead to greater satisfaction, productivity, and success in your chosen creative endeavors. Whether it's in the arts, business, technology, or any other field, understanding your vocational aptitude can provide a valuable framework for pursuing creative endeavors in a purposeful and meaningful manner.

## Vocation vs occupation

It is imperative that we understand that though vocation and occupation are related concepts, they have slightly different meanings. Your vocation generally refers to a person's sense of calling or purpose in life. It goes beyond just a job or career and encompasses the idea of fulfilling a meaningful and significant role or mission. A vocation is often associated with a deep sense of passion, drive, fulfillment, and alignment with your values and talents. Occupation, on the other hand, refers to the specific job or work that a person engages in to earn a living. It involves the tasks, responsibilities, and duties associated with a particular profession or trade. While some individuals may find their vocation and occupation to be closely aligned, this is not always the case. Some people may have a job or occupation that does not fully align with their personal sense of vocation or calling. If this is your situation, you must seek ways to bring your vocation into your occupation by infusing meaning and purpose into your work or exploring alternative career paths that better align with your vocation.

There is nothing wrong with holding down a job to pay the bills until you can fully pursue your vocation, as it can sustain you and your family.

In summary, vocation refers to a broader sense of calling or purpose, while occupation refers to the specific job or work that a person engages in.

When you flip the switch of vocational aptitude, the engines of your creativity will function very efficiently. Many people have gone through tertiary institutions and graduated with flying colors, yet they can't put their hands on the one thing they want to commit their lives to. They lack vocational aptitude. Even when they get a job, they are still confused about whether that is their true calling. Professionals who truly succeed and find fulfillment in the corporate world of work and business do so because they have tapped into their inner genius. They know what they are cut out for and suited for, which gives them an uncanny ability to succeed in their vocation even when others doubt that they will. The key takeaway here is to ensure you are not a square peg in a round hole. Flip the switch for your vocational aptitude and ignite your creativity!

> **SAY THESE WORDS**
>
> I embrace my unique vocational aptitude and recognize it as a powerful switch that ignites my creativity. My vocational aptitude is a valuable asset that allows me to express my creativity in meaningful and fulfilling ways. I trust in my vocational aptitude to guide me towards creative endeavors that align with my passions and strengths. As I explore and develop my vocational aptitude, my creativity flourishes and opens up new possibilities.

## FLIP THE SWITCH EXERCISE #32 - Vocational Aptitude

Instructions: Read the following questions and statements related to vocational aptitude. Reflect on your skills, interests, and values to answer each question or complete each statement. Take your time to consider your responses and be honest with yourself. This exercise will help you gain insights into your vocational aptitude and guide you towards discovering a fulfilling career path.

1. What are your natural talents or abilities that you believe could be valuable in a professional setting?

   _______________________________________________

2. Consider the activities or tasks that you enjoy and find fulfilling. How could these activities be incorporated into a potential career?

   _______________________________________________

   _______________________________________________

   _______________________________________________

3. Reflect on your past experiences, both personal and professional. What tasks or responsibilities did you excel at or find particularly satisfying? Why?

   _______________________________________________

   _______________________________________________

   _______________________________________________

4. Think about the subjects or areas of knowledge that genuinely interest you. How could you leverage these interests in a vocational context?

   _______________________________________________

   _______________________________________________

   _______________________________________________

5. Consider the values that are important to you. What kind of work or profession aligns with those values?

_______________________________________________

_______________________________________________

6. List three potential career paths or industries that you feel drawn to. Why do you believe these areas could be a good fit for your vocational aptitude?

_______________________________________________

_______________________________________________

_______________________________________________

7. Research and explore job descriptions or profiles that align with your interests and skills. What positions stand out to you as potential matches for your vocational aptitude?

_______________________________________________

_______________________________________________

_______________________________________________

8. Connect with professionals or mentors who are working in fields that interest you. Seek their advice and insights on how your skills and interests could be applied in those areas. Write down the names of people you can reach out to for this.

_______________________________________________

_______________________________________________

9. Consider any additional education, training, or skills development that may be necessary to pursue a career aligned with your vocational aptitude. How can you acquire or enhance those skills?

_______________________________________________

_______________________________________________

10. Write a short paragraph describing your current understanding of your vocational aptitude and any initial insights you have gained through this reflection process.

_______________________________________________

_______________________________________________

_______________________________________________

11. Remember, this worksheet is a starting point for self-reflection and exploration. Use your responses as a foundation for further research, career planning, and decision-making as you navigate your vocational journey.

## Intuition:

Once upon a time, I had a tricky puzzle to solve. You see, I had to fix some issues that were causing the company's software to behave unexpectedly. It was a complex problem because there was a small mistake causing trouble, but the tricky part was that the mistake wouldn't show up when anyone wanted to replicate it. It was like trying to catch a sneaky bug that only came out when no one was looking! So, there I was, sitting at my desk, feeling a bit lost because I couldn't figure out where to search for the problem. But then something amazing happened. Suddenly, I heard a tiny voice inside me saying, "check the feature toggle." It was like a whisper, but it grabbed my attention right away. Now, let me explain what that means. You know when you have a button on your phone or computer that turns something on or off? Well, in this case, there was a special button that controlled a specific part of the program I was working on. It was called a "feature toggle." It's like having the power to switch a certain function of the program on or off. When I heard that little voice telling me to check the feature toggle, it was like a light bulb turning on in my head! I had a strong feeling that looking in that direction might just solve the problem. And guess what? It did! You see, sometimes our inner voice or intuition can guide us in the right direction when we are trying to solve a problem, even when things seem confusing or complicated. It's like having a secret helper inside us, giving us clues to find the answers we're looking for. So, with newfound confidence, I followed that intuitive message and examined the feature toggle. And just as I suspected, there was a little switch that was causing the trouble, and no one had a clue about it. By making a small adjustment, I fixed the bug, and everything started working smoothly. This story shows how our intuition can be an invaluable asset. It's like having a smart advisor whispering helpful suggestions to us. And by listening to that inner voice, we can solve problems and find solutions, no matter how complex they may seem. This explains how the switch of intuition can ignite your creativity if leveraged.

Richard Branson once said that he relies far more on gut instinct than researching huge amounts of statistics. In other words, he keeps himself abreast of statistical projections and permutations but ultimately leans toward his gut feeling. Similarly, Steve Jobs once said, "Intuition is a very powerful thing, more powerful than intellect, in my opinion." Oprah Winfrey also shared, "I've trusted the still, small voice of intuition my entire life. And the only time I've made mistakes is when I didn't listen." To the outsider, it looks like these people have been blessed by luck. Everything they touch turns to gold. But the truth is that they've tapped into an intelligence that is rarely wrong. You can call it your gut feeling, your sixth sense, or even just a hunch, but each one of us has that inner voice that seeks to guide us. The trick is learning how to really listen and distinguish between the intuitive guiding hand of your human spirit and your own mental chatter. Intuition refers to the ability to understand or know something instinctively, without the need for conscious reasoning or analysis. It is often described as a "gut feeling" or an inner sense that guides decision-making or problem-solving.

Intuition can manifest as sudden insights, hunches, or a deep sense of knowing. Intuition plays a significant role in the creative process. Creativity involves generating novel ideas, making connections between seemingly unrelated concepts, and finding innovative solutions to problems. Intuition acts as a switch for creativity by facilitating the flow of ideas and allowing the mind to make unconventional associations.

**Here's how intuition can be a switch of creativity:**

1. **Pattern recognition:** Intuition helps you recognize patterns and connections that may not be immediately apparent to your conscious mind. It allows you to see relationships between seemingly unrelated ideas, which can spark creative insights.

2. **Unconscious processing:** Intuition draws on the vast amount of information and experiences stored in your subconscious mind. It taps into this knowledge and brings it to the surface, providing you with new perspectives and ideas.

3. **Rapid decision-making:** Intuition can lead to quick decision-making based on a sense of what feels right or aligns with your goals and values. This rapid decision-making can be essential in creative pursuits where overthinking or excessive analysis can hinder progress.

4. **Authentic expression:** Intuition often taps into your authentic self and helps you express your true thoughts and emotions. It allows you to bypass self-doubt and societal expectations, leading to more original and authentic creative expressions.

5. **Inspiration and ideation:** Intuition can serve as a wellspring of inspiration, providing flashes of insight and innovative ideas. It can help you overcome creative blocks and generate novel solutions by accessing the vast resources in your subconscious mind. While it is an invaluable tool in the creative process, intuition alone may not

guarantee creative success, but it can act as a powerful switch that opens the door to new possibilities and unconventional thinking. This is because creativity is an interplay of various cognitive processes, including critical thinking, domain knowledge, and deliberate practice. That is why the switch of intuition needs to be turned on alongside other triggers of creativity to have the right balance when exploring creative possibilities. The problem some people have is they rely solely on gut feeling without having the other switches of creativity like research and critical thinking turned on.

## The inward light

> *The spirit of a man is the **lamp** of the Lord, searching all the inner depths of his heart.*
>
> *Prov 20:27 NKJV*

The Bible makes it clear that everyone has a human spirit and refers to that spirit as a lamp. This spirit functions like a candle or lamp that can provide some degree of illumination when lit. The author of the verse (Proverbs 20:27) uses the metaphor of a lamp to describe the human spirit because a lamp is ignitable, giving light and heat when lit. Why does the author of that verse (Proverbs 20:27) consider the lamp a suitable metaphor to describe the spirit of man? I believe this is because a lamp is ignitable, and gives light and heat when lit. In Solomon's days, the lamps commonly used were oil lamps, which functioned by burning oil to produce light. These lamps consist of a container for holding oil, a wick, and a means to ignite the wick. When a lamp is lit, it burns the wick. The tip of the wick is ignited with a flame from a separate source, such as a match or a fire. The flame initially burns the exposed portion of the wick. Hear this: you possess a lamp that can be used to communicate with the fourth dimension where creativity lives. So, if everyone has this lamp, which is a metaphorical description of the spirit of man, why is everyone not creative? This is because not everyone has ignited that lamp. When a person's lamp is lit, they can receive insights into their mind from the realm beyond their physical senses of touch, sight, smell, hearing, and taste can interact. Take note, even the atheist who does not believe in God has a candle by which they can receive illumination into their mind. This explains why atheists can also be creative. It's why some of the great inventors of contemporary and ancient times are creative despite being atheists. For these atheists, there is always a limit to their wits, just as the candle or lamp has limits to how much light it can give off and how long it can stay lit until the wick burns away completely. This is what differentiates a creative atheist from someone who believes in God and relies on His Omnificence for their creative endeavors.

The spirit of man, as described in Proverbs 20:27, can be understood as the medium through which intuition is sometimes received. As I have previously established, intuition is often considered a deep inner knowing or a gut feeling that goes beyond logical reasoning. It is a form of guidance that arises from within, providing insights and understanding that may not be readily apparent through your physical senses or conscious thought processes. When we ignite the lamp of our spirit, it becomes a channel for receiving intuitive insights. Just as the flame of a lamp illuminates its surroundings, the awakened spirit illuminates our inner depths, allowing us to tap into a realm beyond our ordinary perception. Intuition can be seen as a form of communication or guidance from the deeper realms of our being, accessed through the awakened human spirit. Through this spirit, we can receive intuitive messages, hunches, or subtle cues that guide us in decision-making, problem-solving, and creative endeavors. The spirit acts as a bridge between our conscious mind and the intuitive wisdom that resides within us. Therefore, when we acknowledge and nurture our human spirit, we create an environment where intuition can flourish. By listening to our intuition and trusting the insights that arise from within, we tap into a wellspring of creativity and wisdom that goes beyond our limited rational thinking. So, the spirit of man can be seen as the medium through which intuition is received. By igniting your spirit and cultivating a connection with your inner self, you open yourself to the flow of intuitive guidance, enhancing your creativity and decision-making abilities.

Today, I challenge you to unlock the untapped potential of your intuition. Amplify the whispers of your inner voice and let it guide you towards inspired decisions and creative breakthroughs. Trust in your intuitive power, for it holds the key to unlocking new realms of innovation and personal growth. Dare to flip the switch of intuition and embark on a transformative journey where your unique brilliance shines brightly.

## How to amplify your intuition

Developing the ability to listen to and trust your inner voice, or intuition, is a valuable skill that can be honed through practice. Here are some ways to train yourself to better listen to your inner voice:

1. **Cultivate self-awareness:** Start by becoming more aware of your thoughts, feelings, and bodily sensations. Notice how your body and emotions react in different situations. Pay attention to the subtle cues or nudges you may experience when faced with decisions or choices.

2. **Quiet your mind:** Create moments of stillness and silence in your daily life. Engage in activities like meditation, mindfulness, or deep breathing exercises to calm your mind and create space for intuition to emerge. Regular practice can help quiet the mental chatter and allow your inner voice to be heard more clearly.

3. **Trust your instincts:** Begin by making small decisions based on your intuition. Take note of the outcomes and whether your intuition was accurate. With time and experience, you will build confidence in your intuitive abilities, which will make it easier to trust your inner voice in more significant decisions.

4. **Reflect and journal**: Spend time reflecting on your experiences and decisions. Consider instances where you followed your intuition and assess the outcomes. Journaling about your thoughts, feelings, and intuitive insights can help you better understand and remember these experiences.

5. **Seek solitude:** Create opportunities to be alone and disconnect from external distractions. Solitude provides a fertile ground for introspection and listening to your inner voice. Take walks in nature, spend time in quiet spaces, or engage in activities that promote introspection, such as journaling or creative pursuits.

6. **Practice mindfulness in decision-making:** When faced with a decision, practice being fully present and tuned in to your intuition. Notice any physical sensations, emotions, or spontaneous thoughts that arise. Take these cues into consideration alongside any rational analysis you may conduct.

7. **Embrace creativity:** Engaging in creative activities can help access and amplify your intuitive abilities. Creative practices like painting, writing, dancing, or playing a musical instrument can stimulate your intuitive faculties and foster a deeper connection with your inner voice.

Remember that intuition is deeply personal, and the process of developing and listening to your inner voice may differ from person to person. It takes time, patience, and trust in yourself. Be open-minded, embrace the journey, and gradually build a stronger relationship with your intuition.

## FLIP THE SWITCH EXERCISE #33 – Intuition

Exercise 1: Intuitive Reflection

1. Take a few deep breaths and relax your body and mind.

2. Reflect on a recent decision or situation where you had to make a choice.

3. Close your eyes and turn your attention inward.

4. Without overthinking, notice any feelings or sensations that arise in your body when you recall that decision or situation.

5. Write down any intuitive insights or gut feelings that come to mind.

6. What does your intuition tell you about that decision or situation?

7. Are there any subtle cues or signals that you picked up on?

8. Trust your initial impressions and write them down without judgment.

Exercise 2: Intuitive Visualization

1. Find a quiet space where you won't be disturbed.

2. Close your eyes and take a few deep breaths to relax.

3. Imagine a situation or problem you are currently facing.

4. Visualize different possible outcomes or solutions in your mind.

5. Pay attention to any emotions, images, or sensations that arise as you imagine each scenario.

6. Which outcome or solution feels most aligned with your intuition?

7. What does your gut instinct tell you about the best course of action?

8. Trust the images and feelings that resonate most strongly and write them down.

Exercise 3: Intuitive Journaling

1. Set aside some time for quiet reflection and journaling.

2. Write down a specific question or problem you would like intuitive guidance on.

3. Take a few moments to relax and clear your mind.

4. Begin writing freely without censoring or overthinking.

5. Allow your thoughts and ideas to flow onto the page, trusting your intuition to guide your writing.

6. What insights or ideas come to you as you write?

7. Are there any recurring themes or patterns in your thoughts?

8. Trust the intuitive nudges that arise and write them down without judgment.

Exercise 4: Intuitive Action

1. Choose a small, low-risk decision or task you need to make or complete.

2. Take a moment to center yourself and get in touch with your intuition.

3. Without overthinking, make a quick decision or take action based on your initial gut feeling.

4. Trust that your intuition will guide you in the right direction.

5. How does it feel to trust your intuition and act upon it?

6. Notice any positive outcomes or insights that arise from your intuitive action.

Reflection Questions:

1. How did it feel to tap into your intuition during these exercises?

   _________________________________________________

   _________________________________________________

2. Were there any surprising insights or discoveries you made through your intuition?

   _________________________________________________

   _________________________________________________

3. How can you incorporate intuitive listening into your daily life?

   _________________________________________________

   _________________________________________________

4. What challenges or barriers do you face when it comes to trusting your intuition?

   _________________________________________________

   _________________________________________________

   _________________________________________________

5. What steps can you take to strengthen your connection with your inner voice?

   _________________________________________________

   _________________________________________________

   _________________________________________________

Remember, intuition is a skill that can be developed and refined with practice. Trust yourself and have faith in your ability to make intuitive decisions.

## Tipping Point

During the creative process, you often grapple with complex problems, explore different avenues, and face obstacles along the way. These challenges can take various forms, such as writer's block when you're unsure how to develop your book idea or technical hurdles encountered during a construction project. It could even be a feeling that the goal you've set is unreachable due to persistent obstacles that arise whenever you try to accomplish it. These moments of struggle and confusion are a natural part of the creative journey and sometimes require you to hang on until you reach the tipping point.

The term "tipping point" was popularized by Malcolm Gladwell in his book titled "The Tipping Point: How Little Things Can Make a Big Difference[14]" A tipping point refers to the critical moment when a small change or event leads to a significant and often unexpected shift or outcome. It represents the point at which a situation or system undergoes a fundamental transformation. The tipping point is a switch that triggers a burst of innovative thinking or a surge in creative output. It is the moment when ideas or influences converge, and the cumulative effect leads to a breakthrough or paradigm shift. **Interestingly, the only way to trigger the "tipping point switch" is by demonstrating staying power. In other words, through persistence**. Staying power refers to the unwavering commitment, resilience, and persistence to push through challenges and setbacks in pursuit of creative breakthroughs. When faced with obstacles or moments of doubt, those with staying power exhibit steadfast determination to keep going. They understand that creativity is not always a linear process but rather a journey with ups and downs. They embrace failures and setbacks as learning opportunities and use them to refine their ideas and approaches.

Staying power, or persistence, fuels the momentum needed to reach the tipping point, where a critical mass is achieved, and ideas gain exponential traction. It is the driving force behind prolonged and focused efforts, enabling you to persevere through the inevitable trials and tribulations of the creative process. By nurturing persistence, you can sustain your creative energy and drive, even in the face of adversity. Do not grow weary of doing all that you need to do to transform your ideas into creative solutions. If you do not faint or pull back, you will get to that point where everything begins to align, and success becomes guaranteed.

## The Walt Disney story

Walt Disney's journey to the tipping point can be seen through his staying power in the face of numerous challenges. He encountered financial difficulties, skeptical investors, and initial setbacks with his early ventures. However, Disney remained committed to his creative ideas and persisted in bringing his vision to reality. Despite the obstacles, Disney continued to refine his craft, learn from his failures, and push the boundaries of animation and storytelling. His breakthrough came with the creation of Mickey Mouse and the success of the first synchronized sound cartoon, "Steamboat Willie." This marked a turning point for Disney, as it showcased his innovative techniques and captivated audiences worldwide. Disney's staying power allowed him to build upon this success and expand his creative empire. He introduced groundbreaking advancements in animation, pioneered the concept of feature-length animated films with "Snow White and the Seven Dwarfs," and later brought Disneyland to life, revolutionizing the theme park industry. Through his determination, perseverance, and willingness to take risks, Walt Disney reached the tipping point. That was when his creations and brand went viral and became deeply embedded in popular culture. His staying power enabled him to leave a lasting legacy, transforming the entertainment industry and inspiring generations of storytellers and dreamers[15].

Creativity itself is a complex process influenced by various factors, including personal experiences, knowledge, external stimuli, and internal states of mind. The tipping point in creativity occurs when these factors align in such a way that they amplify each other, creating a catalytic effect. At the tipping point, there may be a confluence of ideas, inspiration, or insights that push creative thinking beyond its usual boundaries. It could be a sudden realization, a new perspective, or an unexpected combination of elements that ignites the creative process. This shift can result in a burst of innovation, allowing you to generate novel solutions, artistic expressions, or groundbreaking inventions.

> *Just as you cannot understand the path of the wind or the **mystery of a tiny baby growing in its mother's womb**, so you cannot understand the activity of God, who does all things. Plant your seed in the morning and keep busy all afternoon, for you don't know if profit will come from one activity or another—or maybe both.*
>
> *Eccl 11:5-6 NLT*

Take note of how the above verse makes it clear that you need to stay the course and keep taking those steps that lead to the tipping point because you do not know the moment your action will trigger the switch. Also notice how the verse above refers to the formation and growth of a baby in the womb. The procreation process is one of the easiest ways to picture creativity. The gestation period of a baby's growth inside the womb represents the period of accumulation of ideas, skills, experiences, and connections. This is typically referred to as growing pains. In procreation, growing pains refer to the physical and emotional discomforts experienced during pregnancy and childbirth. These pains include the stretching and expanding of the uterus, hormonal changes, and the physical demands of carrying and delivering a baby. Growing pains are a natural part of the reproductive process and are necessary for the development and birth of a healthy baby. Within the context of creativity, these pains may include facing self-doubt, encountering obstacles, making mistakes, and experiencing setbacks. However, these growing pains are essential for growth, as they push you to expand your skills, explore new ideas, and overcome limitations, ultimately leading to greater creativity and innovation. In the birth process, the moment when the pregnant woman's water breaks, and she experiences strong contractions can be seen as the tipping point. This represents a critical defining moment in the creative process. It signifies the transition from the incubation phase to the birthing of the creative idea. Just as the woman must summon all her energy to give birth to the baby, you must put your best effort and commitment to bring your creative ideas to fruition at this critical moment. Your tipping point could be that Aha! Moment, a sudden flash of insight, a moment of clarity, or a breakthrough in understanding, when everything clicks. It may involve the realization of a solution to a problem, the discovery of a new perspective, or the connection between previously disparate ideas. What you do at that moment matters a lot. Many people dovetail into impossibility thinking during their tipping point and start making up excuses for why they cannot release the creative seed within, whose time has come. But for others who end up taking advantage of this switch, this moment of alignment and connection brings a sense of excitement, satisfaction, and progress.

In a nutshell, tipping point could also be seen as the moment when an idea, creative solution or product that has existed before suddenly gains traction in the market and goes viral online. Or that point where a political movement spreads like wildfire. It's important to note that the tipping point in creativity is often preceded by a gradual accumulation of knowledge, experiences, and ideas. The tipping point itself may seem like a sudden change, but it is often the result of an underlying creative process that has been building up over time. This is why you must not undermine the power of baby steps in the creative process. Small changes, insights, or influences can lead to significant shifts in the creative process, unlocking new possibilities and unleashing a wave of innovative thinking. Do not underestimate the power of your ideas, dreams, and aspirations. Embrace the challenges and setbacks as opportunities for growth and learning. Take those baby steps, accumulate knowledge and experiences, and keep pushing forward. Remember that the tipping point is often preceded by a gradual build-up, and it is in those moments of uncertainty and struggle that breakthroughs are born. The world is waiting for what you have to offer. Dare to push past the tipping point, where the miracle happens, and where your dreams become reality. Take that leap of faith and let your creativity shine forth.

## SAY THESE WORDS

I recognize that my creative endeavors have the potential to reach a tipping point, where they gain momentum and make a profound impact. I am open to exploring unconventional approaches and ideas that have the potential to become tipping points in my creative journey. I trust in the process of accumulation, knowing that every small effort contributes to the tipping point of my creativity. I refuse to give up or give in until I see my ideas, dreams, and talents transformed into reality through creativity.

## FLIP THE SWITCH EXERCISE #34 - The Tipping Point

Instructions: Use the following questions and prompts to guide your thoughts and actions. Feel free to jot down your responses and ideas on a separate sheet of paper or in a journal.

1. Understanding the Tipping Point:

a) Define the tipping point in your own words.

b) Why is the tipping point considered a critical moment of transformation?

c) Reflect on a personal experience where you have witnessed or experienced a tipping point. What was the outcome?

2. Exploring Personal Creativity:

a) How do you define creativity? What does it mean to you?

b) Reflect on your creative journey. What challenges have you encountered along the way?

c) Can you identify any moments in your creative process where you have experienced a tipping point? Describe the impact and outcome of those moments.

3. Staying the Course:

a) Reflect on a goal or project you are currently pursuing. Are there any obstacles or challenges you have encountered? List them.

b) How can you stay committed and motivated during times of difficulty or uncertainty?

c) Brainstorm and write down three specific actions you can take to stay the course and move closer to the tipping point in your current endeavor.

4. Recognizing Milestones:

a) Reflect on your past achievements or milestones. What were the moments that marked significant progress or success?

b) How can you identify and celebrate smaller milestones along the way to your tipping point?

c) List three milestones or markers that you would like to achieve on your journey towards the tipping point.

5. Leveraging Resources:

a) Consider the resources available to you, such as knowledge, skills, networks, or tools. How can you leverage these resources to reach your tipping point?

b) Are there any additional resources or support you may need to maximize your chances of success? List them.

c) Identify one specific resource or support system you can seek out or utilize to accelerate your progress.

6. Review and Reflection:

a) Take a moment to review your progress and the insights gained from this worksheet.

b) Are there any adjustments or refinements you need to make to your strategies or approaches?

c) Write down three key takeaways or realizations that you will carry forward on your journey towards the tipping point.

7. Commitment to Action:

a) Based on your reflections and insights, identify one specific action you will commit to taking immediately or soon to accelerate your progress towards the tipping point.

_________________________________________________

_________________________________________________

_________________________________________________

## Yearning

One reason many people fail to unleash their creative potential and leave it untapped is that they lack the inner drive to bring their great ideas to fruition. Your yearning can be like a switch that triggers your creativity. When you yearn for something, it creates a powerful internal motivation and a sense of urgency to find a solution, explore new ideas, or express yourself creatively. This yearning can stem from various sources, such as a desire for self-expression, a need for personal growth, a need to make money from your talents and gifts, or an aspiration to bring about positive change in your world. Yearning refers to a deep longing or intense desire for something. It is a strong emotional or intellectual craving for a particular experience, outcome, or state of being. Yearning often involves a sense of incompleteness or a feeling that something is missing, driving you to seek fulfillment or resolution. Most innovators, inventors, and creators have this burning desire that triggers their curiosity and creativity. One way to identify your creative genius is to recognize that deep-seated desire within you that lingers on until you find an answer to a problem. It is that yearning that can keep you awake at night or make you stay in pursuit of a creative exploration despite rejections or disappointments. This yearning often persists until there is a breaking forth of light, known as the "eureka moment."

Yearning as a switch of creativity is triggered the moment inspiration strikes, and you feel compelled to engage in creative endeavors. Once the yearning switch is triggered, it generates a strong emotional charge that stimulates your imagination, problem-solving abilities, and innovative thinking. It serves as a driving force behind the exploration of new possibilities and the pursuit of novel ideas. The story of Nehemiah teaches us that hunger for a specific outcome or vision can inspire creativity and drive us to find innovative solutions to overcome obstacles. Nehemiah's hunger to see Jerusalem's walls rebuilt compelled him to tap into his creative abilities, rally the community, and navigate challenges along the way.

## Newton's yearning

Newton was a famous scientist and inventor who held Christian beliefs throughout his life. He wrote extensively on theological topics and engaged in biblical studies. He sought to reconcile his scientific investigations with his religious faith, viewing both as paths to understanding God's creation. He believed that studying the natural world through science could provide insights into God's grand design and the underlying order of the universe. Newton was known for his intense curiosity and relentless pursuit of answers to fundamental questions about the natural world. This yearning drove him to engage in extensive research, experimentation, and deep contemplation, leading to his groundbreaking scientific discoveries. One of Newton's most remarkable moments of creativity came when he developed his theory of universal gravitation. While observing an apple falling from a tree, he had a sudden realization that the same force governing the apple's motion also applied to celestial bodies. This eureka moment led to the formulation of his law of universal gravitation and laid the foundation for his revolutionary work on the laws of motion and celestial mechanics. Creativity often arises from a state of tension or a gap between what is and what could be. The yearning to bridge that gap pushes you to tap into their creativity and find unique solutions or create original works. It can lead to new insights, breakthroughs, and artistic expressions that would not have emerged without that deep longing. Therefore, yearning acts as a switch of creativity by igniting the creative process, inspiring individuals to think differently, and providing the motivation needed to pursue imaginative and innovative paths. When someone yearns for a solution or deeply desires to unravel a mystery, they are more likely to engage in dedicated research, brainstorming, and experimentation. This sustained effort and concentration creates the groundwork for the eureka moment to happen.

## How to stimulate Yearning that Births Creativity

1. **Cultivate curiosity:** Foster a sense of wonder and curiosity about the world around you. Embrace a mindset of continuous learning and exploration. Ask questions, seek new experiences, and remain open to different perspectives. Curiosity can ignite the yearning for answers and fuel creative thinking.

2. **Set compelling goals:** Establish clear and inspiring goals that align with your passions and values. Define what you want to achieve and why it matters to you. Having meaningful objectives can ignite a sense of purpose and drive that fuels creativity and motivates you to take action.

3. **Embrace problems and failure:** This can be a great way to stimulate the yearning that ignites creativity. Recognize that challenges and setbacks are opportunities for growth and learning. Use them as catalysts to get into the zone where you can exercise dominion over crisis through creativity.

4. **Use Your Fears as a Driving Force:** For example, the fear of being broke can sometimes be used as a powerful motivator that

stimulates the hunger needed to identify, create, and seize entrepreneurial opportunities.

5. **Practice discipline and consistency:** Cultivate habits of discipline and consistency in your creative pursuits. Set aside dedicated time for creativity, whether it's writing, painting, brainstorming, or any other form of self-expression. Commitment and regular practice can strengthen your drive and deepen your creative abilities.

6. **Seek feedback and collaboration:** Engage in constructive feedback and collaboration with others. Share your ideas, seek input, and embrace different perspectives. Collaborating with others can spark new ideas, provide motivation, and push you beyond your comfort zone.

7. **Reflect and celebrate progress:** Take time to reflect on your creative journey and acknowledge your progress. Celebrate small victories and milestones along the way. Reflecting on your achievements can fuel a sense of accomplishment and drive to continue pursuing your creative endeavors.

---

**SAY THESE WORDS**

I embrace the powerful yearning within me as a driving force for creativity and innovation. I use the passionate hunger within my soul as a guide, nudging me towards new and inspired creations. My yearning serves as a compass, guiding me towards the untapped reservoirs of my lost creativity. A fresh hunger is aroused in me, causing me to transform my ideas, talents, skill and potential into creative solutions. I will not give in until this hunger is quenched! Glory to God.

## FLIP THE SWITCH EXERCISE #35 - Yearning

Instructions:

Reflect on your own aspirations, passions, and areas where you feel a strong desire for growth and change. Use the prompts and questions below to guide your thinking and brainstorming process. Feel free to write down your answers or thoughts in the spaces provided or use a separate sheet of paper.

Section 1: Identify Areas of Yearning

1.  Think about your personal and professional life. In which areas do you feel a strong yearning for improvement, change, or creative expression?

    Area of Yearning: _______________________________________

2.  What specific goals or outcomes do you yearn to achieve in this area?

    Goals or Outcomes: _______________________________________

Section 2: Explore Creative Ideas

3.  Reflect on the area of yearning you identified. Brainstorm creative ideas or solutions that could help you fulfill your yearning and achieve your desired goals. Write down as many ideas as possible.

    Creative Ideas:

    1. _______________________________________

    2. _______________________________________

    3. _______________________________________

    4. _______________________________________

    5. _______________________________________

Section 3: Breaking Through Barriers

4. Consider any barriers or challenges that may hinder you from pursuing these creative ideas or taking action. Identify at least two potential obstacles.

   Barriers or Challenges:

   1. ___________________________________________

   2. ___________________________________________

5. How can you overcome these barriers? Brainstorm strategies or resources that can help you navigate and overcome the challenges you identified.

   Overcoming Strategies:

   1. ___________________________________________

   2. ___________________________________________

Section 4: Develop an Action Plan

6. From the creative ideas you generated, select one idea that resonates with you the most and has the potential to address your yearning. Write it down below.

   Selected Creative Idea: _______________________________

7. Outline three specific action steps you can take to start implementing this creative idea and moving closer to your desired goals.

   Action Steps:

   1. ___________________________________________

   2. ___________________________________________

   3. ___________________________________________

Section 5: Reflect and Commit

8.  Take a moment to reflect on your yearning, the creative ideas generated, and the action steps you outlined. How do you feel about embarking on this journey of creativity and change?

    Reflection: _______________________________________________

9.  Make a commitment to yourself. Write a statement that expresses your dedication to pursuing your yearning, embracing creativity, and taking the necessary steps to bring your ideas to life.

    Commitment Statement:

    _______________________________________________

    _______________________________________________

    _______________________________________________

    _______________________________________________

    _______________________________________________

    _______________________________________________

    _______________________________________________

    _______________________________________________

    _______________________________________________

    _______________________________________________

    _______________________________________________

    _______________________________________________

    _______________________________________________

    _______________________________________________

# CREATIVITY WORKSHEET #4

Instructions:

Use this worksheet to delve into the different switches of creativity discussed in Chapter four. Engage in the activities and reflections below to deepen your understanding of each switch and its impact on your creative journey. This worksheet will help you identify and harness the power of these switches to enhance your creative abilities.

1. Troubleshooting:

a) Reflect on a recent problem or challenge you encountered. How did you approach troubleshooting to find a solution? Write down the steps or strategies you employed.

_______________________________________________

_______________________________________________

_______________________________________________

b) Identify one area of your life or work where you can apply troubleshooting as a creative switch. Write down the specific problem or challenge and brainstorm potential troubleshooting approaches.

Problem/Challenge: _______________________________

Potential Troubleshooting Approaches:

1. _______________________________________________

2. _______________________________________________

3. _______________________________________________

2. Critical Thinking:

a) Think about a recent situation where critical thinking played a crucial role in finding a creative solution. Describe the problem, your thought process, and the outcome.

Problem: _______________________________________________

Thought Process: _______________________________________

Outcome: _______________________________________________

b) Choose a topic or issue that you want to analyze critically. Write a list of questions or thought-provoking prompts to guide your critical thinking process.

Questions/Prompts:

1. _______________________________________________

2. _______________________________________________

3. _______________________________________________

3. Ruthless Execution:

a) Reflect on a project or goal that required you to exhibit ruthless execution. How did you stay focused and committed? Write down the strategies or mindset you adopted.

_______________________________________________

_______________________________________________

_______________________________________________

b) Identify a current goal or project that requires ruthless execution. Write down specific actions or steps you will take to ensure focused and effective execution.

Actions/Steps:

1. _______________________________________________

2. _______________________________________________

3. _______________________________________________

4. Ardent Research:

a) Think about a time when research played a crucial role in your creative process. Describe how research enhanced your understanding and influenced your final outcome.

_______________________________________________

_______________________________________________

_______________________________________________

b) Choose a topic or area of interest for deeper research. Write down a research plan, including the sources and methods you will use to gather information.

Research Topic: _______________________________

Research Plan:

Source 1: _____________________________________

Source 2: _____________________________________

Method 1: _____________________________________

Method 2: _____________________________________

5.  Entrepreneurial Spirit:

a)  Reflect on a situation where your entrepreneurial spirit propelled you to take risks and pursue new opportunities. Describe the experience and the outcomes you achieved.

___________________________________________

___________________________________________

___________________________________________

b)  Identify an area in your life or work where you can embrace an entrepreneurial spirit. Write down a specific idea or opportunity you want to explore and the steps you will take to pursue it.

Idea/Opportunity: _______________________________

Steps to Pursue:

1.  _______________________________________

2.  _______________________________________

3.  _______________________________________

6.  Initiative:

a)  Think about a time when your proactive attitude and initiative led to a creative breakthrough. Describe the situation and the actions you took.

___________________________________________

___________________________________________

___________________________________________

b)  Identify an opportunity or area where you can take initiative to foster creativity. Write down the specific action you will take and the expected impact.

Action: _______________________________________________

Expected Impact: _______________________________________

7.  Vocational Aptitude:

a)  Reflect on your natural talents and strengths that align with your chosen vocation or creative pursuits. Write down three key aptitudes that contribute to your vocational success.

_______________________________________________

_______________________________________________

_______________________________________________

b)  Identify one specific talent or aptitude you want to further develop and leverage in your creative endeavors. Write down the steps or practices you will undertake to nurture this aptitude.

Steps/Practices:

1.  _______________________________________________

2.  _______________________________________________

3.  _______________________________________________

8.  Intuition:

a)  Recall a situation where your intuition guided your creative decision-making process. Describe how you recognized and followed your intuition, and the impact it had on your outcome.

_______________________________________________

_______________________________________________

_______________________________________________

b) Identify an upcoming decision or creative challenge where you want to rely on your intuition. Write down the specific steps or practices you will adopt to enhance your intuitive abilities.

Steps/Practices:

1. _______________________________________________

2. _______________________________________________

3. _______________________________________________

9. Tipping Point:

a) Reflect on a significant turning point or breakthrough moment in your creative journey. Describe the events or factors that led to the tipping point and how it impacted your creativity.

_______________________________________________

_______________________________________________

_______________________________________________

b) Identify a current project or endeavor where you want to reach a tipping point. Write down the specific goals or milestones you aim to achieve, and the strategies you will implement to move closer to the tipping point.

Goals/Milestones:

1. _______________________________________________

2. _______________________________________________

3. _______________________________________________

10. Yearning:

a) Think about a deep yearning or desire that has fueled your creative pursuits. Describe how this yearning has motivated and inspired you along your creative journey.

_______________________________________________

_______________________________________________

_______________________________________________

b) Identify a specific creative goal or aspiration that aligns with your yearning. Write down the steps or actions you will take to bring this goal closer to reality.

Steps/Actions:

1. _______________________________________________

2. _______________________________________________

3. _______________________________________________

Remember, this worksheet is designed to deepen your understanding of the switches of creativity and how they influence your creative journey. Participate in the activities and reflections to discover new insights and ignite your creativity.

# CHAPTER FIVE

# BLOCKERS OF CREATIVITY

Creativity is a remarkable and intrinsic human quality that holds the power to shape your world and ignite the flames of innovation. It enables you to think beyond boundaries, envision new possibilities, and express yourself in unique and meaningful ways. However, despite its abundance and potential within everyone, creativity can sometimes seem elusive, slipping away like a fleeting flame in the wind. This is why many carry their ideas, gifts, and talents to the grave without ever unleashing their creativity. Let us explore some factors that could contribute to the loss of your creative spark or fire and understand how you can navigate these obstacles to reignite your creative energy. Creativity blockers manifest in various forms, ranging from external influences to internal struggles. Below are some blockers we will examine in this chapter:

- Vision Deficit
- Faith Deficit
- Inspiration Deficit
- Knowledge Gap

Let's dive in one after the other.

## Vision Deficit

To create something that transforms and impacts the lives of people, you must see it. Many people have their creative fires extinguished or turned off because they lack a vision of what they could do, be, and experience. If only they would see beyond what already exists! Creativity requires vision, the ability to see what is not visible to others and to make it possible for them to see it too. Without vision, many individuals miss out on opportunities for creativity. Once you can see something, you can create it, but you cannot create what you cannot see. For example, take two men to an empty plot of land overrun with marsh. One of the men would look at the deserted nature of the marshland and say, "Can anything good come out of this place?" While the other one would immediately envision the possibility of turning that deserted piece into a recreational center. The difference between these two men is their vision—one has it, the other does not. Vision, in this context, means seeing with the eyes of the mind, not just what you can see with your optical eyes. Whether it's a physical structure or an intangible concept, you must first have a clear vision or mental image of what you want to create. That's why in developed countries, before any building is approved for development, it must have a detailed architectural drawing.

Let us take a cursory look at how Noah leveraged the power of vision to ignite his creativity. He saw the architectural plan for the large boat before he attempted to build or recreate what God had shown him. God had to tell him to look at what He was showing him so that he would understand the purpose behind the water vessel he was about to create. See what God told him below:

> *Build a large boat from cypress wood and waterproof it with tar, inside and out. Then construct decks and stalls throughout its interior. Make the boat 450 feet long, 75 feet wide, and 45 feet high. Leave an 18-inch opening below the roof all the way around the boat. Put the door on the side, and build three decks inside the boat—lower, middle, and upper. "Look! I am about to cover the earth with a flood that will destroy every living thing that breathes. Everything on earth will die.*
>
> *Gen 6:14-18 NLT*

The words translated as 'build' and 'make' in the above scripture are derived from the Hebrew word 'asah.' This word means to make, produce, fashion, manufacture, create, or build something1. So, it is safe to infer that when God was speaking to Noah, He was telling him to engage his creativity. God made him build an ark by showing him what was required and why it was needed. That was vision in action, stimulating creativity in Noah through the conversation recorded in the above verse. The story of Noah and the ark is a powerful example of how having a clear vision can inspire creativity and lead to great accomplishments. In this story, God showed Noah a vision of the ark he was to build to save his family and the animals from the flood. Noah received specific instructions on the size, shape, and materials of the ark, and he worked tirelessly to bring this vision to life. On the other hand, if Noah had not received a clear vision from God, it is unlikely that he would have been able to build the ark. Without a vision of what he needed to achieve, Noah would not have known where to start or what to do. He would have lacked the direction and focus needed to build, create, or complete such a massive project. Similarly, when we lack a clear vision, we may struggle to be creative and productive in our work. We may feel overwhelmed or unsure of what we need to do, which can lead to procrastination, indecision, or creative blocks. Noah's example teaches us that having a clear vision is crucial for unlocking our full creative potential.

When you have a vision, you can focus your energy and resources on achieving a specific goal. You can overcome obstacles and find innovative solutions to problems. You can work with purpose and determination, even in the face of adversity. Having a clear vision is essential to achieving great things. Without a vision, your creativity and productivity can be hindered, but with a vision, you can accomplish amazing feats and bring about positive change in your life and in the world at large. If you do not have a clear vision of what you want to produce or what problem you want to solve, you will struggle to come up with new and innovative ideas, or you may feel unmotivated to pursue your creative goals. Without a clear vision, it can be challenging to know where to direct your creative efforts or how to turn on your creative switches. You may feel lost or aimless, which can lead to a lack of focus and direction in your creative work. This lack of direction can result in creative blocks, where you struggle to generate new ideas or make progress on your projects.

## Faith Deficit:

When someone embraces an idea that others may not align with initially but remains steadfast in their pursuit to bring that idea to fruition, it showcases a profound sense of belief and faith. It takes faith and conviction to trust in one's vision and persevere despite challenges or skepticism from others. By staying true to your faith and persistently working towards your goals, you can manifest your ideas and inspire others with the power of your unwavering belief. Unfortunately, many people who claim to have faith do not use it to cultivate their creativity. Instead, they focus solely on using their faith to seek miracles or healing for themselves, which is not inherently wrong. However, they are missing an important aspect of faith if they fail to apply it to their creative endeavors. It takes a strong belief in an idea to be creative, sometimes in the face of daunting and visible difficulties. Everyone who has ever created or invented anything had a resolute belief in the fact that they had something worth creating - an idea whose time had come.

If you are reading this and would like to understand more about how faith and creativity are connected, pay attention to the verse that follows:

> *In the beginning, God created the heavens and the earth. The earth was without form and void, and darkness was over the face of the deep...*
>
> *Gen 1:1-2 ESV*

The very first display of creativity recorded in scripture was performed by God. In the very first verse of the Bible, scripture makes it clear that there was no chance that something as beautiful as what we call the earth could come out of the darkness and emptiness that first existed. Yet God created the stars, the moon, sun, plants, animals, and all the wonderful creations we see in nature by faith. In other words, God was not moved by the state of the earth before displaying creativity because He knew the principles of creativity – that to create what can be seen, you must believe in the validity of your unseen ideas and their possibilities. Hence, God created the world out of nothing. When you are creative, sometimes your ideas may not make sense given the reality of what is on ground, and that is where faith or belief becomes important.

> *By faith we understand that the world was created by the word of God, so that what is seen was made out of things which do not appear.*

> *Heb 11:3 ESV*

Keep in mind that any remarkable creation or innovation you see in various fields, such as art, music, invention, or style, began as a simple idea in the mind of its creator. That means everything we now see in the world today that can be classified as a creation of man was once a figment of man's imagination. The same process is what God demonstrated when he created the world. He had an idea in mind, He shared the idea, and turned that idea into tangible reality. This process would not be possible without faith. No wonder the Bible says that faith without works is dead.

> *In the same way, faith by itself, if it is not accompanied by action, is dead.*

> *James 2:17 NIV*

The word 'action,' which is translated as 'works' in other popular Bible translations, comes from a very interesting Greek word, 'ergon.' According to Thayer's Lexicon, this word means 'any product, or anything accomplished by hand, art, industry, or mind.' The word also connotes 'business, employment, enterprise, or that which one undertakes to do[1].' In other words, what James was saying was that faith without action, faith without enterprise, faith without product, faith without creations, is dead.

It takes faith or strong belief to keep trying to develop an invention after multiple failed attempts. That explains why most inventors were able to develop, build, or innovate something unique despite the failures and rejections of naysayers. Sometimes, they go ahead and invent groundbreaking discoveries even when their theory seems not to be working. They just believe there is a way forward and that their ideas can still become a reality. With that mentality, they keep trying, and before long, they get a 'eureka moment' and make a discovery that changes the world. Most times, we listen to the doubts we hear from within and without and allow our inner greatness to die within us. We tell ourselves, 'I have not done it before,' 'no one has done it before in my family, school, organization, or country,' 'everyone who tried to do this failed,' among other excuses. If no one has done it before, then you've got a chance right there to blaze the trail and be a trendsetter. The Wright brothers were only bicycle mechanics when they conceived the idea of making an aircraft in a bid to aid air travel. Notice, they had never built a plane before and did not know how to build one until they built it. People doubted them, did not believe in them, but that did not stop them because they believed they had an idea worth creating. They believed in themselves, and that was all that mattered for them to release their creative genius.

Many people have the next greatest idea sitting in their head, waiting to gain expression through creativity, but for fear and self-doubt, they never allow their creativity to shine through. Many will go to the grave without birthing their brainchildren because they lack faith in what they can be and can do. A lack of belief in your potential leads to feelings of doubt, uncertainty, and even apathy, which can hinder creativity. If one lacks confidence in their abilities or in the possibility of achieving success, they may be less likely to take risks or pursue creative endeavors with enthusiasm. Additionally, if one lacks belief in the value of creativity itself, they may not prioritize it in their lives or put in the necessary effort to develop their skills. This can lead to stagnation in one's creative abilities, as they fail to challenge themselves or seek out new experiences that could inspire fresh ideas.

You may ask, what about great inventors that claim not to have faith in God, would you say they were creative without faith? The principle at play here is not faith in a Deity but faith in one's idea. Having said that, I believe that scientists and inventors who claim not to believe in a Deity as the source of their creativity only do so in self-deceit because whether they admit it or not, it does not change the fact that all wisdom for creativity comes from God. If tomorrow, I announce that I have disowned my father, does that change the fact that I have a father and mother and share some of their attributes in my traits and DNA? No. So, if inventors, creators, or scientists claim that God, who is their source, does not exist, does that make it true? No. Does that also invalidate the fact that they possess creative ability, an attribute that comes from God? Emphatically no!

The Bible says in James 2:18, 'show me your faith without works, and I would show you my faith by my works.' It troubles me when I see people who profess Christ as their Lord and claim to have faith, yet have little or no works of creativity to show. Meanwhile, those who claim to be atheists (who don't even realize that they have faith) demonstrate their faith by their works. By 'works' here, I mean creative solutions that alleviate people's sorrows, poverty, penury, or make life better in any way.

That's why I'm passionate about teaching people how to be creative.

> *By faith Noah, being warned by God concerning events*
> *as yet unseen, in reverent fear constructed an ark for*
> *the saving of his household.*

> *Heb 11:7 ESV*

By faith, Noah believed what God showed him in the unseen and he developed, manufactured, created, or built an ark. That was creativity born out of faith. His faith resulted in creativity. Noah's faith in God's revelation of the future led him to use his creative skills to build an ark. That was an act of creativity stemming from faith. If you have not yet acted on the vision that God has given you or released your own creativity, it is time to wake up!

## Inspiration Deficit:

In the realm of creativity, apathy stands as a blocker, capable of extinguishing even the brightest sparks of inspiration. It is a subtle yet pervasive force that can drain the energy and enthusiasm necessary to bring creative ideas to life. As Thomas Edison once remarked, "Genius is one percent inspiration and ninety-nine percent perspiration." Within this equation (the crucial one percent), inspiration holds immense power, acting as the driving force behind our courage, determination, and willingness to undertake the seemingly impossible. Imagine standing at the precipice of your dreams, armed with a vision that is uniquely yours. You possess a burning desire to transform this vision into reality, to breathe life into your ideas and manifest them in the tangible world. However, the journey towards creative fruition is often paved with obstacles, and it is in the face of these challenges that inspiration becomes crucial.

Many individuals attribute their inability to develop and bring forth their creative ideas to the demands of their hectic or demanding jobs. They blame lack of time as the primary obstacle standing in their way. Yet, the truth lies hidden beneath the surface. It is not time that they lack, but rather inspiration. Without the right dosage of inspiration, the motivation to channel your energy towards your creative endeavor wanes, and your dreams remain dormant. To grasp the power of inspiration, it is important to know that it is cultivated through the consistent devotion of time, effort, and enthusiasm to the creative process. The mistake people make is they expect that their dreams will materialize without understanding the significance of taking small, deliberate steps each day towards their realization. Inspiration acts as the guiding compass, providing the necessary fuel to navigate the complexities of the creative journey. It is the flicker of light in the darkest moments, the force that propels us forward when the path seems uncertain and daunting. One might wonder, where does inspiration reside? How can it be nurtured and harnessed? The answers lie within the details of your daily life, waiting to be discovered. Inspiration can be found in the simplest of moments—a captivating piece of artwork, a soul-stirring melody, or the beauty of nature's tapestry. It can be gleaned from conversations with kindred spirits, who share their own stories of triumph and resilience. Remember the story behind this book? How the inspiration came from a conversation, a gentleman's request? That gives you an idea of how inspiration for creativity can come even when you least expect it. So, stay alert and ready to leverage those moments of inspiration that comes your way daily. By embracing the one percent of inspiration Edison talked about, and allowing it to guide your creative endeavors, you can ignite your creativity and unlock the door to endless possibilities.

## Knowledge Gap

You do not necessarily need to be an erudite scholar to be creative, but you do need to have knowledge. To manifest creativity, you would need to embark on what may seem like adventures into the unknown, in search of ways to bring your ideas into reality. Maya Angelou is a great inspiration today, even though she came from a poor background, grew up in poverty, and dropped out of school at a young age. She suffered abuse as a child and became a single mother, struggling to make ends meet. Through self-education, she became a globally renowned civil rights activist, poet, and award-winning author. Her acclaimed 1969 memoir, 'I Know Why the Caged Bird Sings,' as well as her poetry and essays, earned her well-deserved recognition. Despite the setbacks she faced, Maya Angelou became one of the most influential writers of the 20th century. She even served as a consultant and advisor to several U.S. presidents, including Jimmy Carter, Ronald Reagan, and Bill Clinton. Imagine someone from her background and childhood history becoming an advisor to Presidents in what many refer to as the greatest nation on earth. It doesn't matter where you come from; if you nourish your mind with the right dose of self-education and train yourself to be creative with that information, there is no limit to what you can achieve. Maya Angelou read extensively and educated herself on a wide range of topics, from literature to history to politics. Her diverse knowledge and experiences informed her writing and contributed to her creative genius[2].

*The heart of the discerning acquires knowledge, for the
ears of the wise seek it out.*

*Proverbs 18:15*

Self-education provides the foundation for creativity, giving you the tools and resources needed to generate and develop innovative ideas. Many people do not take ownership of their education and this deficiency is what puts off their innate creativity. The above scripture emphasizes the importance of acquiring knowledge and seeking understanding. It suggests that a wise person is constantly learning and seeking out new information, which can inform and enhance their creativity. By engaging in self-education and actively seeking knowledge, you can cultivate an intelligent heart and expand your creative horizons. When you don't take the time to educate yourself, you limit your perspectives, and the ideas you can generate. The result of this lack of ideas results in a lack of creativity because creativity is simply idea plus execution. Learning about different fields, cultures, and ideas can open you to new ways of thinking and inspire creativity regardless of skin pigmentation, religious creed, or geographical extraction.

*Let the wise listen and add to their learning, and let the
discerning get guidance.*

*Proverbs 1:5 NIV*

If a man is already wise, why does he need to learn? Only fools think they do not need to learn because they already know too much. What this means is that to translate your wisdom into tangible solutions through creativity, you need knowledge that comes from learning. In a nutshell, if you do not make concerted efforts to learn new things, you will have limited solutions and a constrained perspective towards innovation, even when a greater reality is within your reach. When we don't take the time to educate ourselves, we limit our perspectives. Without self-education, you may not have the knowledge or skills to create the things you envision. That's what made men like Richard Branson and Benjamin Franklin make a difference and attain their lofty visions. Despite not having the luxury of traditional education, they became creative despite the odds because they filled their knowledge gaps. Learning about a variety of subjects and skills can provide you with the tools you need to bring your ideas to life. Without self-education, your creativity will stagnate. Learning new things can help you stay engaged and motivated, leading to more creativity..

**SAY THESE WORDS**

I am a visionary, and I use the power of my creative vision to guide my pursuits and bring my God-given ideas to life. I release all doubts and insecurities about my creative abilities, and I confidently embrace my unique talents and gifts. My passion for creativity is unwavering, and I am committed to nurturing and fueling it every day. I fill my knowledge gaps with curiosity and a thirst for learning, continuously expanding my skills and expertise. I release any apathy or resistance, and I approach my creative endeavors with enthusiasm, energy, and a positive mindset. I trust in my creative process and allow my ideas to flow freely, knowing that each step I take brings me closer to my goals. Thank you Lord Jesus!

## CREATIVITY WORKSHEET #5: BLOCKERS OF CREATIVITY

**Instructions:**

This worksheet will help you identify and address the barriers that hinder your creative potential and provide actionable steps to overcome them.

1. Vision Deficit:

a) Reflect on your current creative endeavors or projects. Do you have a clear vision or goal for each of them? If not, why do you think that is?

_______________________________________________

_______________________________________________

_______________________________________________

_______________________________________________

b) What steps can you take to clarify your vision and set clear goals for your creative pursuits?

_______________________________________________

_______________________________________________

2. Lack of faith:

a) Are there specific areas or aspects of your creative abilities that you doubt? Identify the doubts or insecurities that hold you back.

_______________________________________________

_______________________________________________

b) How can you challenge and overcome these doubts? List strategies or actions you can take to build confidence in your creative skills.

___________________________________________

___________________________________________

3.  Lack of inspiration:

a)  Have you ever experienced a lack of motivation or passion for your creative endeavors? If so, when and why did it happen?

___________________________________________

___________________________________________

What strategies can you implement to reignite your passion and overcome apathy? Consider activities, inspirations, or practices that can help you stay motivated.

___________________________________________

___________________________________________

4.  Knowledge Gap:

a)  Reflect on areas where you feel a knowledge gap or lack of expertise in your creative pursuits. What specific knowledge or skills do you feel you need to develop?

___________________________________________

___________________________________________

b)  How can you address this knowledge gap? Identify resources, learning opportunities, or mentorship that can help you acquire the necessary knowledge and skills.

___________________________________________

___________________________________________

5.  Action Plan:

Based on your reflections and insights from this worksheet, create an action plan to overcome the blockers of creativity:

a) Identify one specific action you will take to address each of the blockers discussed (Vision Deficit, Lack of faith, Lack of inspiration, Knowledge Gap).

_________________________________________

_________________________________________

_________________________________________

_________________________________________

Remember, this worksheet is designed to help you recognize and overcome the blockers of creativity that may be hindering your progress. Use it as a tool for self-reflection and personal growth and refer back to it whenever you encounter challenges along your creative journey. Keep pushing through and never lose sight of your creative potential.

# ACKNOWLEDGMENT

$\mathcal{I}$ would like to express my heartfelt gratitude to those who have been instrumental in the creation and completion of "Ignite Your Creativity."

I want to thank my dear wife, Precious, for standing by me throughout this journey.

To my wonderful daughter Amarissa, thank you for filling my life with joy and reminding me of the power of creativity. Your conception, birth, and innocent curiosity have taught me valuable lessons in creativity.

And to you my dear reader, this book will not be a reality without you. Thank you for being the number one reason I wrote this book. I hope that it continues to serve as a guiding light, encouraging you to continue exploring the vast landscapes of your imagination and innovation.

I would like to acknowledge the divine presence of God. His guidance, strength, and grace have guided me through moments of doubt and provided me with the inspiration to delve deeper into the realms of creativity.

To all my friends and family who have supported me along the way, your encouragement and positive energy have been a great source of motivation.

Thank you all for being a part of this incredible journey.

With gratitude,

Iredafe Owolabi,

The Creativity Expert.

# ABOUT ME

Hi there, I'm Iredafenevesho Owolabi, but you can call me 'Dafe.' I'm a creativity coach, author, and professional software engineer based in Canada. My passion lies in unlocking creative potential and inspiring individuals to reach their full capabilities. This is who I am:

1. Author of 17 books and counting.
2. Facilitator of seminars, workshops, and conferences worldwide.
3. Specializes in Creativity, 4D Thinking, Problem Solving, Authorpreneurship, and Kingdom topics.

My goal for writing "Ignite Your Creativity" is to help you develop your creativity skills and guide you on the journey from ideas to creative solutions with the aid of practical insights and exercises.

My books have been read and celebrated in different parts of the world, with countless testimonials of their impact. As a software engineer, I've had the privilege of working in Canadian-based unicorn startups and Fortune 100 US-based firms, which has further amplified my practical, hands-on knowledge on the topic of creativity and more.

To schedule me for a keynote presentation or to have me speak at your seminar, workshop, training, church, or conference, whether in-person or virtually, please visit www.iredafeowolabi.net/invite-me

# REFERENCES

## INTRODUCTION


1.  Vine's Expository Dictionary of Old Testament Words. Vine, W. E., Unger, Merrill F., and White, William. Thomas Nelson Publishers, 1985. Accessed through PC Study Bible.
2.  Strong, J. (1994, 2003, 2006). Exhaustive Concordance of the Bible. In Biblesoft's New Exhaustive Strong's Numbers and Concordance with Expanded Greek-Hebrew Dictionary (7th ed.).
3.  Thayer, J. H. (1889). New Testament Lexicon. In Clavis Novi Testamenti: Being Grimm S., Wilke S. Translated, revised, and enlarged by Joseph Henry Thayer, D.D. Originally published by Harper & Brothers. Accessed through PC Study Bible (Complete and Abridged formats).


## CHAPTER 1


1.  Carson, B., & Murphey, G. (1990). Gifted Hands: The Ben Carson Story. Zondervan.
2.  Kwik, J. (2020). Limitless: Upgrade Your Brain, Learn Anything Faster, and Unlock Your Exceptional Life. Hay House Inc.
3.  Feloni, R. (2015, June 25), "KFC founder Colonel Sanders didn't achieve his remarkable rise to success until his 60s", Business Insider. https://www.businessinsider.com/how-kfc-founder-colonel-sanders-achieved-success-in-his-60s-2015-6

4. Brands, H. W. (2008), "Traitor to His Class: The Privileged Life and Radical Presidency of Franklin Delano Roosevelt", Anchor Books.

5. Huart, W. (2020, December 28), "Stevie Wonder and the Prodigious Imagination of One of Music's Most Inventive Voices", Produce Like a Pro.

6. https://producelikeapro.com/blog/stevie-wonder-and-the-prodigious-imagination-of-one-of-musics-most-inventive-voices/

7. Inspire Yourself. (2020, April 24), "The inspiring story of Nick Vujicic - The man without limbs who became limitless", YouTube. https://www.youtube.com/watch?v=6OAu8SWy6Fc

8. Kaushik, P. (2011, December 29), "The journey of J.K. Rowling and her Harry Potter", Business Insider, https://www.businessinsider.com/the-journey-of-jkrowling-and-her-harry-p-2011-12

9. Smith, D. (2019, April 19), "What everyone gets wrong about this famous Steve Jobs quote, according to Lyft's design boss", Business Insider, https://www.businessinsider.com/steve-jobs-quote-misunderstood-katie-dill-2019-4

10. Strong, J. (1994, 2003, 2006). Exhaustive Concordance of the Bible. In Biblesoft's New Exhaustive Strong's Numbers and Concordance with Expanded Greek-Hebrew Dictionary (7th ed.).

11. Thayer, J. H. (1889). New Testament Lexicon. In Clavis Novi Testamenti: Being Grimm S., Wilke S. Translated, revised, and enlarged by Joseph Henry Thayer, D.D. Originally published by Harper & Brothers. Accessed through PC Study Bible (Complete and Abridged formats).

12. Hotten, R. (2015, December 10), "Volkswagen: The scandal explained. BBC News", https://www.bbc.com/news/business-34324772

## CHAPTER 2

1. Thayer, J. H. (1889). New Testament Lexicon. In Clavis Novi Testamenti: Being Grimm S., Wilke S. Translated, revised, and enlarged by Joseph Henry Thayer, D.D. Originally published by Harper & Brothers. Accessed through PC Study Bible (Complete and Abridged formats).
2. Aristotle. (1976). Metaphysics, Book VIII, Section 3 (Trans. W. D. Ross). Walton St., Oxford, United Kingdom: Clarendon Press.
3. Burger, N. (Director). (2014). Divergent [Film]. United States: Summit Entertainment.

## CHAPTER 3

1. Brown, B. (2015). Daring Greatly: How the Courage to Be Vulnerable Transforms the Way We Live, Love, Parent, and Lead. New York: Avery.
2. McGonigal, K. (2015). The Upside of Stress: Why Stress Is Good for You, and How to Get Good at It. Penguin Random House.
3. Dweck, C. (2006). Mindset: The New Psychology of Success. Ballantine Books.
4. Gilbert, E. (2015). Big Magic: Creative Living Beyond Fear. Riverhead Books.
5. Bandura, A. (1997). Self-Efficacy: The Exercise of Control. W.H. Freeman and Company.

## CHAPTER 4

1. Ben Carson. (2017, October 18). Ben Carson: An Extraordinary Life - Conversations from Penn State [Video file]. Retrieved from https://www.youtube.com/watch?v=4-8NRSfk_a8

2. Shen, L. (2020, November 19), "Meet the unicorn founder that braved war zones and missed meetings to make his mark on the startup world", Fortune, https://fortune.com/2020/11/19/calendly-founder-tope-awotona-startup-unicorn/

3. Steirn, J. (2023, February 14), "Report: Calendly Business Breakdown & Founding Story", Contrary Capital. Retrieved from https://research.contrary.com/reports/calendly

4. Strive Masiyiwa, "How to Build a Multi-Billion Dollar Business in Africa from Scratch", Tenganamba, G. (Compiler). [PDF compilation]

5. Aydin, R. (2019, September 19), "How 3 guys turned renting air mattresses in their apartment into a $31 billion company, Airbnb", Business Insider. Retrieved from https://www.businessinsider.com/how-airbnb-was-founded-a-visual-history-2016-2

6. Kay, C. (2023, June 21), "Elon Musk: The Extraordinary Visionary and Innovator Shaping Our Future", Valiant CEO, Retrieved from https://valiantceo.com/elon-musk/

7. Mostoufi, A. (May 22, 2023), "Startup Almanac — From Idea to Execution", Medium Retrieved from https://medium.com/@alimostoufi/playing-founder-at-the-startups-619501a1494c

8. Clary, S. D. (July 8, 2021), "How Airbnb Hacked Craigslist for Viral Growth", Hackernoon, Retrieved from https://hackernoon.com/how-airbnb-hacked-craigslist-for-viral-growth-24l35eg

9. Maslan, A., "A Few of History's Most Successful Business Collaborations", Pinnacle Global Network, Retrieved from

https://pinnacleglobalnetwork.com/a-few-of-historys-most-successful-business-collaborations/

10. Sikder, T. (2022, November 22), "The Great Amazon Success Story: Journey From A Garage Bookstore To Trillion Dollar Empire", Wedevs, Retrieved from https://wedevs.com/blog/413420/amazon-success-story/

11. Pisano, G. P., & Wheelwright, S. C. (1995), "The New Logic of High-Tech R&D", Harvard Business Review, September–October 1995, From the Magazine. Retrieved from https://hbr.org/1995/09/the-new-logic-of-high-tech-rd

12. Ash Turner (Jul 2023), "How Many Users Are on WhatsApp? User Statistics and Trends", BankMyCell, Retrieved from https://www.bankmycell.com/blog/number-of-whatsapp-users/

13. David Rowan (01 May 2018). "The inside story of Jan Koum and how Facebook bought WhatsApp." Wired, Retrieved from https://www.wired.co.uk/article/whats-app-owner-founder-jan-koum-facebook.

14. Gladwell, M. (2002). The Tipping Point: How Little Things Can Make a Big Difference. Back Bay Books.

15. Williams, P., & Denney, J. (2013), "Walt Disney: The Biography", SaltRiver.

## CHAPTER 5

1. Thayer, J. H. (1889). Old Testament Lexicon. In Clavis Novi Testamenti: Being Grimm S., Wilke S. Translated, revised, and enlarged by Joseph Henry Thayer, D.D. Originally published by Harper & Brothers. Accessed through PC Study Bible (Complete and Abridged formats).

2. The Editors of Encyclopaedia Britannica, "Maya Angelou", Britannica. Accessed 10th July 2023, https://www.britannica.com/biography/Maya-Angelou

www.ingramcontent.com/pod-product-compliance
Lightning Source LLC
Chambersburg PA
CBHW032218050726
47591CB00001B/180